SURVIVING THE EARLY YEARS

United Kingdom Council for Psychotherapy Series

Recent titles in the UKCP Series
(for a full listing, please visit www.karnacbooks.com)

SURVIVING THE EARLY YEARS

The Importance of Early Intervention with Babies At Risk

edited by

Stella Acquarone

KARNAC

First published in 2016 by
Karnac Books Ltd
118 Finchley Road, London NW3 5HT

British Library Cataloguing in Publication Data

A C.I.P. for this book is available from the British Library

ISBN 978 1 78220 278 3

Edited, designed and produced by The Studio Publishing Services Ltd
www.publishingservicesuk.co.uk
email: studio@publishingservicesuk.co.uk

Printed in Great Britain

www.karnacbooks.com

CONTENTS

PART III: VULNERABLE GROUPS COMING FROM
"INTERNAL" FRAGILE CIRCUMSTANCES

I would like to dedicate this book to those individuals who have taught me over the years, as well as those I have taught—some of whom are contributors to this book. I also extend this dedication to all professionals who, through their unyielding commitment and hard work, are helping to shed light on the complex world of the early years. May they continue to survive the challenges that this work brings.

ACKNOWLEDGEMENTS

I would like to thank the School of Infant Mental Health, part of the London-based Parent Infant Centre, for organising the conference on the early years ("Early Years: Importance of Early Intervention for Babies at Risk") in November 2011, which was managed by Claire Rees. I would also like to thank the charity International Pre-Autistic Network (ipAn) for sponsoring the event.

The idea for this book was as a result of that conference. In the months that followed, I asked colleagues and past trainees to contribute a chapter on their area of expertise, in order to highlight the potentially damaging effects of trauma on babies and parents. I would like to thank all for their efforts and courage.

I would also like to thank the institutions that create a space to help parents and babies after they have been through a traumatic experience—be it war, rape, prison, or torture—and especially for allowing a psychotherapist into their premises to help with the understanding, holding, and expression of personal states.

My thanks also go to the staff on neonatal intensive care units, for allowing psychotherapists on to their wards to support the parents and offer advice on how to "be with" their babies during this testing period.

Finally, I would like to thank Caroline Hunt for her admirable proofreading and corrections, and my husband, Don Hughston, for all the help he has provided.

Stella Acquarone is founder and principal of the Parent Infant Centre, London, and is an adult and child psychoanalytic psychotherapist, with a PhD in psychology. She has worked for over thirty years in the NHS, and also works privately. She has presented workshops and conferences all over the world and has published several books, including *Infant–Parent Psychotherapy: A Handbook*; and *Signs of Autism in Infants: Recognition and Early Intervention* (both published by Karnac). She is a member of the Neuropsychology Section of the British Psychological Society, the British Psychoanalytic Council, and the Association of Child Psychotherapists.

Franca Brenninkmeyer is a psychologist with over twenty years of professional adoption experience. She has worked at PAC-UK (formerly the Post-Adoption Centre) since 1996 where she is now Head of the Child and Family Service. She has Masters degrees in Pedagogical Sciences and Counselling Psychology from Belgium and the UK. Franca was instrumental in developing PAC-UK's assessments and (intensive) therapeutic work for adoptive families. She regularly presents on adoption, trauma, and attachment-related topics.

Zack Eleftheriadou is a chartered counselling psychologist, a chartered scientist, and Associate Fellow of the British Psychological Society. She is also a child and adult psychotherapist and has worked with refugees and the area of trauma for over twenty years, in organisations such as The Medical Foundation and the Intercultural Therapy Centre, Nafisyat. She has published widely in this cross-cultural field, including *Transcultural Counselling* and *Psychotherapy and Culture*. She is patron of the multi-ethnic counselling and listening service Mothertongue, in Reading.

Brett Kahr is Senior Clinical Research Fellow in Psychotherapy and Mental Health at the Centre for Child Mental Health in London, and an Honorary Visiting Professor in the School of Arts at Roehampton University. He also works as a training therapist and training supervisor in psychology at the Bowlby Centre, London. In addition, Professor Kahr practises psychotherapy with individuals and couples in Hampstead, north London. He is author or editor of eight books, including *Sex and the Psyche*; *Life Lessons from Freud*; and the forthcoming *Tea with Winnicott*.

Daphne Keen is a consultant in neurodevelopmental paediatrics and an Honorary Senior Lecturer at St George's, London, with a small independent practice in central London. She has worked in the area of autism spectrum conditions and associated developmental disorders for twenty-five years, and has published research and practice articles in major international journals. Dr Keen has had a longstanding involvement with the Royal College of Paediatrics and Child Health in developing the college's mental health sub-speciality, and is an executive member of the Paediatric Mental Health Association.

Julie Kitchener is lead child and adolescent psychotherapist at Greenfields, a therapeutic community in Kent, run by the charity Childhood First. She developed a particular interest in working with children with disabilities and their families during her time at the London Borough of Camden's child and adolescent mental health (CAMH) services. Julie also tutors in Child and Adolescent Psychotherapy at the British Psychotherapy Foundation, and works in private practice.

Magdalena Polaszewska-Nicke is a psychologist and co-founder and president of ZERO-FIVE, Poland. She specialises in therapeutic work with families with infants in Poznań and Warsaw, conducts and designs workshops for parents and training for professionals, and co-operates with local social services in helping hard-to-reach families in rural areas.

Maeja Raicar is a member of the Bowlby Centre, London, and has a private therapy and supervision practice in Essex. She also works part-time as an adult counsellor for the adoption support service, PAC-UK. Maeja has authored two books: *Teenage Pregnancy: The Social Making and Unmaking of Mothers* (Pepar Publications, 1984); *Child-Centred Attachment Therapy* (The CcAT Programme; Karnac, 2009).

Joan Raphael-Leff is both a psychoanalyst (Fellow of the British Psychoanalytical Society) and a social psychologist. Previously Professor of Psychoanalysis at University College London and the University of Essex, she now leads the UCL/Anna Freud Centre Academic Faculty for Psychoanalytic Research. Over the past forty years, her clinical practice and academic work has focused on emotional issues in reproduction (infertility, pregnancy, neonatal loss, early parenting), with over a hundred single-author publications and twelve books in this field. She is consultant to perinatal and women's projects in many different countries, including South Africa, where she is Visiting Professor at Stellenbosch University.

Maria Rhode is Emeritus Professor of Child Psychotherapy at the Tavistock Clinic and the University of East London, where she currently works with toddlers at risk of developing autistic spectrum disorders. She is also a member of the Association of Child Psychotherapists and is Honorary Associate of the British Psychoanalytic Society. She lectures and publishes widely and is co-editor of *Psychotic States in Children* (with Margaret Rustin and Alex & Hélène Dubinsky, 1997); *The Many Faces of Asperger's Syndrome* (with Trudy Klauber, 2004); *Invisible Boundaries: Psychosis and Autism in Children and Adolescents* (with Didier Houzel, 2006). She was awarded the Frances Tustin Memorial Prize in 1998.

Colette Salkeld is a clarinettist, clarinet teacher, and music therapist. She has a special interest in the role of music therapy in developing secure attachments in adopted children. Since 2004, Colette has worked with the Adoption Support Service at Essex County Council, providing music therapy for families, and using an attachment based model in both individual and group work. Colette has also completed Theraplay training to further enhance her work in this area.

Magdalena Stawicka is a psychologist and co-founder of ZERO-FIVE, the Foundation for Infant Mental Health in Poznań, Poland. She works at the Institute of Psychology at Adam Mickiewicz University, teaching and conducting research on attachment in children. In the ZERO-FIVE Foundation, she works therapeutically with young children and their families, develops ideas for supportive programmes, and lectures for specialists. She is also an invited lecturer in postgraduate schools for clinical psychology and early intervention.

Pamela Windham Stewart was born in Texas and moved with her parents to Europe in 1963. After gaining an Honours Degree in History of Art she worked in advertising and publishing until she became a mother. Further study included an MA (distinction) in Infant Observation. Her dissertation "Born inside" (1998) described therapeutic work with mothers and babies in a large British prison. This work continues in her weekly therapy group for mothers and babies in prison, as well as a group for pregnant prisoners. In addition to her forensic work, she has a private psychoanalytic practice, and is the founder of The Saturday Forensic Forum.

Colwyn Trevarthen is Professor Emeritus of Child Psychology and Psychobiology at the University of Edinburgh. He trained as a biologist in New Zealand and gained a PhD in psychobiology at Caltech. After postdoctoral work in France, he was a Research Fellow at the Center for Cognitive Studies at Harvard, where his infancy research began. He has published on brain development, infant communication and child learning, and emotional health. His current research concerns how rhythms and expressions of "musicality" in movement animates communication with children and their development and learning. He holds an Honorary Doctorate in Psychology from the University of Crete, and is a Fellow of the Royal Society of Edinburgh, a Member of the Norwegian Academy of Sciences and Letters, and a Vice-President of the British Association for Early Childhood Education.

Jo Winsland, born in Uganda and medically trained in the UK, has been working since 1998 as a general practitioner in preventative child health and child protection in France, a job that provides intense ongoing observation of child development from birth, under widely varying conditions. Dr Winsland has worked on a study by the French PREAUT association—with Marie-Christine Laznik and Graciela C. Crespin—into detecting the very early warning signs of relating disorders in infants, and has developed a special interest in the preventative measures possible from the age of one to two months.

Lucie Zwimpfer is a registered parent–infant psychotherapist completing her doctorate in pre-term infant affect regulation. She is UK trained and works as a consultant and supervisor for the parent–infant mental health service in Wellington, New Zealand. She is an executive member of the Infant Mental Health Association of Aotearoa NZ (IMHAANZ). Dr Zwimpfer lectures and publishes in infant mental health, and has a particular interest in bringing psychoanalysis into the neonatal intensive care unit setting.

FOREWORD

> "Drink to me only with thine eyes,
> And I will pledge with mine"
>
> (From *Song: To Celia*, Johnson, 1979)

It is a delight to see the mutual attentiveness of mother and infant gazing at each other with love and affection, giving and receiving communication with their eyes and facial mobility. An observer involuntarily smiles with pleasure and does not interrupt the privacy of their intense interaction. As the obstetrician Professor Norman Morris once counselled with caution, "You would not come between a mother bear and her cub, would you!" On his Unit at Charing Cross Hospital in the 1960s and 1970s, mothers could stay on the ward for up to ten days. During this time they had the care of a breastfeeding nurse whose task was to help them be comfortable with their own bodies and find a pleasurable way of feeding their newborn infants, assisting the infant to find the nipple and engulf the areola while positioning himself in the security of the mother's arms. The looking at and the feeding occur simultaneously. Sometimes the infant may suck with closed eyes and could be thought to be temporarily oblivious of the mother's ownership of the breast, experiencing himself as merged with it. The further establishment of a normal, healthy family relationship was enhanced by advising the mother that she should go out for an evening with the father before leaving hospital, thus allowing the midwives to give the missed feed with the mother's own expressed breast milk.

This thoughtful care was very different to that provided in some other institutions where the mothers who had decided not to breastfeed were left to get on with feeding their babies on their own. Prepared bottles were placed in front of them by busy nurses who had other tasks on the ward; one might think that these were perhaps the mothers who were most in need of attentive support and guidance.

As obstetric and medical skill and technology has expanded so remarkably there has been a proper concentration on getting "an alive mother and a live baby". There is now the possibility that premature infants born at twenty-three weeks might survive, due to the skilled and determined neonatologists and nurses in specialised units. These tiny infants require tremendous input to survive physically, but also a huge amount of support to establish their emotional pleasure in their mother and her delight in them. The mothers of these fragile beings need help with sustaining their loving attention when their infants are incapable of the gratifying responsiveness of the full-term infant.

The exquisite reciprocal attunement of mother and child changes and develops over the years depending on the maturation of the child and the capacities of the mother. This development does not proceed without difficulties and is dependent on the growing ability of the child to initiate interactions and on its mother's wellbeing with the father's support and understanding. Times of inevitable dysjunction, painful and distressing, short term or long term, can be mitigated by the thoughtfulness and sensitivity of the clinicians who might be involved in caring for the families: doctors, health visitors, midwives, nurses, physiotherapists, psychologists. It is these clinicians who will find much of interest in this book that will stimulate discussion and point the ways to attending to such dysjunctions practically, with early interventions helping to limit the long-term effects of what can seem to be a heartbreaking impasse.

The effectiveness of the interventions described in this book has implications for all those planning and financing the mental health of the nation, since we now know that early intervention can lead to the lessening of the cost of treatment or institutionalisation in the future. Managers and those responsible for strategic planning within the National Health Service (NHS), including members of the government, will enjoy reading what can be done and will understand that there is a public health element in the work described: that proper funding now will inevitably produce savings in the future if a long-term view is taken.

In this volume we have a distillation of years of work by experienced clinicians who have helped mothers with their infants and growing children, and, of course, children with their mothers, within different settings. This difficult work is movingly described. The rationales and the theories sustaining the interventions are clearly explained, and there are good references to the classic texts on infant and child emotional growth and behaviour.

From my own perspective of over fifty years of clinical work, I found it satisfying to read these chapters contributed by admired colleagues and friends, as well as others who are referenced with whom I was in contact and who formed a great part of my own learning experiences. I hope others will take such pleasure in the book and still learn new things, as I did.

I have one further thought. This book brought to mind all the videos of detailed observations that should be compulsory viewing for those engaged in work with mothers and children—"seeing is believing".

Marcus Johns,
Psychoanalyst and Fellow of the Royal
College of Psychiatrists, and Trustee of ipAn

Reference

Johnson, B. (1979). The Forest. Song: To Celia. *Oxford Dictionary of Quotations*. Oxford: Oxford University Press.

Introduction

Stella Acquarone

> There passed a weary time. Each throat
> Was parched, and glazed each eye.
> A weary time! a weary time!
> How glazed each weary eye.
> (From *The Rime of the Ancient Mariner*, Coleridge, 1996 Part III, p. 86)

A young man walking to a wedding is detained by the "glittering eye" of a grizzled old sailor who transfixes him with a strange tale of agony and survival. Fearing the Ancient Mariner, who reassures the Wedding Guest that there is no need for dread, the young man—now late to the wedding and imagining that the groom has already entered the hall—sits on a stone and hears the dreadful retelling of a ship set out "into a sunny and cheerful sea" soon pushed into a frigid water where it is hemmed inside a maze of mast-high ice.

Coleridge's *The Rime of the Ancient Mariner* is an epic tale of despair that can also be read as an emotionally accurate allegory of the despair resulting from the unmet needs of infants, parents, and carers (with their little albatross) and the "sea" of society in the early years. Despite the strong imagery of a dead albatross hung round the neck of the

mariner and the many dead sailors, the point of Coleridge's epic "rime"
is that mariners (and carers)—clinging only to hope—can survive.

The early years experienced by many infants, parents, and carers
can be a grim tale. Like the Ancient Mariner, simply surviving the early
years—and living to tell their tale to other "wedding guests"—is the
entire point: they managed to survive. However, often they survived
without hope; they could not find any; the journey was grim indeed.

This book is about the hope underlying the ability to survive the
early years.

It is no secret that not all early years are voyages "into a sunny and
cheerful sea". Some are long voyages into horror and weariness that
can last for years: babies born into difficult families, into conflict-
ridden countries, or into difficult circumstances. These babies are
pretty much alone, because their mothers might be too ill to look after
them and nurses might be too few or too busy to fulfil the maternal
function other than changing and feeding them. They might have
been born in war zones, or in prisons, or have been in intensive neonatal premature units. Unlike mothers who recall the early years with
their babies as a dance of understanding and development, other
carers do not recall hearing the music at all. They slog through the
early years with only hope as a compass. Like the Ancient Mariner,
theirs is a poignant search of the horizons for hope in any form:

> With throats unslaked, with black lips baked,
> We could nor laugh nor wail;
> Through utter drought all dumb we stood!
> I bit my arm, I sucked the blood,
> And cried, A sail! a sail!
>
> (Coleridge, 1996, Part III, p. 86)

It is this image of something possibly good that enables the Mariner
to hang on. Along with parents and carers, babies look for sails, too.
Strapped to a painful and dreary reality, they seek some external
humanity that might represent a first home; they search for a womb in
the middle of the water where they float in oblivion, desperate to link
to voices and a beating heart. Whether they are floating in a sea of
domestic violence, or drugs, or alcohol, they scour the horizon for a
womb—an overall container—for which they can set their sails.

In this book, I set out to sail straight into the different calamities
that some infants (and their parents) endure. Throughout my career, I

have accompanied parents into all seas of despair, thinking with them about where the winds of hope are hiding, and, in finding it, help them and their babies set sail out of their misfortune. This book will bring us face to face with the wonderful capacities of the newborn and the great potential for parents (both mother and father) and child to continue growing together in a society that cares for them. My own career is a long and continuous effort to help parents form their own networks of help in institutions and in everyday life, enriched by the cyberspace that links countries and their solutions with problematic conditions and new preventative practices.

But for this book to be successful in helping infants and parents survive the early years, I set out to do more. I asked other professionals to join me.

Together with the School of Infant Mental Health and the International pre-Autistic Network (ipAn) charity, we organised a conference so that we could all talk, discuss, and present our collective breakthroughs in thinking and understanding the perils of the early years. Too often, my colleagues and I sit transfixed by the glittering eyes of infants and parents who find themselves in perilous waters without any hope of seeing "a sail!"

This book emerged from the strength and comradely synthesising of different disciplines and accounts professionals give of the horrors and pain endured by the early years' survivors who walk into our clinics. It is a book written in three parts.

Part I: Thoughts in search of a thinker. In the first three chapters of this book, we consider a particular dialogue of emotions: the principal physical and psychological ideas and thoughts of what happens to parents from the moment they conceive.

Joan Raphael-Leff gives us imagery of the womb-as-habitat, gleaned from more than forty-five years of working with (and writing about) pregnancy. She explains how the differing roles of generator, expectant mother, woman, and lover destabilise a pregnant woman's self-image and prepare the ground for the new relationship. This process can be easier or more difficult, depending upon the experiences that she had growing up. The same is true of the father. In Raphael-Leff's own words, "The intensity relates to images of one's baby-self in the mind of the archaic primary carers, including their unwitting reactions to, and projective distortions of, that baby".

For Raphael-Leff, pregnancy is a shared emotional experience between parents, the strength and presence of them as a couple, and a new experience in their lives. Pregnancy recycles and reactivates the supercharged past of both partners and helps them to face the growing foetus in a new light. She also tells us how the foetus moving inside the womb influences the mother physically (through hormones and other generated substances, sleep patterns, etc.) and emotionally. We accompany the foetus on its journey of development, even towards perinatal difficulties and how to prevent them, watching it grow and observing how parents prepare themselves for its arrival.

Colwyn Trevarthen, perhaps the world's foremost authority in the communication of experience and emotion from infancy, describes the effects of caring in a developing newborn who arrives with the desire to fully interact. He begins the chapter by giving us a primer on the marvellous and extraordinary ways babies communicate through movement:

> A newborn baby's body is expressive of its personality. It tells us that the young mind anticipates the pleasure of moving coherently and well, and that it feels anxiety about having difficulty or pain in fulfilling its functions and intentions. Eyes, head, and hands shift with intricate curiosity, signalling purposes and feelings for others' attention. Right from the start a baby has a special sensitivity for how the movements of another person transmit the quality of their feelings . . , They . . , do not have to be learnt after birth.

Trevarthen then gives us a succinct summary of all views of infancy from Darwin onwards. He tells us that today's rich communication between disciplines, whether from observation, description, or careful reflection, exploring all of the innate and environmental forces at play that give rise to an infant's imagination, aesthetics, and mortal affections can be a strong foundation for recovery from neglect. He shows us how psycholinguistics is filling in the gaps in understanding why musicality is at the core of relationships. In addition, almost as a bonus, he gives us his own "Theory of infant intersubjectivity by tracing changes in motives and interests" as a consequence of maternal factors (such as depression), and shows us how music and song help promote attachment and intimate relationships.

Trevarthen carefully explains the evolution of emotional expressions and how hope and pride of early childhood can be betrayed by deprivation of love. He points to research showing how recovery is more difficult when the neglect starts very early. He ends the chapter with his compelling thoughts about autism—that it should no longer be considered a genetic disorder. Because infants must find a live partner to interact with, epigenetic factors that influence development during gestation—and the quality of the relationship with the parent after birth—means that autism is a product of the parent–child relationship and company in play. Trevarthen strongly suggests that this relationship is the place where hope can be found.

Brett Kahr presents his contribution on infanticide, "'Happy birthdeath to me': surviving death wishes in early infancy", which he divides into three sections. The first section provides a review of the ideas about unconscious death wishes towards infants from the time of the ancient Greeks. The second section analyses the clinical scenario: how "psychological infanticide" (the sense of being killed off and yet remaining alive) presents itself. He describes the style of interaction as "infanticidal attachment", a type of disorganised attachment that provides no safety for the child and could stimulate severe psycholopathology. Kahr then develops a typology of psychological infanticide that is exemplified with clinical cases. Finally, in the last section, he provides a working model for mental health workers to use in order to identify death wish symptoms in adults and, thereby, avoid potential catastrophes in children.

Part II: Reaching the vulnerable at risk from "external" circumstances. Chapters 4–9 discuss the mothers who have become vulnerable due to "external" circumstances, such as external trauma. For the mothers to be able to become reflective and insightful about their babies and themselves, they need to overcome the trauma, and here we look at different models used to help this process and develop a helpful relationship with therapists, which allows the essential provision for babies to develop in a healthier way.

Zack Eleftheriadou's chapter, "Creating a safe space: psychotherapeutic support for refugee parents and babies", uses the concepts of Winnicott (holding environment), Bion (containment), and Stern (different points of entry in the parent–infant relationship) when considering how to help refugee mothers and their babies. She describes, in a very skilful and compassionate way, how there are different stages in the development of a psychotherapist's relationship with the shocked and traumatised mother and baby. She highlights the importance of creating a safe environment for the mothers to share their trauma, pain, and hatred, thus relieving them from the unaccompanied past experience. In so doing, Eleftheriadou enables the mother's reflective function to become operative, thereby allowing her to cease projecting her lived horrors to the infant, and to receive the infant's new and raw feelings. This important early intervention helps mother and child to bond by providing a good holding environment and containment that is culturally respectful.

Pamela Windham Stewart describes the challenges faced by mothers and babies in prisons. The mothers live in a closed and contrived space, and although they have access to psychotherapeutic help, they only have controlled access to their babies, if any at all. They have the opportunity to develop a relationship with their babies, but only if they are helped. Despite the challenges, Stewart describes working with her weekly mother and baby group. She recounts how the mothers develop a new and different relationship with the therapist, as well as with the other mothers in the group. She offers the women a different model of parenting, encouraging them not to merely repeat the family history, but to offer their babies love, and to think, and be curious, about them. In this way, the mothers learn to feel, acknowledge feelings, mourn loss, and reflect on their experiences. Theirs are poignant accounts of these processes.

In her chapter, Lucie Zwimpfer gives us a psychoanalytic viewpoint of relationships in the neonatal intensive care unit (NICU), specifically the aspects of "talking to" and "being with" babies. We now know that preterm infants in the NICU can experience a great deal of pain. Being born immature and before their time, preterm babies can suffer in other ways, too. They lose precious months in the mind of the parents who, because of their early arrival, are also premature as parents, and might not be sufficiently ready or equipped to deal with parenthood. They feel guilt that their child is suffering because of them. Despite a team of carers that includes parents and nurses, the parents are often not available and the nurses are overworked and overwhelmed with all the tasks involved. Zwimpfer examines this dynamic, exploring if and how psychoanalytic treatment methods can be useful in improving infant–carer relationships in the NICU, describing, for example, a model of attuned vocal soothing as a pain management tool during certain procedures.

Magdalena Stawicka and Magdalena Polaszewska-Nicke's chapter shows us how a small group of young professionals in Poland is making great strides in changing the country's attitudes towards the idea of infant mental health. The authors set up their programme, "Toward the baby", to provide psychological support to parents-to-be and new parents in order to develop healthy parent–infant relationships and, thus, avoid possible future emotional and behavioural disorders in the child.

Stawicka and Polaszewska-Nicke explain that, in Poland, after so many wars and social difficulties, the very concept of infant mental health did not exist, and so they improvised. The idea was that after the birth of their babies, new parents would receive individual consultations on psychological, physiotherapeutic, lactation, and feeding issues. What surprised Stawicka and Polaszewska-Nicke was the change in the perceived value of psychological support. At the beginning, parents came for the physiotherapy and lactation classes, but in their end evaluations they expressed their liking for, and usefulness of, the psychological elements most of all. The programme evolved into a type of preventative tool for all kinds of parents, not just multi-risk families. They added workshops with an idea of scaffolding parents' mentalizing abilities (which they describe as a reflective function of the yet-unborn and, later, the born child and the process of attunement). For parents who needed more, they offered parallel individual sessions. The results were promising, creating a mentality around the importance of paying attention to mothers and babies.

Maeja Raicar helps us think about adoption and fostering, and the centrality of the concepts of loss and mourning. She takes up the shadow dynamics of the adopted or foster child's birth parents, as well as the types of help needed by the adoptive and foster parents. She describes how the family generates a circle of security as well as vicious circles that become repetitive and pathological. For this purpose, she acknowledges the lifelong hurt for the growing child and adult and offers alternative help for them to attune to the child and create new attachments to promote emotional development.

The chapter includes contributions from Colette Salkeld, an accomplished music therapist who helps mother and babies and small children to attach securely through well-thought music activities, and Franca Brenninkmeyer, who has developed an integrative approach to tackling the effects of chronic and pervasive neglect and abuse in early

life. Brenninkmeyer describes the PAC programme of intensive therapeutic work for under-fives and their adoptive families, which uses
the ARC (attachment, regulation, and competencies) model, with its
ten "building blocks", for therapeutic intervention.

Julie Kitchener tells us that, in cases of special needs, it is important to keep in mind that these babies have to deal with their deficit
and that, in general, the parents feel overwhelmed and disorientated,
due to their unbearable feelings of loss, dislocation, rage, and anger
about what they had expected in their new child and what they
received. Kitchener examines the part played by trauma (birth, diagnosis, stress, or cumulative—e.g., intergenerational or repeated
medical interventions and assessments, etc.). questions of integration
and disintegration, and what leads to the need for psychotherapeutic
support. She tells us how these factors could collude against facing up
to the real child.

The special needs child and parent require an imaginative engagement to strengthen the quality of their relationship, as well as enable
the child to gain a sense of self and other (like any other child). She
also considers the implications for the child to have parents or carers
that are aware of their disillusions and uncomfortable thoughts
caused by the child's own disability. Kitchener shows us that, through
disability, child and parent can find a relationship that is fulfilling and
happy for both.

Part III: Vulnerable groups coming from "internal" fragile circumstances. In the final part of the book, we look at vulnerable groups
of babies—their vulnerability due to "internal" fragile circumstances—and learn what is essential for them to develop in a healthier way. Not only do we have to keep up with new developments in
applied psychoanalysis and neuropsychology, we also have to review
what has worked in the past. Overall, we need to recognise the power
of the relationship and be grateful for the ways we can prevent the
occurrence of disorders and difficulties that can be avoided.

Daphne Keen explores, from the viewpoint of the neurodevelopmental paediatrician, the importance of recognising the condition as
early as possible. She helps us understand the impact of co-existing
medical and developmental conditions on delay in diagnosis. She
shows us how the diagnosis is made: via a thorough recognition of
sensory impairment, psychosocial deprivation, selective mutism,
attention and hyperactivity deficit disorders, and intellectual disability

and developmental syndromes. She also describes how professional and service responses can cause delays to early recognition. Dr Keen writes eloquently about the "competent infant" and how the different areas of competence develop from social understanding to joint attention and mentalizing. With clear examples, she invites the reader to submerge themselves in the realms of the diverse pathways in pathological development through play, language, and sensory processing.

My chapter (Stella Acquarone) is a focus on the extraordinary power to be found in focusing on the relationship. Through clinical observations, we see how children who pursue an avoidant way of relating—no matter the contributing factors—can be rescued to varying degrees by an early understanding of the causes of retreating. These children can be integrated into mainstream education with a secure attachment arising from this understanding of underlying causes. The most important thing is to find out what is impeding relationship development.

I look at the concept of an "autistic evolution", when, for example, infants and children retreat to a world of their own. Based on neuropsychology and brain growth and the impact of relationships on neural connections with their positive implications for cognition and emotions, I describe a programme we devised to help these processes become more "normal". I also present a clinical case to illustrate the various elements that must be taken into account when helping little children form relationships that could save them from jeopardy.

Jo Winsland draws our attention to the important role of the informed paediatrician in listening to parents' concerns about their infants when there is nothing physically wrong with them. These parents simply have a gut feeling that their child's emotional development is being hampered by unknown causes, and Winsland underlines the importance of listening to, sharing, and monitoring these concerns with possible solutions. She explains clearly the context of her work in France, and the ready availability and generally welcoming environment of the PMI (Protection Maternelle et Infantile), coupled with the French tradition of frequent follow-up from birth, which creates a context for well-trained infant mental health professionals to recognise early signs of alarm and offer an important preventative service.

Winsland presents some clinical cases, including one in detail that shows how early intervention, skilfully and sensitively done, can make a huge difference—so much so that it should convince all paediatricians to train further in observation and sensitive interaction with parents to use this powerful timing in early infancy.

Maria Rhode, in the final chapter, talks about working with toddlers at risk of autism in a National Health Service setting. She describes a research programme she is involved in where toddlers that are at risk of developing autistic behaviours are offered an infant observer to visit them at home.

Although similar to parent–infant psychotherapy, the difference with Rhode's programme is the absence of insight-based interpretation. Instead, the therapist's function as observer is primarily to make links between parents and child, as well as providing acceptance and understanding of what the parents are going through

She goes on to describe in detail the case of Isabel, who needed to be treated at seventeen months after presenting various signs of alarm and who was assessed by the CHAT (checklist for autism in toddlers). Rhode's working methods included collaborating with the parents to establish the "good grandmother transference", which works as a means of supporting them through the process so that they can help their child to progress. In addition, she points out that, in this case, she did not experience the despair felt by the parents, as the co-operation and support she received from colleagues helped her not to become disheartened by the manifestations of the autistic part of the child.

Rhode's work with autistic children and their families includes overcoming the "vicious circle of discouragement", which has such a powerful effect on parents and professionals. The fact that Isabel did not receive the diagnosis of autism often brings us to the power to help the relationship "no matter what", maintaining an active and perseverant attitude of hope in the everyday life of the family.

What can we do for babies and parents in trouble and troubled babies and parents? With this question in mind, we begin our journey. We learn to understand them through the relationships they have built. Working through these relationships, we are able to "re-start" development so that it re-emerges and evolves in a more hopeful way.

Reference

Coleridge, S. T. (1996). *Selected Poems. The Rime of the Ancient Mariner*. Harmondsworth: Penguin Classics.

PART I

THOUGHTS IN SEARCH
OF A THINKER

In the first three chapters, we consider a particular dialogue of emotions: the principal physical and psychological ideas and thoughts of what happens in parents from the moment they conceive.

CHAPTER ONE

The emotional dialogue: womb to walking

Joan Raphael-Leff

M uch of the research literature over the past decades focuses on the infant's cognitive and emotional development within the primary intersubjective dyad. In this chapter, I focus on the maternal perspective—the mother's mental representations and her own emotional contribution to the primary relational system.

The way we mother is rarely our optimal choice. Women's needs have changed dramatically over the past few decades, but a young baby's needs have changed little over the millennia. In the west, educational parity and legislation grant women greater access to economic resources and higher occupational status. This creates new dilemmas and compromises for women, who realise that their ambitions and workplace demands are discordant with baby care. In Europe, some 12–20% of educated women decide to forego reproduction altogether. Facilitated by effective contraception or safe abortion, many young women delay childbearing in pursuit of a career, and some even decide to freeze their eggs. Pregnancy might occur naturally, but those whose fertility is compromised by postponement need assistance to conceive when the time feels right to have a child. On the other hand, earlier sexual activity and destigmatisation of non-marital births result in a high incidence of teenage pregnancies, and very young, often unsupported, single mothers.

Pregnancy

Pregnancy may be defined as an intertwining of three systems—physiological, emotional, and sociocultural. When first conception takes place within a stable couple, the period of transition to parenthood involves emotional upheaval. The partners' twosome is reproducing a third. For the woman, two people now occupy one body—hers—which could be a bizarre and disturbing experience. Her external body image changes in response to visible alterations (the shape of her breasts and swelling belly), while internal configurations expand to include the newly occupied bodily cavity, new physiological symptoms, and a new organ—the placenta. Parameters of the couple's previous relationships are destabilised with the pregnant woman's greater vulnerability and dependence. As future co-parents, facets of their respective generative identities must be reformulated, and her self-image as expectant mother, worker, and lover changes. In addition, the couple's sexual relationship is affected by bodily reappraisal and conceptualisation of the womb's inhabitant, and their changed selves. While imminent parenthood draws some partners closer, for others, their divergent roles in gestating the baby might feel incongruous with previous equality, leading some women to feel privileged to carry the baby and others to feel resentful at having to do so. Similarly, in some couples, the man might feel grateful, while others might feel envious and deprived of this experience, leading to acrimony or even abandonment. Intimate partner aggression and direct foetal abuse are known to increase during pregnancy.

Many factors are involved in an expectant mother's antenatal attachment to the baby, such as whether the conception was planned, wanted, and timely, and with the right impregnator. Pregnancy could be complicated by physical illness, disability, or multiple gestations. Sudden and incapacitating life events (such as bereavement, eviction, miscarriage, foetal diagnosis, etc.) or socio-economic problems (such as unemployment, poor housing, and poverty) can be devastating. Needless to say, the risk of antenatal as well as post natal emotional disturbance is elevated by a past psychiatric history or post traumatic stress disorder (TSD), but most studies stress the importance of current emotional support in boosting resilience in the face of adversity.

Previous perinatal experiences influence how this conception is perceived, as do unmourned reproductive losses from the past—her own or within her family of origin (Raphael-Leff, 1993). Similarly, fertility treatment and assisted conception, especially with donated gametes, can engender powerful fantasies and evoke feelings that the singularity of conception has been violated, which affect the internal dialogue with the foetus (Fine, 2014).

Antenatal emotional disturbance

In addition to the distress experienced by the suffering woman and her family, maternal disturbance during pregnancy has implications for the unborn child. In the mother, depression, paranoia, phobias, anxiety, and childhood abuse are associated with smoking, self-medication, recreational drug-taking, self-harm, and even suicide. Risk-taking behaviours and enactments have complex meanings, and could signify disregard for, or rejection of, an unwanted baby, or might challenge the baby to prove his/her capacity to withstand maternal failure. A pregnant woman's state of mind, thus, has an indirect impact on the unborn baby through her behaviour.

We have long had evidence that emotional aversion to pregnancy and negative representation of the baby during pregnancy affect the postnatal mother–infant relationship, and predict insecure future attachment patterns (Fonagy et al., 1991; Raphael-Leff, 2011; Zeanah et al., 1994). Twenty to forty per cent of antenatally depressed mothers also report obsessional thoughts of harming the child. Maternal anxiety and PTSD (often linked to early emotional deprivation or childhood abuse of the expectant mother) indirectly affect the unborn baby through poor antenatal clinic attendance, unhealthy eating, or risk-taking during pregnancy—all of which are associated with interuterine growth retardation, smaller babies, and preterm delivery with long-term consequences.

The "foetal origins hypothesis" finds that the lower one's weight at birth, the higher the risk for coronary heart disease, hypertension, stroke, type-2 diabetes, osteoporosis, and more fragile "homeostatic" settings in adulthood (Barker, 1999; Copper et al., 1996; Teixeira et al., 1999). Epidemiological studies suggest this might be attributable to increased uterine artery resistance index in the mother during pregnancy, with long-term effects on the child. Foetal under-nutrition has also been found to predispose men to depression in late adult life, suggesting a neuro-developmental aetiology of depression, possibly mediated by programming of the hypothalamic–pituitary–adrenal (HPA) axis. Interestingly, the odds ratios for depression among men, but not women, rise incrementally with decreasing birth weight (Thompson et al., 2001).

Although long considered an "old wives' tale", research findings now suggest that maternal emotions have a direct effect on the gestating foetus. Emotion can be as toxic as alcohol, nicotine, and opiates imbibed by the mother. Exposure in the womb to chronic maternal stress has been linked in later life with depression, hypertension, psychosis, hyperactivity, and alcoholism, possibly resulting from damage due to prolonged activation of brain opiates during gestation.

A growing body of work finds that maternal distress in pregnancy is associated with later behavioural problems in the offspring. Antenatal as well as postpartum maternal stress are correlated with the temperament of their three-year-olds (Susman et al., 2001). One longitudinal study of over 10,000 women isolated antenatal from post natal disturbance, finding that anxiety in late pregnancy posed an independent risk associated with behavioural/emotional problems into pre-adolescence (O'Connor et al., 2005).

The mechanism of transfer is unclear, but it is postulated that emotion has an impact through associated biochemical and physiological transmission. Foetal cerebral circulation is affected by maternal anxiety (Sjöström et al., 1997) through high cortisol levels, which, when transmitted to the foetus, increase the baby's hyper-reactivity (Wadha et al., 1993). Obstetric complications are also associated with both heightened maternal anxiety and perinatal distress.

Clearly, as prophylactic treatment is indicated, midwives, health visitors, and other perinatal practitioners are in a prime position to identify distress and refer women for psychotherapy, ideally during pregnancy. But what does such "distress" consist of?

Placental paradigm

Depending on the "emotional climate" of her inner world, a pregnant woman views her inmate as vulnerable or thriving, damaged or demanding, perfect or potentially harmful (Figure 1.1). Concurrently, she might see herself as bountiful or deficient, hospitable or invaded. Accordingly, their emotional connection is deemed reciprocal, while at other times it feels asymmetrical, incongruous, or antithetical, a one-way process that privileges either herself (as generous, withholding, or exploited), or focuses on the baby (as greedy, or needy, malevolent or benign, etc.). Depending on her own psycho-history, current mood, physical condition, and the baby's movements, one pregnant woman may oscillate several times a day, alternating between both positive and negative fantasies, while another maintains a "fixed" idea of the primal interchange.

Thus, one pregnant woman might experience the give-and-take between herself and her unknown baby as a pleasurable communion, while another is filled with a sense of alarm at the foetus pumping

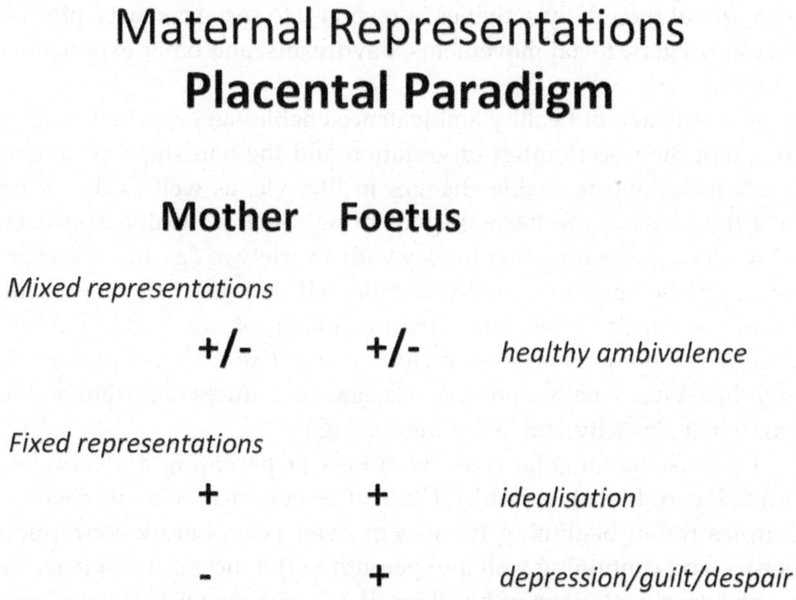

Maternal Representations
Placental Paradigm

Mother   Foetus

Mixed representations

+/-	**+/-**	*healthy ambivalence*

Fixed representations

+	**+**	*idealisation*
-	**+**	*depression/guilt/despair*

Figure 1.1.   Maternal representations.

waste into her. Endangered by the foetus leaching her internal resources, an expectant mother might be unable to stop binging or smoking
to assuage her escalating anxiety. Another feels guilt-ridden, believing
she is insufficiently nurturing to sustain the pregnancy or produce a
normal, viable baby. Experiencing persecutory feelings of invasion or
dissipation and exploitation, yet another resorts to retaliatory behaviour, such as bashing or starving the "parasitic" foetus.

Clearly, her personal stance, with its underpinning mental config-
uration, reflects a woman's self-esteem and generative psycho-history
(including previous miscarriages or abortions, painful experiences
of disappointment or betrayal, or happy ones of love and trust). A
woman with a robust sense of self, who has self-reflectively come to
terms with her own parents' human fallibility, will be resilient enough
to tolerate the discomforts and risks of pregnancy through trust in her
own "good-enoughness" now, and as mother to a less-than-perfect
future baby.

Observations of non-clinical groups (for instance, childbirth education classes and community samples) indicate that pregnant women
who are confident in their capacities and more secure in their attachments experience a rich mixture of feelings and fantasies. These vary
throughout their daily activities in response to social contacts, physiological triggers, foetal movements, daydreams, and other experiential
stimuli.

This attitude of healthy ambivalence enables an expectant mother
to accept the uncertainties of gestation and the hardships of parenthood, including inevitable changes in lifestyle, as well as the many
joys (and losses) motherhood will bring. Such a flexible approach
allows an expectant mother to play with a variety of daydream scenarios about her unknown baby and herself as a mother, during the
course of which further digestive processing of her own childhood
experiences occurs. However, maintaining a "fixed" idea of pregnancy
and the foetus, whether positive or negative, reduces the likelihood of
emotional elasticity and "working through".

Preconscious mental representations of parenting are complex,
multi-layered, and variable. Clinical experience with women or
couples (often beginning months or even years before conception
occurs, and continuing well into parenthood) indicates that a person's
mental representations of him/herself as carer are multi-determined.
Imagery consists of a composite schema related to one's own emo-

tional experience (or "internal model") of being parented. Childhood events and recollections of early care mingle with subsequent encounters with nurturing or rejecting others. Adult expectations, hopes, and conscious wishes join less conscious configurations, including identifications with the baby, and with past carers and/or aggressors.

However, in addition to such residues, during the emotional upheaval of pregnancy and early motherhood, unresolved past issues are powerfully reactivated.

"Contagious arousal"

For all of us, our sense of self is constituted through reflective mirroring (Winnicott, 1967), and "affective biofeedback" provided by sensitive carers (Gergely & Watson, 1996), which forms the basis of our capacity for our understanding of mental states in ourselves and others (Fonagy et al., 1991). Such parental "mentalization" echoes the "metabolisation" of acute preverbal anxieties, which paves the way to internalisation of a capacity for self-containment (Bion, 1962). Parenting revives this procedural experience with an intensity that relates to intentional and unwitting "messages", including projective distortions. Emotional understanding is also composed of residues of the archaic carer's own unconscious sense of self—as mother, sexual woman, and agential person—in the world beyond domesticity. All this might or might not have been processed along the way, both by the original carer and the current (expectant) mother whose composite representations of motherhood also reflect imagery of her own baby-self in the mind of her archaic primary carers, thus replicating the emotional climate of her own primary care.

Those of us who work with couples know that each partner brings to the relationship their own early attachment experience, which affects expectations of sexual intimacy and parenting styles. Thus co-parenting partners' "orientations" differ, with discrepant or dovetailing facets. The degree to which each partner can meet the other's need for trust, responsiveness, and protection will be affected by, and in turn influence, their own current internal models of parenting.

A new baby is intensely disturbing. For a couple, the arrival of a needy, vulnerable being alters the emotional balance that sexual partners worked out between themselves. Sibling alliances, too, change,

altering the family constellation as the new baby becomes the young-
est, and the focus of special attention. For inexperienced primary
carers, and young siblings, exposure to the infant's preverbal raw feelings and neediness resonates with primitive substrates within the
internal world. In addition, unmediated contact with primal substances (amnion, lochia, colostrum, urine, baby faeces, mucus, breast
milk, posset, etc.) also evokes non-verbal procedural memories reacti-
vating sub-symbolic experience (Raphael-Leff, 2003). Such "contagious arousal" is further exacerbated by sleep deprivation, hormonal
fluctuations, and disconcerting unpredictability, especially for mothers who receive little practical support and replenishment of their own
emotional resources (Raphael-Leff, 2003).

Further destabilisation occurs due to dispersal of extended families and community networks for pregnant women and new parents
in westernised societies. Social stratification, urbanisation, and insula-
tion/isolation of smaller nuclear units result in intense dyadic relationships. However, in such close quarters there are few significant
members of extended families of origin to mitigate super-saturated
representations. In small isolated units, lack of intimate contact with
babies while growing up deprives people of opportunities to work
through their own unformulated infantile experiences in the presence
of siblings or cousins before becoming parents. Hence, the intensity of
arousal in first-time parents, who have had little close contact with
young babies before being given full responsibility for their own. Not
only are they inexperienced, but they are also ill-prepared for the
emotional impact of parenting, which retriggers unresolved early
issues pertaining to situations of abandonment and helplessness in
their own childhoods, traumatic states, including unmourned losses,
experiences of cruel goading, violence, or sexual abuse, and chronic
states of emotional deprivation or material adversity. Once again, the
more the archaic relationships and past events are subjected to a
process of evaluative self-reflection—able to be digested, updated,
and integrated into the fabric of daily life—the less obstructive are
these preconscious registrations in the present.

Orientations

While traditional societies provide guidelines for gestation and mothering, in accommodating to pregnancy and motherhood western women manifest a diversity of "orientations" (Raphael-Leff, 2005, 2011). These differing approaches to pregnancy and mothering reflect the complex internal emotional preoccupations and mental representations of self and baby. For instance, among "Facilitators" (as I named one group), a pregnant woman treats pregnancy as the pinnacle of her feminine identity, tending to identify with both the mother of her own gestation and the foetus inside her, with whom she feels in constant "communion". Post natally, she adapts to the baby, and opts for exclusive care, believing that she, the biological mother, is uniquely qualified to fathom the baby's communications. Having been primed by pregnancy and breastfeeding, she alone can really understand and gratify her baby's every need.

A contrasting response is that of a "Regulator", for whom pregnancy entails unavoidable discomfort necessary to get a baby. Aiming to disrupt her lifestyle as little as possible, the mother resolves to forego introspection, maternity clothes, and "mummy brain". She expects the baby to adapt to the household, and designates her maternal role as socialising the asocial baby. As mothering is seen as a learnt skill, and the baby as non-differentiating, she resolves to share care and provide continuity between carers by introducing a routine.

A third orientation is that of the "Reciprocator", who maintains mixed feelings about the joys and constraints that pregnancy and parenting entail. Experiencing the ambiguity and ambivalence (rather than defending against it through idealisation, like the Facilitator, or detachment, like the Regulator), this expectant mother remains open to all eventualities and, post natally, rather than adapting or expecting the baby's adaptation, negotiates each incident as it arises. A fourth "conflicted" group alternates inconsistently between the first two modes, during both pregnancy and labour, and post natally.

Responses to intervening factors, such as employment, differ according to orientation. Thus, for Facilitator working mothers, enforced separation from the young baby is excruciatingly painful, as they cannot envisage a replacement babyminder. Conversely, for a Regulator, distress lies in unmitigated contact, so that unemployment leads to enforced togetherness with the infant, and lack of meaningful adult company. Today, when economic recession results in high levels of male unemployment, the non-earning baby's father might involuntarily become drawn into primary childcare, thereby changing persistent patterns of female child-rearing. Fathers will respond according to their own orientations—"Participators" and "Reciprocators" rejoice while "Renouncers" could feel humiliated. The degree of commensurability of maternal and paternal orientations and ways in which they support each other or conflict alleviates or exacerbates post natal distress (Raphael-Leff, 1985, 2010).

Perinatal emotional disturbance

In the twenty-first century, the incidence of parental disturbance is very high. Close to half of western expectant and new parents experience some form of emotional disorder. Around a quarter of fathers, too, are prone to post natal disturbance (Ballard & Davies, 1996; Dudley et al., 2001). As noted above, precipitants of disturbance vary according to parental orientation, linked to an inability to fulfil one's own anticipated mode of parenting. Perinatal distress (between conception and the child's toddlerhood) reflects the discrepancy between a mother or father's expectations and their implementation. Also, in a two-parent family, the degree to which their respective orientations dovetail or conflict influences the level of friction within each couple.

Despite the current clinical focus on post natal depression (with guilt, anxiety, pervasive low mood, a sense of worthlessness, tendency to self-harm, and possible suicide), there is a wide spectrum of other potentially dangerous perinatal disorders that professionals ignore at their peril, especially where the baby is part of a delusional system. Antenatally as well as post natally, these range from persecutory disorders, including paranoia, phobias, and anxiety states (with a threat of punitive caring patterns and retaliatory enactments), obsessionality with incapacitating compulsive rituals and a tendency to break through intrusive thoughts possibly leading to inordinate control and/or violent reactions, and dissociative disorders underpinning neglect and/or sexual abuse. Residues of abusive childhood experience manifest in a variety of presenting symptoms that range from mild to acute depressive or persecutory feelings, chronic anxiety, and manic disorders including promiscuity, sleep and eating disorders, alcohol, substance and drug abuse, fears about birth, and foetal or baby abuse.

To some parents, watching their baby thrive might, paradoxically, reactivate old grievances. In the context of social fragmentation and isolation, a father or mother might actually envy the good care their own baby receives, comparing it with their own perceived experience. The sense of injury manifests in syndromes of self-pity and desire for compensation for infantile deprivation, or fury and vengefulness over past humiliations. Unprocessed dissatisfactions tend to leak out in disruptive or repetitious behaviours between partners and with the baby, as tensions from each carer's internal world scenarios are played out externally.

Despite the common desire to be better parents than one's own, revitalised conflicts from the past are powerful impositions when the new baby is inserted into an old script and made to suffer its painful aspects. Insufficient emotional support and lack of choices constitute an important factor in post natal disturbance. It is well known that, when coupled with childhood adversity and/or lack of emotional support, parental vulnerability is increased. In addition, issues that were particularly antagonistic in a given family of origin (such as conflicts over autonomy and control, intimacy and psychic/bodily boundaries, triangulation and inclusion–exclusion, etc.) form weak links that are retriggered acutely for parents when their own child reaches a specific developmental phase. For many, preverbal infancy is difficult. For others, it is toddlerhood. This is particularly so with teenage parents for whom the newly walking child can be especially problematic. The exuberant toddler intent on omnipotently exploring the world at a time when motherhood or fatherhood hampers the teen in their own exploration is aggravating. Like the toddler, a young parent is still engaged with his/her own developmental tasks and anxiety-laden preoccupations about novelty and sameness, difference and separateness, bodily changes, loss of control, and containing aggression. In such cases, both toddler and teen experience internal struggles between emotional vulnerability and a sense of invincibility. When synchronised, similarities can create a bond of mutual excitement; however, when their intentions clash, a terrible battle of wills erupts, fuelled by furious frustration or intense despair (Raphael-Leff, 2012a,b).

But new parents of all ages find themselves susceptible to contagious arousal. To cope with a revival of unresolved childhood issues at the very time of the greatest demand on their adult capacities, some rigidify their defences by utilising primitive mechanisms of projection, heightened control, and denial. Others succumb to the onslaught of their own unresolved emotions, finding themselves overwhelmed at times by self-pity, or fury and vengefulness, self-loathing and worthlessness, or fears of being smothered or exploited, as they felt they were in childhood.

Unprocessed dissatisfactions tend to erupt in disruptive or repetitious parental behaviours and projections that inevitably affect the child in their care. The child's own symptoms (such as sleep disorders, feeding problems, and persistent crying, or behavioural disturbances during toddlerhood) both reflect family dynamics and further contribute to family symptomatology.

Perinatal psychotherapy

On the positive side, psychotherapeutic treatment can be effective with early referrals during the first thousand days "from womb to walking". Even a few sessions to address perinatal difficulties can achieve a great deal, precisely because unconscious issues have risen so close to the surface. As a by-product of retriggered unprocessed hurts, a major turning point occurs with recognition of one's own fallibility, and forgiveness of one's archaic carers' frailties and transgressions. Individual, parent–infant, or family therapy are all effective treatments in mitigating distress, and perinatal groups also form support networks.

Ideally, many parenting difficulties can be pre-empted by providing therapeutic space before the birth, thus establishing some insight before the onset of a connection to the baby that becomes pathological. Whether cohabiting or not, even weekly couple therapy is often sufficient to restore the balance in a troubled relationship between expectant partners, or defuse an unendurable situation between co-parents. Cases of profound insecurity involving a deeper sense of betrayal and fewer good internal resources necessitate longer-term individual sessions, and sometimes prolonged treatment, ideally beginning during pregnancy for the expectant parent to work through the cumulative transgenerational disturbance before it invades the relationship with the baby and/or partner.

Finally, to end on a practical note, when resources are scarce (as they are increasingly becoming in the National Health Service), it is my contention that mental health priorities must centre on three focal areas: prevention; detection of high-risk groups; early referral for treatment.

Conclusions

- Given the growing evidence that antenatal parental disturbance affects the baby, it is important to increase perinatal mental health provisions. "Talking cures" during pregnancy explore unprocessed issues, prophylactically modifying fixed internal representations and emotional suffering before the birth.
- Women's ubiquitous use of antenatal services, including breast-feeding and well-baby clinics, offer screening opportunities and educational enhancement to understand infant non-verbal communication and emotional states.
- Midwives and health visitors can be trained to identify perinatal disturbance and to provide support built up through trust in continuity of care.
- Perinatal therapy that pre-empts and resolves distortions in emotional contact with the baby reduces future difficulties and the cost of treating established conditions.
- Finally, personal orientations are indicative of specific needs and associated with diverse pathogenic experience, vulnerabilities, and protective factors. It is, therefore, important to help women achieve their own birth plans and preferred mode of parenting, and to provide choices tailored to these subgroups.

To sum up, precisely because the period from womb to walking is a time of heightened passion and contagious arousal, with help it can potentially foster an empathic parent–infant emotional dialogue and a chance of healthy growth.

References

Ballard, C., & Davies, R. (1996). Postnatal depression in fathers. *International Review of Psychiatry*, 8: 65–71.
Barker, D. J. P. (1999). Early growth and cardiovascular disease. *Archives of Disease in Childhood*, 80: 305–307.

Bion, W. R. (1962). A theory of thinking. *International Journal of Psychoanalysis, 43*: 306–310.

Copper, R. I., Goldenberg, R. L., Das, A., Elder, N., Swain, M., Norman, G., Ramsey, R., Cotroneo, P., Collins, B. A., Johnson, F., Jones, P., & Meier, A. M. (1996). The preterm prediction study: maternal stress is associated with spontaneous pre-term birth at less than 35 weeks gestation. *American Journal of Obstetrics & Gynecology, 175*: 1286–1292.

Dudley, M., Roy, K., Kelk, N., & Bernard, D. (2001). Psychological correlates of depression in fathers and mothers in the first postnatal year. *Journal of Reproductive & Infant Psychology, 19*: 187–202.

Fine, K. (2014). *Donor Conception For Life: Psychoanalytic Perspectives on Building a Family With Donor Conception*. London: Karnac.

Fonagy, P., Steele, M., Moran, G., Steele, H., & Higgitt, A. (1991). The capacity for understanding mental states. The reflective self in parent and child and its significance for security of attachment. *Infant Mental Health Journal, 13*: 200–217.

Gergely, G., & Watson, J. S. (1996). The social biofeedback theory of parental affect-mirroring. *International Journal of Psychoanalysis, 77*: 1181–1212.

O'Connor, T. G., Ben-Shlomo, Y., Heron, J., Golding, J., Adams, D., & Glover, V. (2005). Perinatal anxiety predicts individual differences in cortisol in pre-adolescent children. *Biological Psychiatry, 58*: 211–221.

Raphael-Leff, J. (1985). Facilitators and regulators, participators and renouncers: mothers' and fathers' orientations towards pregnancy and parenthood. *Journal of Psychosomatic Obstetrics and Gynaecology, 4*: 169–184.

Raphael-Leff, J. (1993). *Pregnancy: The Inside Story*. London: Karnac.

Raphael-Leff, J. (Ed.) (2003). *Parent–Infant Psychodynamics: Wild Things, Mirrors and Ghosts*. London: Whurr.

Raphael-Leff, J. (2005). Psychotherapy in the reproductive years. In: G. Gabbard, J. Beck, & J. Holmes (Eds.), *The Concise Oxford Textbook of Psychotherapy* (pp. 367–380). Oxford: Oxford University Press.

Raphael-Leff, J. (2010). Parental orientations: mothers' and fathers' patterns of pregnancy, parenting and the bonding process. In: S. Tyano, M. Keren, H. Herman, & J. Cox (Eds.), *Parenthood and Mental Health: A Bridge Between Infant and Adult Psychiatry* (pp. 9–30). London: Blackwell-Wiley.

Raphael-Leff, J. (2011). *Psychological Processes of Childbearing* (4th edn). London: Anna Freud Centre.

Raphael-Leff, J. (2012a). "Terrible twos" and "terrible teens". The importance of play. *Journal of Infant, Child, & Adolescent Psychotherapy, 11*(4): 299–315.

Raphael-Leff, J. (2012b). *Working with Teenage Parents: Handbook of Theory & Practice.* London: Anna Freud Centre.

Sjöström, K., Valentin, L., Thelin, T., & Marsál, K. (1997). Maternal anxiety in late pregnancy and fetal hemodynamics. *European Journal of Obstetrics & Gynaecology and Reproductive Biology, 74*: 149–155.

Susman, E. J., Scheelk, K. H., Ponirakis, A., & Gariepy, J. L. (2001). Maternal prenatal, postpartum and concurrent stressors and temperament in 3-year-olds: a person and variable analysis. *Developmental Psychopathology, 13*: 629–652.

Teixeira, J. M. A., Fisk, N. M., & Glover, V. (1999). Association between maternal anxiety in pregnancy and increased uterine artery resistance index: cohort based study. *British Medical Journal, 318*: 153–157.

Thompson, C., Syddall, H., Rodin, I., Osmond, C., & Barker, D. J. P. (2001). Birth weight and the risk of depressive disorder in late life. *British Journal of Psychiatry, 179*: 450–455.

Wadha, P. D., Sandman, C. A., Porto, M., Dunkel-Schetter, C., & Barite, T. J. (1993). The association between prenatal stress and infant birth weight and gestational age at birth: a prospective investigation. *American Journal of Obstetrics & Gynecology, 169*: 858–865.

Winnicott, D. W. (1967). Mirror-role of mother and family in child development. In: P. Lomas (Ed.), *The Predicament of the Family: A Psychoanalytical Symposium.* London: Hogarth Press.

Zeanah, C. H., Benoit, D., Hirshberg, L., Barton, M. L., & Regan, C. (1994). Mothers' representations of their infants are concordant with infant attachment classifications. *Developmental Issues in Psychiatry and Psychology, 1*: 9–18.

CHAPTER TWO

Sharing joyful friendship and imagination for meaning with infants, and their application in early intervention

Colwyn Trevarthen

"In healthy families, a baby forms a secure attachment with her parents as naturally as she breathes, eats, smiles and cries. This occurs easily because of her parents' attuned interactions with her. Her parents notice her physiological/affective states and they respond to her sensitively and fully. Beyond simply meeting her unique needs, however, her parents "dance" with her. Hundreds of times, day after day, they dance with her. There are other families where the baby neither dances nor even hears the sound of any music. In these families she does not form such secure attachments. Rather, her task – her continuous ordeal – is to learn to live with parents who are little more than strangers. Babies who live with strangers do not live well or grow well"

(Hughes, 2006, p. ix)

Introduction

Help for young children in trouble and their distressed families needs to recognise and support impulses of natural sympathy that are in every human being from the start, and that try to grow with motives and feelings that need warm human company. Any intervention should attempt to find and encourage this eager joy for shared affection and fun when there is confusion and defensiveness, fear and anger, or when there has been hurt and the result is silence.

Research into how a person grows from conception proves that we each create a proactive and imaginative Self, one that is ready to live with a hopeful sense of purpose (Trevarthen et al., 2006). A newborn baby's body is expressive of this personality. It tells us that the young mind anticipates the pleasure of moving coherently and well, and that it feels anxiety about having difficulty or pain in fulfilling its functions and intentions. Eyes, head, and hands shift with intricate curiosity, signalling purposes and feelings for others' attention. Right from the start a baby has a special sensitivity for how the movements of another person transmit the quality of their feelings. Many expressive signs of human self-awareness and readiness for communication can be observed in foetuses (Piontelli, 1992), and they respond to human vitality. They and their sensibility do not have to be learnt after birth (Trevarthen, 2011a).

The infant's signs of human feeling can powerfully attract the sympathetic affection of a parent and promote attachment. If these signs are not known and responded to with warmth and joy, the signals of the positive emotions that cause them can turn to expressions of withdrawal and distress. They are special adaptations of the human spirit for sharing experience in play, and for proudly creating and learning habits that can become meaningful social events in the company of many friends. Eventually, the infant's acts of communication lead to the learning of words, so the expressions of self-confident agency and adventure can become stories in the ancient language of a community. From birth, a contented and lively baby can entertain with "projects of moving" that are felt by mother and father to be interesting "stories", and the baby can imitate expressions of others and exchange them with variation in dialogue. Absence of companions and unkindness inhibit the infant's curiosity and learning, causing shame (Trevarthen, 2001a, 2005a). The stories become bitter and avoidant.

We have made studies of how infants develop the skill of sharing intimate rhythmic moving with persons whom they love and trust (Trevarthen, 1999, 2005b). These have led to a theory of story-making "communicative musicality". A baby has innate motives regulated by different emotions (Frank & Trevarthen, 2012; Trevarthen, 1998, 2009a), and through the first year of life these open the way to different interests and skills. There are three kinds of innate motives:

- those that regulate feelings of vitality and security inside the body as it grows in size, strength, and skill;
- Those that give rise to aesthetic apprehension of objects and curiosity that leads to learning of their uses by body movements;
- Those that lead to moral emotions of love and admiration that guide co-operative action and playful rivalry in sharing intentions and meanings with companions, or of fear and anger that guard against, or resist, unfriendly attentions (Trevarthen, 2011b).

The different emotions so clearly displayed by infants inform us about forms of therapy that do not need words (Trevarthen, 2005b). They tell us about the causes of pain in the hopelessness of depression (Panksepp & Watt, 2011), and they advise how therapy might help (Fosha et al., 2009; Trevarthen, 2003).

My account supports the eighteenth-century theory of Adam Smith concerning "innate motives of sympathy" leading to the intuitive learning of self-conscious and self-critical habits and co-operative moral sentiments, and also Darwin's nineteenth-century theory of the evolution of emotions and their social functions. It refers to the concept of the human being that Charles Sherrington developed from his physiological research in the early twentieth century, and his account of the innate "zest for life" that every organism has from its beginning and how it is expressed in human actions.

We have abundant evidence now that sympathetic regulation of rhythms and narrations of human relationships has evolved as a foundation for *intimate* family life and development of self-confidence in society, for *inventive* discovery of artful experience in a community, for *informative* communication in mastery of technical co-operation, and for acceptance of *instructive* or *imperative* principles to ensure harmony in society and its more formal rules and rituals. Language is a late player in this game of shared expressive movement and participation in cultural meaning, and it has musical/poetic precursors that remain as basic syntactic forces.

I hope to clarify the limitations of current theories of automatic one-way reactions of "empathy" that are said to give us understanding *about* another person's feelings, and how impressions of these are supposed to be transformed by a process of learning or education into "interpretations" *about* other people's expressions to construct representations *about* "mentalizing" and an articulate "theory of mind" (Trevarthen, 2009a). The "aboutness" is too preoccupied with the outside conditions and facts to be taken in. The behaviours of infants are better understood as actively motivated, from within, by a desire for two-way sympathy *with* others.

It is important also to note that evidence from experimental brain science and the effects of severe deprivation of experience on the "plasticity" of the young child's brain needs balancing with information concerning the "constructive and creative processes" of emotion by which the brain is formed, that are active in it from the start, and that become part of communication (Trevarthen, 2001b, 2009b). How the brain develops depends first on the child's imaginative and passionate curiosity and hope for experience that makes satisfying sense, and second on their responses to the sympathy of loving company. All forms of therapy and teaching need to respect both these motives.

How to intervene to help a young child in trouble

"Intervention" means coming in between an unwanted cause and its effect. Surgeons intervene by operating on a person's body to remove or unblock a cause of suffering, and teachers intervene to overcome lack of knowledge by instructing the learner's mind. However, in each case, the intervention needs to recognise and attempt to use a "two-way", or interpersonal, approach with respect for vitality and emotions. Phoebe Caldwell, who works with profoundly disabled people, teaches that we have to meet the feelings and urges of the person in intimacy if we want to help them escape their isolation (Caldwell & Horwood, 2007).

Yet, institutions and experts are preoccupied with their structures, rules, and instruments. They might lack attention to the complex expectancies and hope of a young life. If the belief is that the human being at birth is a mindless creature, we need think only of protecting it from injury and feeding it when it is hungry. If the newborn self is purely organic in this limited sense, then all that is required, when development or the environment are defective, is to correct anatomical or physiological faults, to administer to the reflex needs for comfort and nourishment, and to train "state regulation". This has been the dominant scientific, medical, or psychological model of the inexperienced human being, and the map for any search for "evidence of good practice".

However, that model, we now know, is far from an accurate description of the state of vitality in newborn human nature.

A new psychology discovers surprising talents and expectations in naïve human life

The old model of thinking of the newborn infant as helpless and ready to be shaped by his environment prevented us from seeing his *power as a communicant* in the early mother–father–infant interaction. To see the neonate as chaotic or insensitive provided us with the capacity to see ourselves as acting "on" rather than "with" him. (Brazelton, 1979, p. 79, my italics)

Paediatric medical practice, by taking a different approach open to discover neglected innate powers of self-creation and self-expression, has found that a newborn normally has a well co-ordinated body that moves its many parts with elegant precision, engaging external events selectively with sight, touch, or hearing. The baby also has an adventurous mind and expressive movements of emotion that seek human company. The newborn cannot talk and knows nothing of the world, but knows her own body and how it feels in movement, and she can be awake to share it with another's vitality and friendship. The baby is intelligent, and can think and imagine and make intentions clear by communicating with what Daniel Stern (1985, 1993) calls "implicit relational knowing" with "relational emotions", which, moreover, become essential for learning language (Lüdtke, 2012).

The change of understanding about what an infant can do and can feel was due to influences from four directions, which came to life in the 1960s—the result of rich communications between disciplines that used observation, description, and careful reflection to explore the depths of innate human motives.

The post Freudian paediatrics and child psychiatry of Brazelton (1973) and Daniel Stern (1985) made doctors more aware of the sensibilities and needs of infants. They clarified the rich communication of the emotional bond, the vital importance of which had been revealed by the shocking effects of loss of maternal care described by Rene Spitz (1945) and John Bowlby (1951). They found institutionalised infants failed to speak and died early, and that a hospitalised baby became deeply depressed when separated from maternal care. For such children, the appropriate "intervention" has to be immediate removal from the institution and placement in the affectionate and responsive attention of those who can act as a warm and playful family. Brazelton (1961, 1979) made a revolution in care of newborn infants, using the baby to teach new parents about communication, and Stern fostered attention to the pleasures of play with a young infant in response to a mother's affectionate attunement (Stern, 1974, 1977).

A post Piagetian infant psychology developed by Jerome Bruner (1968), Margaret Donaldson (1978), and others perceived young children as both curious and sociable, seeking not only how to handle and perceive objects, but how to share perceptions of the world by joint imagination for objects and their usefulness with other people, and by intimate communication of interests and emotions. It became clear that for both psychoanalytic understanding of therapy and for Piaget's theory of how epistemological awareness develops from the way a child uses objects for herself, knowledge of the original richness of human motives was needed. An infant was seen to have thoughtful imagination and strong aesthetic and moral affections, and to be sensitive to how other people seek to be in relation with these talents. The same primary talents are a strong foundation for recovery from neglect or maltreatment.

Ethology and anthropology had discovered important life principles in animals that psychologists had been neglecting; how their natural intelligence drives learning and how their social life—from insects to birds and mammals—depends on semiotic behaviours. In other words, on the animals' imaginative signalling by rituals of movement and imitation of them (Darwin, 1872; von Uexküll, 1957). Research on human postural communication of Albert Scheflen (1972), and "kinesics" of Ray Birdwhistell (1970) traced from film how, in casual conversations between adults, the gestures, facial expressions, and vocalisations are "orchestrated" with intricate precision of timing as non-verbal "body language" (Bullowa, 1979a). At the same time, English readers received news of the pioneering motor physiology of the Russian scientist Nicholai Bernstein (1967), who, by analysing films, had made evident how all motor tasks carried out by a complex human body require prospective co-ordination by "motor images" with sensitive proprioceptive regulation of the muscle actions of the whole body in the context of changing forces from the environment.

William Condon and Lou Sander (1974) demonstrated inter-synchrony and "interactional participation" between adult and infant, while Mary Catherine Bateson (1971, 1979), using insights from anthropology and comparative linguistics, discovered, just after her own daughter was born how kinesics could be richly applied to examine the "exquisite ritual courtesy" of "proto-conversations" between mothers and infants. She revealed, with the aid of detailed study of a single film of a mother with a nine-week-old baby, the complexity and finesse of their non-verbal communication. The inter-synchrony she describes is really an inter-sympathy, a joining in time of feelings for and with each other.

All these developments constitute a radical departure from mechanistic, inanimate, explanations of human actions as behaviour triggered by stimuli, from a psychology that only searched for ways to teach or "condition" human behaviour for social purposes. They announced that the natural powers of the human spirit in action, from which adult skills grow, are present from birth, with their motives and affective regulations. Human curiosity does not come about as a product of social learning or out of the articulation of cognitive "theories of mind", although acquired habits of action, awareness, and belief certainly grow to elaborate them.

Nearly all the important actors in this new infant psychology contributed to a book entitled *Before Speech*, published in 1979, in which the editor, Margaret Bullowa, who had been using film to study language development, recruited many researchers from the USA and the UK to explain their exciting findings about non-verbal communication (Bullowa, 1979b). However, Stern and Bruner were two names missing from that particular book.

Daniel Stern and colleagues in New York had applied William Condon's demonstration of inter-synchrony between the speech of an adult and the limb movements of a newborn in their analysis of the co-ordination of vocalisations in mother–infant play (Beebe et al., 1979; Jaffe & Felstein, 1970). Stern (1985) used this work to transform psychoanalytic theory of the development of the self into a new view of the interpersonal awareness and motivated self of the baby. He explained the collaborative support a mother gives for progressive stages in development that are motivated from the baby. This has led to a theory of the core process of interpersonal awareness in arts and all cultural achievements through direct transmission of "forms of vitality" (Stern, 2010). A complementary account has been offered by the Norwegian sociologist and cybernetics expert, Stein Bråten (2009), who speaks of "felt immediacy" as a foundation for intersubjective awareness and the acquisition of language.

Bruner (1972, 1977, 1983, 1986, 1990) expanded and enriched our view of human nature and its imaginative powers. He combined a view of the practical use of perceptual discrimination to serve personal and social needs, and anthropological insights into the processes that transmit knowledge, shifting developmental psychology from its obsession with detection and discrimination about facts in the world to a more alive appreciation of the "story-telling" of human nature— the imaginative making of meaning. His entry into infancy research (Bruner, 1968), which redirected psychology at the Harvard Center for Cognitive Studies, making it more culture-sensitive, inspired me to occupy myself fully with research on the development of agency and communication in companionship between the infant and his family, and how this leads to awareness of rituals, tools, and language. I applied ideas and methods from my previous work on the psychobiology of action and visual awareness and, with Bruner, Brazelton, and Martin Richards (an ethologist of maternal behaviour of mammals), applied film to a detailed recording and analysis of how infants a few weeks old move to make sense of objects and people, distinguishing the affordances.

Developing a theory of infant intersubjectivity
by tracing changes in motives and interests

In Bullowa's book, I described how the work started in Harvard was continued in Edinburgh with a group of very talented students (Trevarthen, 1979). I proposed that analysis of the "chats" we had filmed between two-month-olds and their mothers proved that the babies could communicate with the motives and feelings of their mothers by an immediate innate sense of what lay behind their facial expressions, eye movements, hand gestures, and vocalisations. We found evidence that the babies were active as expressive persons and strongly motivated to share mutual awareness. Following Joanna Ryan, who described a philosophy of a "communicative competence" that leads to the learning of language (Ryan, 1974), I called their ability to pick up mental states by sensing motives and feelings in another's movements "primary intersubjectivity", using a term to describe the first stage in the development of the shared experience of all human engagements, whether mediated by language or not.

Through longitudinal studies with film, we traced how expressive movements and playful communication developed as the baby's body grew, and how habits developed for being part of daily life with the mother. Within a few months the mother's special attention led her to guide the infant's less emotional "scientific" interest in mastery of objects, which develops greatly after three months, so that it became part of shared games and meanings (Trevarthen, 1977, 1998). We tested the feelings of babies for what they were trying to do, including the effects of interrupting or "perturbing" the mother's contact with her baby (Murray & Trevarthen, 1985; Trevarthen et al., 1981). In this way, Lynne Murray clarified how a mother's postnatal depression could affect the baby's development (Murray, 1992). Study of the emotional "musicality" of the mother's speech and the baby's vocal responses has helped us comprehend the intimate emotional relationship between them, and how it is affected by the mother's emotional health (Gratier & Apter-Danon, 2009; Marwick & Murray, 2009).

Our subjects showed different attitudes to people and inanimate objects from the start, and their attentive mothers changed their play to meet and support the infant's changing curiosity as the motor and perceptual capacities grew. With affection and joy, the mothers grew with their babies' interests. They played games with them using exaggerated and gently "teasing" tricks of expression, and when the baby was engrossed in an object, they tried to capture this impulse in carefully measured and often repeated games. Together, they developed pleasure from habits of communication, which benefited the self-confidence of both of them, and the babies happily became "show-offs", watching carefully how their families responded (Reddy, 2008; Trevarthen, 1990).

A crucial change in "co-operative awareness" was discovered in 1974 by Penelope Hubley. She was following play between an infant girl, Tracy, and her mother on film, and observed that, at nine months old, Tracy started to be curious in a new way about her mother's ideas and ways of using objects (Trevarthen, 1977; Trevarthen & Hubley, 1978). She would even "assist" her mother to complete her intentions if something was getting in the way. Mother and daughter began to exchange and build on ideas of how to use objects in systematic constructive ways, not just for fun, but more "seriously" to invent and to collaborate in joint projects. Up until then, Tracy had been happy to follow her mother in games invented to amuse her. Now, she took more initiative and began to be very willing to take "instructions" or "directions" of how to perform a simple co-operative task, to accept invitations to build with objects, to put them in an indicated container, or to accept that an object needed to be moved or displayed in a particular way. Her mother intuitively detected this new willingness for sharing purposes, and started to give indication how Tracy might complete part actions she made, or how her pointing movements could be complied with. The change in her baby transformed what the mother said. Instead of asking "questions" and trying to attract Tracy's attention, she simply pointed or gave instructions or "directives" about what to do (Trevarthen & Marwick, 1986). She spontaneously became a teacher as well as a companion in discovery.

In the preceding five months, Tracy had been a spirited and wilful playmate, enjoying the artfulness of games; first in body movement, taking part in "person–person" games her mother invented, then in "person–person–object" games involving chasing and teasing with a toy that Tracy wanted to use. Now, at nine months, she was a confident co-worker in what we called "Secondary intersubjectivity" or "person–person–object" tasks where practical intentions and social gestures were shared in a co-operative and knowing "business-like" way. Hubley followed up her discovery with a longitudinal video study of five infant girls through the critical ages from eight to twelve months. All babies changed at nine months, just as Tracy had done. They began to be eager to "share a task" (Hubley & Trevarthen, 1979).

Gradually, I have built on our findings to develop a theory of how experience is shared in dialogues and in lively games, and how what the linguist Michael Halliday (1975) calls "acts of meaning" are performed and understood before words are learnt (Trevarthen, 1987, 1998). Clearly, language is learnt within or from the narratives of intimate communication ruled by shared emotions. Speaking is not the start of meaningful communication, and neither is it the beginning of artful story-making. The stages of development of self–other consciousness and the meanings that can be created from it correspond with those identified by Stern (1985), and we confirm his representation that they are added like geological strata, the later ones building on and extending the competence practised from the start, which continue to be important.

Using stages of infant intelligence as a frame for assisting development

We can summarise the important strata of activity, understanding, and sociability as follows to trace how the baby learns new ways of mastering and exploiting the self-conscious and other-conscious embodied mind he or she is born with (Frank & Trevarthen, 2012; Trevarthen, 1998, 1990).

In the first three months, beginning with intimate sharing of feelings and imitation of marked expressions from birth, the baby joins in proto-conversations, showing, and sharing, emotions of affection or mistrust, and begins to take part in play and teasing. If the mother fails to respond and just looks on with a blank face, the baby is disturbed and worried. By four months, the baby explores the nearby world and reaches for objects, and the games become more lively. This is a time when infants show interest in watching themselves in a mirror, and sometimes they are "self-conscious" in response to close attention from another, or from their own gaze reflected in a mirror (Reddy, 2008). They also begin to be wary of strangers or to feel shy. Five months is a time of growing curiosity and pleasure for sharing ritual play in action games and baby songs. Some of the baby's behaviours with a familiar person seem to be "joking" or "mocking" (Trevarthen, 1990).

Six- to eight-month-olds are cleverer and more self-possessed. They show off more and tease, but are also more fearful of strangers. They are becoming attached to the habits of their life with the family, and share jokes with the mother, father, or siblings as special friends. They are learning "how to behave", because they want to be part of the customs others respect, but they are quite capable of making fun of the rules. At nine months, an infant loves clowning and teasing and can show strong independence of will and intense interest in mastering objects, or using them "properly" by imitation. They act ashamed when with a stranger, worried that he or she does not understand what, for the baby, is felt to be important because it can be shared with the family.

At ten to twelve months comes the breakthrough in co-operative awareness and great interest in sharing meanings. With it comes a readiness for learning words to name people, objects, and actions, which begins in the child's second year.

Throughout life, the foundation for sharing life experiences and building relationships is the intimate and immediate *love* of the first narratives composed between a parent and a newborn. As the energy and agility of the infant's body grows, and the head is strongly supported and more mobile, the special senses of sight, touch, and hearing become sharper and more discriminating. The baby is enabled to be a more lively and self-conscious playmate, and, in turn, becomes more acutely aware of needing special people who appreciate the clever tricks the baby has learnt. Now the routine of an action game, like "Clappa, clappa handies", can be displayed with an intent look and smile of "pride" to a familiar person who can be trusted to give a confirming response (Trevarthen, 1990, 2008). However, with this self-awareness as an actor "on stage" comes a sense of vulnerability to misunderstanding of "how to fit in". That is why a stranger is regarded with doubt and caution, and the baby might seem timid and show "shame" (Trevarthen, 2005a). Then, after the appearance of secondary intersubjectivity near the end of the first year, the baby, now nearly a toddler, is seriously interested in meaningful *work*, treating objects as tools with proper uses.

The progress from *love*, to *play* and then to *work* seems to be a formula for an effective therapy, one that builds companionship from affection and trust (Trevarthen, 2011c). This therapy will need to be artful, not just corrective or instructive, as, for example, in the cognitive behaviour therapies advised for autism. Music therapy, drawing on the innate musical appreciation found in infants, can be very effective in helping a young autistic child or a child with a severe developmental disorder to be more open and happier in engagement (Wigram & Elefant, 2009). It can also be used by a skilled practitioner to bring peace to a traumatised child (Robarts, 2009), to raise shared joy in a community (Pavlicevic & Ansdell, 2009), or to overcome terrors resulting from the traumatic effects of war (Osborne, 2009).

The different self-created events and life experiences of a baby and their essential steps in sharing new ideas with a loved one are potential guides for a therapist (Frank & Trevarthen, 2012). They give indications of how to meet the problems a child might have when life has been too difficult for normal growth of understanding and self-confidence in acting and in communicating (Brazelton, 1993; Trevarthen & Aitken, 2003). Sometimes, the infant or young child feels it is necessary to address the self-conscious interest and method of doing things alone with objects, to assist self-mastery and growth of knowledge, as Geoffrey Waldon advised (Solomon, 2012), practice with which inspired the method of "functional learning" to help children with autism and other disorders of movement that affect their relating to people (Stroh et al., 2008). The stages of development have provided a frame for developing video interaction guidance to aid emotional development and learning (Kennedy et al., 2011; Trevarthen, 2011c), which Hughes (2006) has also found important for assisting adoptive teenagers and their parents overcome conflicts and misunderstandings.

Defining precisely the parameters of creative musicality in communication with infants

In recent years, the dynamic emotional foundations for sharing stories of action and awareness that we have found in infancy, for building joint experience in creative "artful" play (Trevarthen, 2012a), have been examined closely with the help of insights from the science of music. A violinist and expert in musical acoustics, Stephen Malloch, has helped me analyse the rhythmic patterns, melodies, and narratives of baby songs and action games with infants (Malloch, 1999; Trevarthen, 1999, 2008, 2012b). We have edited a book on the theory of communicative musicality that grew from this work, in which experts from many fields of research and practice find evidence of the power of musical sound to carry appealing messages (Malloch &

Trevarthen, 2009). There is an abundance of information now on the musical awareness of infants and on their abilities to participate in games of musicality, following pioneering work by Hanuš and Mechtild Papoušek (Papoušek, H. 1996; Papoušek, M., 1994; Papoušek & Papoušek, 1981).

Musical analysis of baby songs, to which infants older than four months respond enthusiastically (Mazokopaki & Kugiumutzakis, 2009; Trevarthen, 1999), has revealed both that their affective tone is detected and that young infants attend to, and move with, the rhythms and narrative patterns or melodies of sound made by human movement (Trainor, 1996; Trevarthen, 1993, 1999). The baby soon learns certain cultural features of their parents' speech or music, mainly clearly intoned expressions of feeling, such as vowels and their presentation in rhyming pairs in the phrases of poetry or song. Infants share and learn the ways the mother "belongs" to her family and its culture (Custodero & Johnson-Green, 2003; Gratier & Trevarthen, 2007, 2008). A universal time pattern and pitch range of the notes or syllables, phrases, and verses of baby songs indicate that they are adapted to engage with innate bio-chronological and affective principles of human movement and self-regulation, to which the infant's listening is "attuned" (Stern et al., 1985). Innate properties of co-ordinated polyrhythmic body movement express the intrinsic motive pulse (IMP) of a human brain, and these rhythms carry the emotionally charged messages of communication, making it possible for minds to become affectively "in sync" (Gratier, 2008; Panksepp & Trevarthen, 2009; Trevarthen, 1999).

We have found that the human body is innately co-ordinated in rhythmic ways that both express thoughtful and aesthetically appreciated vitality of moving, and are powerfully adapted to communicate. Thus, music may be defined as the innate ability to make and hear sounds of the human body moving in communicable ways. The infants confirm Bruner's claim that we are "story making creatures" (Bruner, 1990), for babies can join with delight in poetic and musical story-making many months before they can name anything in words. Ellen Dissanayake (2000) calls this "art and intimacy", and considers it the source of all human cultural inventiveness. Peter Hobson (2002) describes communication with infants as "the cradle of thought". Neither art nor thinking requires the specification of reference in language, though they may be greatly extended and enriched by verbal or "declarative" memory (Tulving, 2005; Vandekerckhove & Panksepp, 2011).

"Story-making" with mother from birth, and the making of an infant's autobiography

Recently we have, through close observation of the attuned behaviours of a mother and her son, collected evidence that a newborn baby, if not sleepy or distressed by hunger or pain, can "share a story", enjoying the unfolding plot or "project" of imagining with a sensitive and "interested" parent (Trevarthen & Delafield-Butt, 2012). In the video, the baby clearly has an urge to move body, limbs, head, mouth, and eyes through self-generated time in coherent "propositional" and "dramatic" ways, and these creations or compositions are attractive and seductive to the mother, giving her wonder and joy. His right hand is particularly active and some of its delicate gestures "describe" and synchronise precisely with expressive phrases of the mother's admiring speech. This demonstrates how it is that an adult can become part of the self-sensing human vitality of a young child, and how the child's sensitivity to the mother could be a clear pointer for how to give support and encouragement to a baby in difficulty, as Brazelton (1973, 1979) has long proclaimed and demonstrated. One has to be ready to feel and to enjoy the pulse and dancing compositions of the wakeful human spirit as expressed by how the body moves, as a loving mother or father naturally is.

Even before birth, in the mother's womb, both a closely regulated physiological co-operation with her vital functions and a communication by movements and perceptions that anticipate the rhythms and its emotional evaluations of human conversation are possible for a foetus. Birth gives prospects for a much wider experience of the world in which many events and objects can be recognised and emotionally valued, but the initial state of human experience is generated within the self, and in intimate co-operation with the vitality of a special other, primarily the mother. Within a few weeks, the baby is mastering the theatrical conventions of action songs. In joyful games of teasing and joking, the baby tests the prospects of shared play enthusiastically, humorously, and provocatively (Reddy, 2008). Bruner used analysis of the game of "peek-a-boo" to illustrate the joy of "story-making" as a bridge to learning how to talk (Bruner & Sherwood, 1975). There is a marvellous readiness for creativity and cultural learning (Trevarthen, 2012a), and this grows in self-confidence quickly if supported.

Making the story of one's self, with moral values

In the middle of the first year, the fun of story-telling games is strengthened by the development of a more extensive memory that expands the mind's "locus of concern" (Donaldson, 1992), and the baby has a sharper sense of self or "character", and is clearly developing a "personal history". Vandekerckhove and Panksepp (2011), building on Tulving's theory of the development and evolution of memories from "procedural" to "declarative" and "episodic" (Tulving, 2005), describe this as the passage from anoetic, or autonomic, "knowledge-less" consciousness to "noetic", "knowledge based" consciousness with development of an articulate or "semantic" memory, giving an account of the child's consciousness of "being in the world" and of sharing it with known others. Reddy (2008) has shown how a four-month-old might act "coy" when held up to see his face in a mirror, and has documented babies of this age beginning to appreciate being teased and to be capable of showing off to family members or teasing them. She has collected much evidence that this is the time when the social "me" is becoming strong, and also vulnerable to confusion if it is treated unkindly.

Playfulness is a powerful emotional state that generates relationships among all social animals, and it leads to appreciation of the accepted social place of different individuals and how collaborative groups may form and change (Bekoff, 2000; Panksepp, 2005). Research on development of companionship between infants and all family members and their acquaintances outside the family (Perry, 2002; Panksepp, 2012; Trevarthen, 2012a) and studies of the social life of rhesus monkeys both give clear evidence that sharing experiences with a family or social group depends on emotions for sharing playful adventure and discovery.

Older infants learn customary expressions of their family, and they make fun of them, seeking appreciation of their wittiness. Reddy takes these convivial behaviours as proof of a self-and-other awareness, or "second person intentionality", and she demonstrates its importance for the development of the "self-consciousness-in-the-eyes-of-the-other": the I–Thou relationship of Buber (1923[1970]), and the "Social Me" of Mead (1934). From this intimacy and mutual appraisal develops the capacity to share practical attentions to the world and to participate in the purposes and emotions of "acts of meaning" before language. With it, the child grows a more or less self-confident individuality (Frank & Trevarthen, 2012).

To understand the infant's appreciation of a social place in the community of the family and its daily activities, we must accept that the list of "simple basic emotions" attributed to the individual, the classical six described from photographs of face expressions—anger, disgust, fear, happiness, sadness, and surprise (Ekman, 1972)—do not adequately describe feelings of relating between persons. A more expanded list (Ekman, 1999), closer to the one Charles Darwin recognised in his book *Expression of the Emotions in Man and Animals* (1872), includes more subtle interactive or "moral" emotions: amusement, contempt, contentment, embarrassment, excitement, guilt, pride in achievement, relief, satisfaction, sensory pleasure, and shame. Stern describes the feelings of being with other persons as "relational emotions", and Draghi-Lorenz and colleagues (2001) consider the "basic complex emotions", such as pride, shame, jealousy, to be primary regulators of relations between persons and their social achievements from infancy. Moreover, such social functions are certainly basic for the neural regulations of "primary process" emotional states in animals, which Panksepp names as seeking, rage, fear, sexual lust, maternal care, separation-distress, panic/grief, and joyful play (Panksepp, 2003). Of course, in humans, as in most animals, emotions are expressed not only in facial movements, but as the manners of moving the whole body or any of its parts, which Stern (2010) calls "vitality dynamics", and most richly among humans, in vocal cries that we cultivate as song and music (Panksepp & Trevarthen, 2009).

We find clear evidence that infants have strong and clearly expressed emotions of pride and shame, and we believe they should be regarded as primary innate emotions in interpersonal relations and in social life and learning and the development of a moral character (Trevarthen, 1990, 2005a, 2011b). Sue Carter and Stephen Porges explain the evolution of emotional expressions from movements of self-regulation of vital states that are commanded by the brain in readiness for finding the benefits of engagements with the environment, including the love that motivates attachment and maternal care, or the fear and aggression that initiate reactions of flight or fight in self-defence (Carter & Porges, 2012; Porges, 2001).

How the hope and pride of early childhood can be betrayed

Studies of childhood abuse and neglect have important lessons for considerations of nature and nurture. While each child has unique genetic potentials, both human and animal studies point to important needs that every child has, and severe long-term consequences for brain function if those needs are not met. The effects of the childhood environment, favorable or unfavorable, interact with all the processes of neurodevelopment . . .

While technology has raised opportunities for children to become economically secure and literate, more recent inadvertent impacts of technology have spawned declines in extended families, family meals, and spontaneous peer interactions. The latter changes have deprived many children of experiences that promote positive growth of the cognitive and caring potentials of their developing brains. (Perry, 2002, p. 79)

One person who has reviewed the evidence that the clever and sociable brain of a newborn is seriously damaged by neglect or abuse is Bruce Perry, a neuroscientist who has made it his task to educate those concerned with care of the early years, and administrators responsible for management of medical and social services, about the serious long-term effects on intelligence and socio-emotional life if the brain is stressed or deprived of affection in infancy (Perry, 2002; Perry & Szalavitz, 2010). He demonstrates that recovery is more difficult if the neglect starts very early in the life of the child, when the brain is growing fastest, and that the effects show better response to care if the neglect comes in later years. He makes a case that one factor putting many infants at risk in the modern world is the isolation of nuclear families and the stresses upon parents trying to cope with poverty and mental distress on their own. The evidence in extreme cases of a damaged and stunted brain that fails to thrive and learn and long-term emotional problems indicates that a modern urban environment might not be one that a young child and its family are adapted to live in. It is an inadequate nurture against nature. Human brains are built to grow in a different kind of community, with different, more extended families, different, more artful social rituals, and peer environments that are not entirely regulated for school instruction. Human self-awareness and wellbeing is a capacity of the brain and body to communicate sympathetically with other human imaginations and purposes, and with their emotions (Panksepp, 2012). Psychopathology impairs the abilities to contribute to work in society (Heckman, 2007) and to share the community of experience created in the history of a culture, which shapes the growing brain (Han & Northoff, 2008).

From birth, the infant's motives and emotions are adapted for a rich evolving experience within a happy family supported by an intimate caring community of friends and neighbours who have a secure and creative traditional way of life (Trevarthen, 2012a). If these impulses are weakened in the child because of a disturbance at some stage in the formation of body and brain, or if the normal expectations are not given the support from the human environment for which they are adapted, their energy can generate chronic stress and psychopathology that blocks the path to pleasure in human company and to meaning for future life (Trevarthen, 2001a; Trevarthen & Aitken, 2001). The infant's psychic powers are to be regulated in intimate and lively relationships—they suffer disorder or trauma from destructive events in these relationships (Hughes, 2006; Perry & Szalavitz, 2010). They are, however, not weak, and are capable of impressive self-corrective reactions to distress. They also respond readily to sensitive forms of therapeutic communication, and especially to any improvements in contact and emotionally and practically satisfying engagement with the carer (Trevarthen & Aitken, 2001; Trevarthen & Malloch, 2000; Frank & Trevarthen, 2012).

An infant is an animal being evolved to become part of a universe that has been shaped by the thoughts, actions, beliefs, and moral attitudes of past generations of human adults and children, and his or her fate depends on the ways the society of adults manages life and work in the whole community with its language, technology, and many conventions of belief and social conduct, and with its stresses (McEwen, 2001). The causes of child psychopathology, and their potential for creating suffering in adult life, cannot be understood without relating them, not just to the regulations or disorders of the child as an individual organism, but also to his or her impulses as a person who wishes to share the emotions and practicalities of life intimately with other persons (Trevarthen et al., 2006).

Critical steps to a healthy and pleasurable life in company, and opportunities for change

Stages in the development of the human mind bring a series of transformations that carry promise of advance in intelligence, skills, and social relationships. The power of action and range of understanding are repeatedly transformed from within the child's brain and body and through engagement with a responsive human environment (Trevarthen & Aitken, 2003). Each change brings new opportunities for companionship and new needs for the energy of adventurous action to be balanced against nurturing care and mutual emotional regulation (Brazelton, 1993). Failure in these regulations at any stage can lead to stressful and unhappy consequences.

These changes are products both of changes in the child and the responses of the parents. What infants require at each period in which their initiative and experience are expanding is the company of a wilful, aware, and emotional person who is playfully ready to gently tease, or be teased, and extend a "reaching out for fun" (Reddy, 1991, 2005). However, we do not understand well enough how joy affects the growing brain and what it contributes to the formation of satisfying and effective child—parent relations, how it fosters further child development and how it motivates the kind of learning that makes the life of a young person in society full of emotional rewards and achievements, and secure and realistic hopes and ambitions.

There have been clear calls for research on the nature of joyful play and its value for development (Emde, 1992; Panksepp, 2012; Panksepp & Burgdorf, 2003; Reddy, 2008; Stern, 1990). Play, with its exuberant rivalry and immediate imitation of extravagant expressions, has benefit for the regulation of the positive use of near stressful "flow" in activity, and, above all, for joint or collaborative activity. In the centre of all such celebratory behaviours are rhythmic rituals of action modulated by cycles of energy expenditure and recovery, which Victor Turner (1982) calls "the human seriousness of play". There is an improvised dance of life in every collaborative enterprise, even in one that seems to have a most serious practical purpose.

Attachment-based therapy for neglected or abused children, and parents who foster or adopt them

Knowledge of how infants develop self-confidence in intimate relations with their parents can advise care for older children who have been given a family by foster parents. The experience of those who offer support for disturbed children and their families, and, in particular, those rebellious or resistant children who have been removed from their biological parents because they have been mistreated, or because their parents cannot cope, is that it is necessary to get into immediate responsive engagement with the child using the same kind of intuitive forms of communication that affectionate and happy parents use with their infants and toddlers (Archer & Burnell, 2003; Hughes, 1997, 1998). In this communication, sympathy for what the child is feeling, genuine emotional response that is accepting and flexible, and good humour in play are essential. Emotions of shame and pride must be accepted and respected, and forms of playful and joyful escape to more spontaneous and trusting communication can be developed.

Play means interaction with any impulses for adventurous and enjoyable movement and experience. It means sharing expressions of joy and surprise (Panksepp & Burgdorf, 2003). It draws on the basic emotions for pleasure in attachment. As ethologists have discovered by studying the instinctive movements of young animals chasing and "pretend fighting", play is affiliative (Bekoff, 2000). It strengthens and develops social bonds while sorting out social hierarchies. Play therapy draws on these psychobiological principles in a systematic way (Jernberg & Booth, 2001). For a troubled child, making happy and trusting friendships in playful and intimately affectionate responsive ways is key to positive learning and emotional security.

Video evidence of the emotional nature and patterning of this kind of communication, used as a detailed record of interacting behaviours and a prompt for more supportive and constructive communication, is beneficial not only for therapists or teachers, but also for parents attempting to guide a child to better emotional health (Beebe, 2003;

Gutstein & Sheeley, 2002; Kennedy et al., 2011; Schechter, 2004). Spontaneous and creative art therapies, in dramatic acting, dance, or music, all engage with the timing and expressiveness of intuitive communication in the present, bypassing the rationalised detachment of verbal explanations and not relying wholly on an attempt to trace the generation of fantasy in one mind (Karkou & Sanderson, 2006; Malchiodi, 2011). Play in any medium is creative as interpersonal improvisation in which partners are both free to be expressive in themselves and instantly reactive to what others do, and, therefore, open to guidance and learning. Real intuitive engagement is necessary for positive emotions to flourish, as it is with infants (Reddy & Trevarthen, 2004), and is a basis for practical, realistic co-operation, too.

The fundamental motives for active engagement in shared activities, identified by research on the development of co-operative behaviours of infant and mother, have profound importance for all supportive or humane interventions, whether they are for therapy or education. Indeed, there have been clear recommendations for change in psychiatry and education to counter excessive use of impersonal assessment of the individual by diagnosis of disorder, and application of teaching by instruction with assessment of outcomes according to a prescribed curriculum for improvement. Correction of these practices reflects both a radical transformation in the hypotheses about the nature of mental illness and how it should be treated as a problem in expression of natural social capacities of persons for sharing experience and its values (House & Portuges, 2005; Meares, 2005; Ryle & Kerr, 2002), and a redefinition of the means by which teachers may best guide the eagerness of a pupil to learn what society expects him or her to know (Bruner, 1996; Dewey, 1927; Rogoff, 2003; Vygotsky, 1978; Whitehead, 1929).

Older people use specific and realistic memories and verbal explanations to guide their awareness and direct their interests. In normal life, these cognitive components, built up through experiences in established relationships, strengthen the prospective control of attentions and intentions and lead to more knowledgeable and skilful action. In psychopathology, the cognitive contents of memory are entangled with emotions of self-doubt, anxiety, and anger. These feelings about the self and relationships intrude into the imagination and block effective consciousness and action. Therapy for adults requires work with these cognitive contents. At the same time, engaging directly with the emotions and a clear focus on the interpersonal motives that direct movements in the present can regulate disturbing or inhibiting material from memory and imagination, opening the way to more rewarding and creative purposes in relationships that are affectionate and trusting (Kerr, 2005; Kohut, 1984). A therapist aiming to help a child with developmental psychopathology through more intimate intersubjective or interpersonal therapy has responsibility to stay with the child through periods of resistance or rejection to find this path to self-confidence and trust (Archer & Burnell, 2003).

Premonitions of autism in infancy, and the communication that develops between child and parent: advice for intervention

Infantile autism was first defined by Leo Kanner in 1943, and his description remains the basis for diagnosis of autism in young children. He described childhood autism as "a biological disturbance of affective contact", and noted, in addition to the child's inability to establish social relatedness or "aloneness" and a failure to use language normally for the purpose of communication, an obsessive desire for the maintenance of sameness, and a fascination for certain kinds of stimulating objects and gadgets. Many of his cases appeared to have good, even superior, cognitive potentialities of particular kinds, and this has been confirmed by studies of the very wide range of intelligence in young people who are diagnosed as autistic. Some show exceptional talents in visuo-spatial skills, or in music performance and memory for melodies. Clearly, there are many transformations of different parts of the motive processes that regulate individual action and awareness, social co-operation, and cultural learning, and "autism spectrum disorders" overlap with other developmental disorders.

Kanner identified the age of appearance of infantile autism as "before 30 months", a crucial stage when a normally developing child is in a major developmental transition from preverbal communication, social self-consciousness, imitation, and co-operative and imaginative play to rapid acquisition of language with narrative memory, and mimetic identification with many conventional ways of understanding and acting (Trevarthen et al., 1998). Levels of language and of cognition or intelligence are generally lowered, but vary widely. The ritualistic, stereotyped exploration of objects and insistence on sameness seem to be manifestations of a restricted investigative or executive motivation, or they might be motivated as defences, protecting the child from invasive experiences or novel situations that he or she cannot understand or predict and that precipitate anxiety or panic. The vulnerability of an autistic child to invasive sensations and confusion of awareness point to a fault in generation and regulation of the rhythms of movement that animate attention and the picking up of experience (Trevarthen, 2000).

Kanner did not have information on the progress of an autistic child through infancy. It is clear now, mainly as a result of research on home videos made by parents, that signs of disordered perception and movement, and inattention to other people's attempts at communication, can be detected from before a baby is six months old (Muratori & Maestro, 2007a; Saint-Georges et al., 2010) and that these can be disturbing to parents, causing them to attempt engagement with the baby in more intrusive ways that could further weaken emotional engagement and play (Muratori & Maestro, 2007b; Mahdhaoui et al., 2011).

We have studied home movies of two genetically identical twin girls, only one of whom received diagnosis of autism in the third year (St Clair et al., 2007; Trevarthen & Daniel, 2005). The differences in early development of these girls proves, first, that autism might not be a straightforward genetic disorder, but can be a consequence of epigenetic factors influencing development during gestation, and second, that the restricted responses of the affected infant has immediate effects on how a parent engages with that child in dialogue or games, complicating the sharing of experience. This indicates that the development of autism is a product of changes in the parent–child *relationship*; between the developing foetus and the mother's body, and then between the infant and parent as attachment figure and companion in play.

Recent studies of the speaking of parents to infants later diagnosed as autistic children proves that distinctive characteristics of the expressive quality and communicative content of the parent's infant-directed speech, or "motherese", can assist early diagnosis (Muratori & Maestro, 2007b; Mahdhaoui et al., 2011). It also indicates that guidance towards more receptive and less directive ways of responding to the infant's subdued signs of willingness or enjoyment in communication and play could reduce the probability that the child will be severely affected by autism. This research is encouraging forms of therapy or support for the parents that protect the child from developing more serious social isolation and dependence (Acquarone, 2007).

Identification with the intentions of the child in ways that avoid coercion or "reinforcement" and that seek to offer tasks that match the level of mastery and interest for handling objects and arranging them spontaneously, as recommended by Geoffrey Waldon, might also reduce the difficulty experienced by the child, and can lead to positive orientation towards the person offering subdued aid (Solomon, 2012). Similar responses are observed to sensitive interactive music therapy by children with autistic or other disorders of communication and sensori-motor development (Gold et al., 2006; Robarts, 1998; Wigram, 2004; Wigram & Elefant, 2009).

The clear message is that development for infants and young children with disabilities is best fostered by methods that attend to and support the motives and emotions expressed by the child. It is necessary to give them the lead and to encourage feelings of achievement for what they intend to do, just as for the education of a young child who is developing with no diagnosis of a problem (Trevarthen, 2011d).

References

Acquarone, S. (Ed.) (2007). *Signs of Autism in Infants: Recognition and Early Intervention*. London: Karnac.

Archer, C., & Burnell, A. (2003). *Trauma, Attachment and Family Permanence: Fear Can Stop You Loving*. London: Jessica Kingsley.

Bateson, M. C. (1971). The interpersonal context of infant vocalization. *Quarterly Progress Report of the Research Laboratory of Electronics*, 100: 170–176. Boston, MA: MIT.

Bateson, M. C. (1979). The epigenesis of conversational interaction: a personal account of research development. In: M. Bullowa (Ed.), *Before Speech: The Beginning of Human Communication* (pp. 64–77). London: Cambridge University Press.

Beebe, B. (2003). Brief mother–infant treatment using psychoanalytically informed video microanalysis. *Infant Mental Health Journal*, 24(1): 24–52.

Beebe, B., Stern, D., & Jaffe, J. (1979). The kinesic rhythm of mother–infant interactions. In: A. W. Siegman & S. Feldstein (Eds.), *Of Speech and*

Time; Temporal Speech Patterns in Interpersonal Contexts (pp. 23–34). Hillsdale, NJ: Lawrence Erlbaum.

Bekoff, M. (2000). Animal emotions: exploring passionate nature. *BioScience*, 50: 861–870.

Bernstein, N. (1967). *Coordination and Regulation of Movements*. New York: Pergamon.

Birdwhistell, R. L. (1970). *Kinesics and Context: Essays on Body Motion Communication*. Philadelphia, PA: University of Pennsylvania Press.

Bowlby, J. (1951). *Maternal Care and Mental Health*. World Health Organization Monograph (Serial No. 2).

Bråten, S. (2009). *The Intersubjective Mirror in Infant Learning and Evolution of Speech*. Amsterdam: John Benjamins.

Brazelton, T. B. (1961). Psychophysiologic reactions in the neonate. I: The value of observations of the neonate. *Journal of Pediatrics*, 58: 508–512.

Brazelton, T. B. (1973). *Neonatal Behavioural Assessment Scale* (Clinics in Developmental Medicine, 50. Spastics International Medical Publications). London: Heinemann Medical Books.

Brazelton, T. B. (1979). Evidence of communication during neonatal behavioural assessment. In: M. Bullowa (Ed.), *Before Speech: The Beginning of Human Communication* (pp. 79–88). Cambridge: Cambridge University Press.

Brazelton, T. B. (1993). *Touchpoints: Your Child's Emotional and Behavioral Development*. New York: Viking.

Bruner, J. S. (1968). *Processes of Cognitive Growth: Infancy* (Heinz Werner Lectures, 1968). Worcester, MA: Clark University Press with Barri.

Bruner, J. S. (1972). The nature and uses of immaturity. *American Psychologist*, 27: 687–708.

Bruner, J. S. (1977). Early social interaction and language acquisition. In: H. R. Schaffer (Ed.), *Studies in Mother–Infant Interaction: The Loch Lomond Symposium* (pp. 271–290). London: Academic Press.

Bruner, J. S. (1983). *Child's Talk. Learning to Use Language*. New York: Norton.

Bruner, J. S. (1986). *Actual Minds, Possible Worlds*. Cambridge, MA: Harvard University Press.

Bruner, J. S. (1990). *Acts of Meaning*. Cambridge, MA: Harvard University Press.

Bruner, J. S. (1996). *The Culture of Education*. Cambridge, MA: Harvard University Press.

Bruner, J. S., & Sherwood, V. (1975). Early rule structure: the case of peek-aboo. In: J. S. Bruner, A. Jolly, & K. Sylva (Eds.), *Play: Its Role in Evolution and Development* (pp. 277–285). London: Penguin.

Buber, M. (1923)[1970]. *I and Thou*, W. Kaufmann (Trans.). Edinburgh: T. & T. Clark.

Bullowa, M. (1979a). Introduction. Prelinguistic communication: a field for scientific research. In: M. Bullowa (Ed.), *Before Speech: The Beginning of Human Communication* (pp. 1–62). Cambridge: Cambridge University Press.

Bullowa, M. (Ed.) (1979b). *Before Speech: The Beginning of Human Communication*. Cambridge: Cambridge University Press.

Caldwell, P., & Horwood, J. (2007). *From Isolation to Intimacy: Making Friends without Words*. London: Jessica Kingsley.

Carter, C. S., & Porges, S. W. (2012). Neurobiology and the evolution of mammalian social behavior. In: D. Narvaez, J. Panksepp, A. Schore, & T. Gleason (Eds.), *Human Nature, Early Experience and Human Development* (pp. 132–151). Oxford: Oxford University Press.

Condon, W. S., & Sander, L. S. (1974). Neonate movement is synchronized with adult speech: interactional participation and language acquisition. *Science, 183*: 99–101.

Custodero, L. A., & Johnson-Green, E. A. (2003). Passing the cultural torch: musical experience and musical parenting of infants. *Journal of Research in Music Education, 51*(2): 102–114.

Darwin, C. (1872). *The Expression of Emotion in Man and Animals*. London: Methuen.

Dewey, J. (1927). *The Public and its Problems*. New York: Holt.

Dissanayake, E. (2000). *Art and Intimacy: How the Arts Began*. Seattle: University of Washington Press.

Donaldson, M. (1978). *Children's Minds*. Glasgow: Fontana/Collins.

Donaldson, M. (1992). *Human Minds: An Exploration*. London: Allen Lane/Penguin.

Draghi-Lorenz, R., Reddy, V., & Costall, A. (2001). Re-thinking the development of "non-basic" emotions: a critical review of existing theories. *Developmental Review, 21*(3): 263–304.

Ekman, P. (1972). Universals and cultural differences in facial expression of emotion. In: J. Cole (Ed.), *Nebraska Symposium on Motivation, 1971, Volume 19* (pp. 207–283). Lincoln: University of Nebraska Press.

Ekman, P. (1999). Basic emotions. In: T. Dalgleish & M. Power, *Handbook of Cognition and Emotion* (pp. 45–60). Chichester: John Wiley.

Emde, R. N. (1992). Positive emotions for psychoanalytic theory: surprises from infancy research and new directions. In: T. Shapiro & R. N. Emde (Eds.), *Affect: Psychoanalytic Perspectives* (pp. 5–54). Madison, CT: International Universities Press.

Fosha, D., Siegel, D. J., & Solomon, M. F. (Eds.) (2009). *The Healing Power of Emotion: Affective Neuroscience, Development, and Clinical Practice.* New York: Norton.

Frank, B., & Trevarthen, C. (2012). Intuitive meaning: supporting impulses for interpersonal life in the sociosphere of human knowledge, practice and language. In: A. Foolen, U. Lüdtke, T. P. Racine, & J. Zlatev (Eds.), *Moving Ourselves, Moving Others: The Role of (E)Motion For Intersubjectivity, Consciousness and Language* (pp. 261–303). Amsterdam: John Benjamins.

Gold, C., Wigram, T., & Elefant, C. (2006). Music therapy for autistic spectrum disorder (Cochrane Review). *The Cochrane Library, Issue 2.* Chichester: John Wiley.

Gratier, M. (2008). Grounding in musical communication: evidence from jazz duet performances. *Musicae Scientiae, Special Issue, "Expression and Narrative",* 71–110.

Gratier, M., & Apter-Danon, G. (2009). The improvised musicality of belonging: repetition and variation in mother–infant vocal interaction. In: S. Malloch & C. Trevarthen (Eds.), *Communicative Musicality: Exploring the Basis of Human Companionship* (pp. 301–327). Oxford: Oxford University Press.

Gratier, M., & Trevarthen, C. (2007). Voice, vitality and meaning: on the shaping of the infant's utterances in willing engagement with culture. Comment on Bertau's "On the notion of voice". *International Journal for Dialogical Science,* 2(1): 169–181.

Gratier, M., & Trevarthen, C. (2008). Musical narrative and motives for culture in mother–infant vocal interaction. *Journal of Consciousness Studies,* 15(10–11): 122–158.

Gutstein, S. E., & Sheely, R. K. (2002). *Relationship Development Intervention with Young Children. Social and Emotional Development Activities for Asperger Syndrome, Autism, PDD and NLD.* London: Jessica Kingsley.

Halliday, M. A. K. (1975). *Learning How to Mean: Explorations in the Development of Language.* London: Edward Arnold.

Han, S., & Northoff, G. (2008). Culture-sensitive neural substrates of human cognition: a transcultural neuroimaging approach. *Nature Reviews, Neuroscience,* 9: 646–654.

Heckman, J. J. (2007). *Invest in the Very Young.* Ounce of Prevention Fund and the University of Chicago Harris School of Public Policy Studies.

Hobson, P. (2002). *The Cradle of Thought: Exploring the Origins of Thinking.* London: Macmillan.

House, J., & Portuges, S. (2005). Relational knowing, memory, symbolization, and language: commentary on the Boston Change Process Study

Group. *Journal of the American Psychoanalytic Association*, 53(3): 731–744.

Hubley, P., & Trevarthen C. (1979). Sharing a task in infancy. In: I. Uzgiris (Ed.), *Social Interaction During Infancy: New Directions for Child Development*, 4: 57–80. San Francisco, CA: Jossey-Bass.

Hughes, D. (1997). *Facilitating Developmental Attachment: The Road to Emotional Recovery and Behavioral Change in Foster and Adopted Children*. New York: Jason Aronson.

Hughes, D. (1998). *Building the Bonds of Attachment: Awakening Love in Deeply Traumatized Children*. Northvale, NJ: Jason Aronson.

Hughes, D. A. (2006). *Building the Bonds of Attachment: Awakening Love in Deeply Troubled Children* (2nd edn). Lanham, MD: Rowman & Littlefield.

Jaffe, J., & Felstein, S. (1970). *Rhythms of Dialogue*. New York: Academic Press.

Jernberg, A. M., & Booth, P. B. (2001). *Theraplay: Helping Parents and Children Build Better Relationships Through Attachment-Based Play* (2nd edn). San Francisco, CA: Jossey-Bass.

Kanner, L. (1943). Autistic disturbances of affective contact. *The Nervous Child*, 2: 217–250 [reprinted in *Acta Paedopsychiatria*, 35(4): 100–136, 1968].

Karkou, V., & Sanderson, P. (2006). *Arts Therapies: A Research-Based Map of the Field*. Oxford: Elsevier Health Sciences.

Kennedy, H., Landor, M., & Todd, L. (2011). *Video Interaction Guidance A Relationship-Based Intervention to Promote Attunement, Empathy and Wellbeing*. London: Jessica Kingsley.

Kerr, I. (2005). Cognitive analytic therapy. *Psychiatry*, 4(5): 28–33.

Kohut, H. (1984). *How Does Analysis Cure?* Chicago, IL: University of Chicago Press.

Lüdtke, U. M. (2012). Relational emotions in semiotic and linguistic development: towards an intersubjective theory of language learning and language therapy. In: A. Foolen, U. Lüdtke, J. Zlatev, & T. Racine (Eds.), *Moving Ourselves, Moving Others: The Role of (E)Motion for Intersubjectivity, Consciousness and Language* (pp. 305–346). Amsterdam: John Benjamins.

Mahdhaoui, A., Chetouani, M., Cassel, R. S., Saint-Georges, C., Parlato, E., Laznik, M. C., Apicella, F., Muratori, F., Maestro, S., & Cohen, D. (2011). Computerized home video detection for motherese may help to study impaired interaction between infants who become autistic and their parents. *International Journal of Methods in Psychiatric Research*, 20(1): e6–18.

Malchiodi, C. A. (2011). *Handbook of Art Therapy* (2nd edn). New York: Guilford Press.

Malloch, S. (1999). Mother and infants and communicative musicality. In: I. Deliège (Ed.), *Rhythms, Musical Narrative, and the Origins of Human Communication. Musicae Scientiae, Special Issue, 1999–2000* (pp. 29–57). Belgium: European Society for the Cognitive Sciences of Music.

Malloch, S., & Trevarthen, C. (Eds.) (2009). *Communicative Musicality: Exploring the Basis of Human Companionship*. Oxford: Oxford University Press.

Marwick, H., & Murray, L. (2009). The effects of maternal depression on the "musicality" of infant-directed speech and conversational engagement. In: S. Malloch & C. Trevarthen (Eds.), *Communicative Musicality: Exploring the Basis of Human Companionship* (pp. 281–300). Oxford: Oxford University Press.

Mazokopaki, M., & Kugiumutzakis, G. (2009). Infant rhythms: expressions of musical companionship. In: S. Malloch & C. Trevarthen (Eds.), *Communicative Musicality: Exploring the Basis of Human Companionship* (pp. 185–208). Oxford: Oxford University Press.

McEwen, B. S. (2001). From molecules to mind. Stress, individual differences, and the social environment. *Annals of the New York Academic Sciences, 93*: 42–49.

Mead, G. H. (1934). *Mind, Self, and Society*. Chicago, IL: Chicago University Press.

Meares, R. (2005). *The Metaphor of Play: Origin and Breakdown of Personal Being*. London: Routledge.

Muratori, F., & Maestro, S. (2007a). Early signs of autism in the first year of life. In: S. Acquarone (Ed.), *Signs of Autism in Infants: Recognition and Early Intervention* (pp. 21–45). London: Karnac.

Muratori, F., & Maestro, S. (2007b). Autism as a downstream effect of primary difficulties in intersubjectivity interacting with abnormal development of brain connectivity. *International Journal for Dialogical Science, 2*: 93–118.

Murray, L. (1992). The impact of post-natal depression on infant development. *Journal of Child Psychology and Psychiatry, 33*: 543–561.

Murray, L., & Trevarthen, C. (1985). Emotional regulation of interactions between two-month-olds and their mothers. In: T. M. Field & N. A. Fox (Eds.), *Social Perception in Infants* (pp. 177–197). Norwood, NJ: Ablex.

Osborne, N. (2009). Music for children in zones of conflict and post-conflict: a psychobiological approach. In: S. Malloch & C. Trevarthen

(Eds.), *Communicative Musicality: Exploring the Basis of Human Companionship* (pp. 331–356). Oxford: Oxford University Press.

Panksepp, J. (2003). An archaeology of mind: the ancestral sources of human feelings. *Soundings, 86*: 41–69.

Panksepp, J. (2005). Beyond a joke: from animal laughter to human joy? *Science, 308*: 62–63.

Panksepp, J. (2012). How primary-process emotional systems guide child development: ancestral regulators of human happiness, thriving and suffering. In: D. Narvaez, J. Panksepp, A. Schore, & T. Gleason (Eds.), *Human Nature, Early Experience and the Environment of Evolutionary Adaptedness* (pp. 74–94). New York: Oxford University Press.

Panksepp, J., & Burgdorf, J. (2003). "Laughing" rats and the evolutionary antecedents of human joy? *Physiology and Behavior, 79*: 533–547.

Panksepp, J., & Trevarthen, C. (2009). The neuroscience of emotion in music. In: S. Malloch & C. Trevarthen (Eds.), *Communicative Musicality: Exploring the Basis of Human Companionship* (pp. 105–146). Oxford: Oxford University Press.

Panksepp, J., & Watt, D. (2011). Why does depression hurt? Ancestral primary-process separation-distress (PANIC/GRIEF) and diminished brain reward (SEEKING) processes in the genesis of depressive affect. *Psychiatry, 74*(1): 5–13.

Papoušek, H. (1996). Musicality in infancy research: biological and cultural origins of early musicality In: I. Deliège & J. Sloboda (Eds,), *Musical Beginnings: Origins and Development of Musical Competence* (pp. 37–55). Oxford: Oxford University Press.

Papoušek, M. (1994). Melodies in caregivers' speech: a species specific guidance towards language. *Early Development and Parenting, 3*: 5–17.

Papoušek, M., & Papoušek, H. (1981). Musical elements in the infant's vocalization: their significance for communication, cognition, and creativity. In: L. P. Lipsitt & C. K. Rovee-Collier (Eds.), *Advances in Infancy Research, 1*: 163–224. Norwood, NJ: Ablex.

Pavlicevic, M., & Ansdell, G. (2009). Between communicative musicality and collaborative musicing: a perspective from community music therapy. In: S. Malloch & C. Trevarthen, (Eds,), *Communicative Musicality: Exploring the Basis of Human Companionship* (pp. 357–376). Oxford: Oxford University Press.

Perry, B. D. (2002). Childhood experience and the expression of genetic potential: what childhood neglect tells us about nature and nurture. *Brain and Mind, 3*: 79–100.

Perry, B. D., & Szalavitz, M. (2010). *Born for Love: Why Empathy Is Essential—and Endangered*. New York: HarperCollins.

Piontelli, A. (1992). *From Fetus to Child*. London: Routledge.

Porges, S. W. (2001). The polyvagal theory: phylogenetic substrates of a social nervous system. *International Journal of Psychophysiology, 42*: 123–146.

Reddy, V. (1991). Playing with others' expectations; teasing and mucking about in the first year. In: A. Whiten (Ed.), *Natural Theories of Mind: Evolution, Development and Simulation of Everyday Mindreading* (pp. 143–158). Oxford: Blackwell.

Reddy, V. (2005). Feeling shy and showing off: self-conscious emotions must regulate self-awareness. In: J. Nadel & D. Muir (Eds.), *Emotional Development* (pp. 183–204). Oxford: Oxford University Press.

Reddy, V. (2008). *How Infants Know Minds*. Cambridge, MA: Harvard University Press.

Reddy, V., & Trevarthen, C. (2004). What we learn about babies from engaging with their emotions. *Zero to Three, 24*(3): 9–15.

Robarts, J. Z. (1998). Music therapy for children with autism. In: C. Trevarthen, K. Aitken, D. Papuodi, & J. Z Robarts (Eds.), *Children with Autism. Diagnosis and Interventions to Meet Their Needs* (pp. 172–202). London: Jessica Kingsley.

Robarts, J. Z. (2009). Supporting the development of mindfulness and meaning: clinical pathways in music therapy with a sexually abused child. In: S. Malloch & C. Trevarthen (Eds.), *Communicative Musicality: Exploring the Basis of Human Companionship* (pp. 377–400). Oxford: Oxford University Press.

Rogoff, B. (2003). *The Cultural Nature of Human Development*. Oxford: Oxford University Press.

Ryan, J. (1974). Early language development: towards a communicational analysis. In: M. P. M. Richards (Ed.), *The Integration of a Child into a Social World* (pp. 185–213). Cambridge: Cambridge University Press.

Ryle, A., & Kerr, I. B. (2002). *Introducing Cognitive Analytic Therapy: Principles and Practice*. Chichester: John Wiley.

Saint-Georges, C., Cassel, R. S., Cohen, D., Chetouani, M., Laznik, M. C., Maestro, S., & Muratori, F. (2010). What the literature on family home movies can teach us about the infancy of autistic children: a review of literature. *Research in Autism Spectrum Disorders, 4*: 355–366.

Schechter, D. S. (2004). How post-traumatic stress affects mothers' perceptions of their babies: a brief video feedback intervention makes a difference. *Zero to Three, 24*(3): 43–49.

Scheflen, A. E. (1972). *The Stream and Structure of Communication Behavior*. Bloomington, IN: University of Indiana Press.

Solomon, W. (Ed.) (2012). *Autism and Understanding*. London: Sage.

Spitz, R. A. (1945). Hospitalism—an inquiry into the genesis of psychiatric conditions in early childhood. *Psychoanalytic Study of the Child, 1*: 53–74.

St Clair, C., Danon-Boileau, L., & Trevarthen, C. (2007). Signs of autism in infancy: sensitivity for rhythms of expression in communication. In: S. Acquarone (Ed.), *Signs of Autism in Infants: Recognition and Early Intervention* (pp. 21–45). London: Karnac.

Stern, D. N. (1974). Mother and infant at play: the dyadic interaction involving facial, vocal and gaze behaviours. In: M. Lewis & L. A. Rosenblum (Eds.), *The Effect of the Infant on its Caregiver* (pp. 187–213). New York: Wiley.

Stern, D. N. (1977). *The First Relationship: Infant and Mother*. Cambridge, MA: Harvard University Press.

Stern, D. N. (1985). *The Interpersonal World of the Infant: A View from Psychoanalysis and Development Psychology*. New York: Basic Books.

Stern, D. N. (1990). Joy and satisfaction in infancy. In: R. A. Glick & S. Bone (Eds.), *Pleasure Beyond the Pleasure Principle* (pp. 13–25). Newhaven, CT: Yale University Press.

Stern, D. N. (1993). The role of feelings for an interpersonal self. In: U. Neisser (Ed.), *The Perceived Self: Ecological and Interpersonal Sources of Self-Knowledge* (pp. 205–215). New York: Cambridge University Press.

Stern, D. N. (2010). *Forms of Vitality: Exploring Dynamic Experience in Psychology, the Arts, Psychotherapy and Development*. Oxford: Oxford University Press.

Stern, D. N., Hofer, L., Haft, W., & Dore, J. (1985). Affect attunement: the sharing of feeling states between mother and infant by means of intermodal fluency. In: T. M. Field & N. A. Fox (Eds.), *Social Perception in Infants* (pp. 249–268). Norwood, NJ: Ablex.

Stroh, K., Robinson, T., & Proctor, A. (2008). *Every Child Can Learn: Using Learning Tools and Play to Help Children with Developmental Delay*. London: SAGE (with CD-Rom/DVD).

Trainor, L. J. (1996). Infant preferences for infant-directed versus non-infant-directed play songs and lullabies. *Infant Behavior and Development, 19*: 83–92.

Trevarthen, C. (1977). Descriptive analyses of infant communication behavior. In: H. R. Schaffer (Ed.), *Studies in Mother–Infant Interaction: The Loch Lomond Symposium* (pp. 227–270). London: Academic Press.

Trevarthen, C. (1979). Communication and cooperation in early infancy. A description of primary intersubjectivity. In: M. Bullowa (Ed.), *Before*

Speech: The Beginning of Human Communication (pp. 321–347). Cambridge: Cambridge University Press.

Trevarthen, C. (1987). Sharing makes sense: intersubjectivity and the making of an infant's meaning. In: R. Steele & T. Threadgold (Eds.), *Language Topics: Essays in Honour of Michael Halliday, Volume 1* (pp. 177–199). Amsterdam: John Benjamins.

Trevarthen, C. (1990). Signs before speech. In: T. A. Sebeok & J. Umiker-Sebeok (Eds.), *The Semiotic Web, 1989.* Berlin: Mouton de Gruyter.

Trevarthen, C. (1993). The function of emotions in early infant communication and development. In: J. Nadel & L. Camaioni (Eds.), *New Perspectives in Early Communicative Development* (pp. 48–81). London: Routledge.

Trevarthen, C. (1998). The concept and foundations of infant intersubjectivity. In: S. Bråten (Ed.), *Intersubjective Communication and Emotion in Early Ontogeny* (pp. 15–46). Cambridge: Cambridge University Press.

Trevarthen, C. (1999). Musicality and the intrinsic motive pulse: evidence from human psychobiology and infant communication. In: *"Rhythms, Musical Narrative, and the Origins of Human Communication", Musicae Scientiae, Special Issue, 1999–2000* (pp. 157–213). Liège, Belgium: European Society for the Cognitive Sciences of Music.

Trevarthen, C. (2000). Autism as a neurodevelopmental disorder affecting communication and learning in early childhood: Prenatal origins, post-natal course and effective educational support. *Prostoglandins, Leucotrines and Essential Fatty Acids, 63*(1–2): 41–46.

Trevarthen, C. (2001a). Intrinsic motives for companionship in understanding: their origin, development and significance for infant mental health. *Infant Mental Health Journal, 22*(1–2): 95–131.

Trevarthen, C. (2001b). The neurobiology of early communication: intersubjective regulations in human brain development. In: A. F. Kalverboer & A. Gramsbergen (Eds.), *Handbook on Brain and Behavior in Human Development* (pp. 841–882). Dordrecht: Kluwer.

Trevarthen, C. (2003). Neuroscience and intrinsic psychodynamics: current knowledge and potential for therapy. In: J. Corrigall & H. Wilkinson (Eds.), *Revolutionary Connections: Psychotherapy and Neuroscience* (pp. 53–78). London: Karnac.

Trevarthen, C. (2005a). Stepping away from the mirror: pride and shame in adventures of companionship. Reflections on the nature and emotional needs of infant intersubjectivity. In: C. S. Carter, L. Ahnert, K. E. Grossman, S. B. Hrdy, M. E. Lamb, S. W. Porges, & N. Sachser

(Eds.), *Attachment and Bonding: A New Synthesis* (pp. 55–84). *Dahlem Workshop Report 92*. Cambridge, MA: MIT Press.

Trevarthen, C. (2005b). First things first: infants make good use of the sympathetic rhythm of imitation, without reason or language. *Journal of Child Psychotherapy, 31*(1): 91–113.

Trevarthen, C. (2008). Intuition for human communication. In: S. Zeedyk (Ed.), *Promoting Social Interaction for Individuals with Communication Impairments* (pp. 23–38). London: Jessica Kingsley.

Trevarthen, C. (2009a). The functions of emotion in infancy: the regulation and communication of rhythm, sympathy, and meaning in human development. In: D. Fosha, D. J. Siegel, & M. F. Solomon (Eds.), *The Healing Power of Emotion: Affective Neuroscience, Development, and Clinical Practice* (pp. 55–85). New York: Norton.

Trevarthen, C. (2009b). The intersubjective psychobiology of human meaning: learning of culture depends on interest for co-operative practical work and affection for the joyful art of good company. *Psychoanalytic Dialogues, 19*(5): 507–518.

Trevarthen, C. (2011a). What is it like to be a person who knows nothing? Defining the active intersubjective mind of a newborn human being. *Infant and Child Development, 20*(1) (*Special Issue*): 119–135.

Trevarthen, C. (2011b). Innate moral feelings, moral laws and cooperative cultural practice. In: J. J. Sanguineti, A. Acerbi, & J. A. Lombo (Eds.), *Moral Behavior and Free Will: A Neurobiological and Philosophical Approach* (pp. 377–411). Morolo, Italy: IF Press.

Trevarthen, C. (2011c). Confirming companionship in interests, intentions and emotions: how video interaction guidance works. In: H. Kennedy, M. Landor, & L. Todd (Eds.), *Video Interaction Guidance: A Relationship-Based Intervention to Promote Attunement, Empathy and Wellbeing* pp. 198–212). London: Jessica Kingsley.

Trevarthen, C. (2011d). What young children give to their learning, making education work to sustain a community and its culture. *European Early Childhood Education Research Journal, 19*(2) (*Special Issue, "Birth to Three"*): 173–193.

Trevarthen, C. (2012a). Born for art, and the joyful companionship of fiction. In: D. Narvaez, J. Panksepp, A. Schore, & T. Gleason (Eds.), *Human Nature, Early Experience and the Environment of Evolutionary Adaptedness* (pp. 202–218). New York: Oxford University Press.

Trevarthen, C. (2012b). Communicative musicality: the human impulse to create and share music. In: D. J. Hargreaves, D. E. Miell, & R. A. R. MacDonald (Eds.), *Musical Imaginations: Multidisciplinary Perspectives* on *Creativity, Performance, and Perception* (pp. 259–284). Oxford: Oxford University Press.

Trevarthen, C., & Aitken, K. J. (2001). Infant intersubjectivity: research, theory, and clinical applications. *Annual Research Review. Journal of Child Psychology and Psychiatry and Allied Disciplines*, 42(1): 3–48.

Trevarthen, C., & Aitken, K. J. (2003). Regulation of brain development and age-related changes in infants' motives: the developmental function of "regressive" periods. In: M. Heimann (Ed.), *Regression Periods in Human Infancy* (pp. 107–184). Mahwah, NJ: Lawrence Erlbaum.

Trevarthen, C., & Daniel, S. (2005). Disorganized rhythm and synchrony: early signs of autism and Rett syndrome. *Brain and Development*, 27: S25–S34.

Trevarthen, C., & Delafield-Butt, J. (2012). Biology of shared experience and language development: regulations for the inter-subjective life of narratives. In: M. Legerstee, D. W. Haley, & M. H. Bornstein (Eds.), *Developing Infant Mind: Integrating Biology and Experience* (pp. 167–199). New York: Guilford Press.

Trevarthen, C., & Hubley, P. (1978). Secondary intersubjectivity: confidence, confiding and acts of meaning in the first year. In: A. Lock (Ed.), *Action, Gesture and Symbol: The Emergence of Language* (pp. 183–229). London: Academic Press.

Trevarthen, C., & Malloch, S. (2000). The dance of wellbeing: defining the musical therapeutic effect. *Norwegian Journal of Music Therapy*, 9(2): 3–17.

Trevarthen, C., & Marwick, H. (1986). Signs of motivation for speech in infants, and the nature of a mother's support for development of language. In: B. Lindblom & R. Zetterstrom (Eds.), *Precursors of Early Speech* (pp. 279–308). Basingstoke: Macmillan.

Trevarthen, C., Aitken, K., Papuodi, D., & Robarts, J. Z. (Eds.) (1998). *Children with Autism. Diagnosis and Interventions to Meet Their Needs* (2nd edn). London: Jessica Kingsley.

Trevarthen, C., Aitken, K. J., Vandekerckhove, M., Delafield-Butt, J., & Nagy, E. (2006). Collaborative regulations of vitality in early childhood: stress in intimate relationships and postnatal psychopathology. In: D. Cicchetti & D. J. Cohen (Eds.), *Developmental Psychopathology, Volume 2, Developmental Neuroscience* (pp. 65–126). New York: Wiley.

Trevarthen, C., Murray, L., & Hubley, P. (1981). Psychology of infants. In: J. Davis & J. Dobbing (Eds.), *Scientific Foundations of Clinical Paediatrics* (2nd edn) (pp. 235–250). London: Heinemann Medical Books.

Tulving, E. (2005). Episodic memory and autonoesis: uniquely human? In: H. S. Terrace & J. Metcalfe (Eds.), *The Missing Link in Cognition: Self-*

Knowing Consciousness in Man and Animals (pp. 3–56). New York: Oxford University Press.

Turner, V. (1982). *From Ritual to Theatre: The Human Seriousness of Play*. New York: Performing Arts Journal.

Vandekerckhove, M., & Panksepp, J. (2011). The neural evolution of consciousness: from anoetic affective experiences to noetic and autonoetic cognitive awareness. *Neuroscience and Biobehavioral Reviews*, 35(9): 2017–2025.

Von Uexküll, J. (1957). A stroll through the worlds of animals and men: a picture book of invisible worlds. In: C. H. Schiller (Ed. and Trans.), *Instinctive Behavior: The Development of a Modern Concept* (pp. 5–80). New York: International Universities Press.

Vygotsky, L. S. (1978). *Mind in Society: The Development of Higher Psychological Processes*, M. Cole, V. Steiner, S. Scribner & E. Souberman (Eds.). Cambridge, MA: Harvard University Press.

Whitehead, A. N. (1929). *Process and Reality: An Essay in Cosmology*. New York: Macmillan.

Wigram, T. (2004). *Improvisation: Methods and Techniques for Music Therapy Clinicians, Educators and Students*. London: Jessica Kingsley.

Wigram, T., & Elefant, C. (2009). Therapeutic dialogues in music: nurturing musicality of communication in children with autistic spectrum disorder and Rett syndrome. In: S. Malloch & C. Trevarthen (Eds), *Communicative Musicality: Exploring the Basis of Human Companionship* (pp. 423–445). Oxford: Oxford University Press.

CHAPTER THREE

"Happy birthdeath to me": surviving death wishes in early infancy

Brett Kahr

Section 1: The perils of early infancy: physical survival vs. psychological survival

On the morning of 28 September 1928, while working in his laboratory in the basement of St Mary's Hospital in London, Professor Alexander Fleming, the Scottish-born physician and bacteriologist, first discovered the medicinal properties of a fungus from the genus *Penicillium*, which seemed capable of destroying the staphylococcus bacteria (e.g., Ludovici, 1952; Macfarlane, 1984). By 1942, Fleming's initial observational research, developed further by the pathologist Professor Howard Florey and by the biochemists Dr Ernst Chain and Dr Norman Heatley, resulted in the manufacture of penicillin as the world's very first antibiotic (e.g., Macfarlane, 1979); in consequence, the work of these pioneering scientific researchers would help to save countless millions, if not billions, of human lives (Bud, 2007; Hare, 1970).

The labours of Alexander Fleming and his successors in the fields of bacteriology, microbiology, and pharmacology ultimately eradicated numerous illnesses not only in sickly adults but also among infants and young children. Indeed, prior to the proliferation of antibiotics and other medicaments in the mid-twentieth century, a substantial number of babies died before their first birthday, victims of such diseases as cholera, scarlet fever, tuberculosis, typhoid fever, and many others (e.g., Ashby, 1915; Engels, 1984; Meyer, 1921; Newman, 1906; Titmuss, 1943; Woods, 2009). In ancient times alone, some 30–40% of infants died in the first year of life (Frier, 1982; Golden, 1988), prompting the eminent classicist Professor Sir Moses Finley (1981, p. 159) to conclude that, "Any Greek or Roman who reached the age of marriage could look forward to burying one or more children, often very small ones".

Fortunately, as a result of advances in both pure medicine and in hygiene, rates of infant mortality have continued to plummet steadily over the last three-quarters of a century. Today, thankfully, less than 1% of neonates in the Western world will die during infancy, prompting most neonatologists and medical historians to agree that newborn babies have never had a better chance of surviving.

Not only will more than 99% of infants live to celebrate the first anniversary of their birth but, for many, the early weeks and months of postpartum existence might well be experienced as a time of magical fulfilment of bodily needs and psychological wishes, especially for those born into mentally healthy families. Consider the fortunate infant son or daughter of a sane, robust mother who had embarked upon a planned pregnancy and who had enjoyed an uncomplicated labour and delivery, supported throughout by the ministrations of a loving spouse or partner. For infants born into such blessed circumstances, satisfaction and contentment might well be described as the rule rather than as the exception. For instance, if a baby in a healthy family should experience hunger, then *hey presto*, as if by magic, a milky breast will appear, or if a newborn should feel a chill, then, once again, *hey presto*, as if by magic, a warm blanket will materialise.

The provision of such basic needs, whether food, clothing, shelter, cuddles, eye contact, smiles, cooing, humming of lullabies, and so forth, depends, in large measure, upon the presence of one or more primary carers who devote themselves reliably and generously to the baby's wellbeing (e.g., Winnicott, 1949a, 1966). In other words, such parents will look after their babies in this loving way because they had always *wanted* to have babies, and because they have continued to want their babies even after the challenges of pregnancy, birth, and the multitudinous demands of parenting, whether providing late-night feeds that interrupt sleep or the copious changes of nappies.

But what about newborns who might be described as *unwanted*? Such young people have received very scant attention in the psychological literature (e.g., Bowley, 1947; Chesser, n.d., *ca* 1945; cf. Wilkins, 1985). In certain instances, parents will wish that they had never given birth to a baby at all, or, in more perverse scenarios, will enjoy having given birth to a baby in order to have someone to hate. We might even describe the offspring of such mothers and fathers as the recipients of parental *death wishes*, often conscious, but more often unconscious, in nature.

Do death wishes really exist? Indeed they do.

Every human being will, from time to time, harbour hateful wishes, feelings, and fantasies towards another person (e.g., Strean & Freeman, 1991). For instance, when one fails to receive a promotion at the office, it would not be at all unusual for the spurned employee to indulge in a brief private fantasy that his or her boss might one day trip and fall down a steep flight of stairs. In fact, Professor David Buss (2005), an American research psychologist, published a landmark study of the ubiquity of death wishes that adults harbour towards one another. Buss has demonstrated that the vast majority of human beings have entertained often quite detailed murderous fantasies towards one or more people.[1] My own research on violent sexual fantasies, which will often be fuelled by early trauma, underscores the work of Buss by demonstrating not only the pervasiveness of death wishes but also the erotic pleasure that such wishes will often engender (Kahr, 2007a, 2008).[2]

David Buss's work on aggressive fantasies, and my own study of sexual fantasies, focused predominantly on hateful wishes and feelings directed principally towards adults. But what happens when a grown-up expresses death wishes towards a baby?

We know that a very tiny percentage of parents experience such profound hatred towards their offspring that they will actually murder their babies, a phenomenon known in forensic mental health as neonaticide or infanticide (e.g., Brouardel, 1897, 1909; DiMaio & Bernstein, 1974; Emery et al., 1988; Hrdy, 1999; Kirk, 1887; McKee, 2006; Overpeck, 2003; Scrimshaw, 1984; Tardieu, 1868; cf. Masters, 1990). Such parents often suffer from a profound depression, or postpartum psychosis, or from a personality disorder (e.g., Asch & Rubin, 1974; Bender, 1934; Campion et al., 1988; Green & Manohar, 1990; Spinelli, 2001, 2003), and, like Medea of ancient Greek legend, many kill their babies as an attack on an abusive or violent spouse.

Psychiatric workers have devoted extensive research to the study and prevention of neonaticide and infanticide. They have found that, in the contemporary western world, only a very tiny number of parents will actually end the lives of their babies by suffocation, stabbing, poisoning, smothering, throttling, drowning, strangulation, battery, or other forms of gross, murderous abuse (e.g., d'Orbán, 1979, 1990; Funayama & Sagisaka, 1988; Harder, 1967; Kaplun & Reich, 1976; Resnick, 1969, 1970; Scott, 1973; Wilczynski, 1997).

Regrettably, mental health professionals and child care professionals alike have devoted infinitely less attention to the problem of parents who do *not* kill their babies but who, nevertheless, convey murderous wishes to their offspring, by virtue of their actions and speech and fantasies. Throughout the history of psychotherapy and psychoanalysis, few clinicians have studied the problem of unwanted children, let alone that of unwanted *babies*, in any great detail. Two contributors, however, do stand out as pioneers: the Hungarian physician and psychoanalyst Dr Sándor Ferenczi and the British physician and psychoanalyst Dr Donald Winnicott.[3]

In 1929, Ferenczi published a vital, but still infrequently cited, essay on "The unwelcome child and his death-instinct" in *The International Journal of Psycho-Analysis*. In it, he addressed head-on, perhaps for the very first time in the history of psychoanalysis, the vexing problem of those who had grown up as "unwelcome guests of the family" (Ferenczi, 1929, p. 126). Referring to the case of an unwanted child (the tenth born to the mother), Ferenczi observed that such youngsters will become only too aware of their parents' impatience and, indeed, hatred towards them, and that such perceptions will contribute to the child's wish to die. Ferenczi (1929, p. 127) commented boldly that, "children who are received in a harsh and disagreeable way die easily and willingly", and that further, those with "an aversion to life acquired at an early stage" (Ferenczi, 1929, p. 129) will often lose their appetite in an attempt to die, or will develop such conditions as epilepsy, asthma bronchialis, or infantile glottal spasms, as unconscious attempts at self-strangulation. Although Ferenczi's brave and creative paper has received scant attention, this important work now deserves much more serious consideration by contemporary infant mental health specialists and psychotherapeutic practitioners.

Twenty years after the appearance of Ferenczi's work, Winnicott (1949b) produced an equally brazen paper, the better-known "Hate in the counter-transference"—also published in *The International Journal of Psycho-Analysis*—in which he wrote about the burdens experienced by mental health workers in caring for psychotic patients. In consequence of this encumbrance, clinicians will often experience hateful feelings towards their analysands that must be verbalised in a safe way (albeit *not* to the patient), in order to minimise the likelihood of acting out that hatred in a concrete manner by subjecting the patient to electrical shock or to a leucotomy.

Although predominantly an essay about countertransferential hatred in the mind of the mental health clinician, provoked by the psychotic patient, Winnicott devoted a considerable portion of his now classic paper to the way in which such unconscious feelings between a psychiatrist and patient will mirror those experienced by the overburdened mother towards her baby. Winnicott (1949b, p. 73) observed that even the healthy, ordinary, newborn will make so many demands upon the mother's mind and body that, "the mother, however, hates her infant from the word go". He then listed no fewer than eighteen reasons why the ordinary devoted mother might harbour hateful feelings towards her baby, not least because the baby displays a certain ruthlessness towards the mother, treating her "as scum, an unpaid servant, a slave" (Winnicott, 1949b, p. 73). He even went so far as to characterise the needy baby as "ruthless" (Winnicott, 1949b, p. 73), having caused the mother pain during delivery, as well as forcing the mother to love the baby, "excretions and all" (Winnicott, 1949b, p. 73).

First presented to his colleagues at the British Psycho-Analytical Society in 1947 (Kahr, 2011, 2016), Winnicott might have unsettled his audience with the arguably shocking observation that even a healthy mother can convey hateful feelings and wishes to her baby through a seemingly ordinary lullaby, such as the perennial "Rockabye Baby". Although most parents would regard this little musical offering as an expression of tenderness, which might soothe a child to sleep, Winnicott averred that in reality this song offers the mother a vehicle through which she might express hatred towards her baby by crooning "When the bough breaks the cradle will fall", thus fantasising about the infant's death. In other words, Winnicott came to regard "Rockabye Baby", in actuality, as a paean to infanticide, which allows the mother to manage her hatred in the countertransference.

As a matter of both bibliographical–historical interest and clinical interest, it may be noteworthy that in the references to "Hate in the

counter-transference", Donald Winnicott had failed to cite Sándor
Ferenczi's paper on "The unwelcome child and his death-instinct",
published twenty years earlier in the very same journal. Winnicott had
never distinguished himself as a scholar, and sometimes called upon
others to prepare his citations on his behalf (Winnicott, 1958; cf. Kahr,
2003), but it might be of further significance that he did not refer to
Ferenczi's paper, at least in part, because of its truly unbearable contents and its recognition that a child might not be at all welcome in his
or her own home, and, as a result, that child might wish to die.
Indeed, Ferenczi's essay, as well as Winnicott's, both force us all to
confront the horrible reality that even ordinary parents might hate
their offspring, and that, often, they might do so without any
conscious awareness of this fact.

Parents have murdered infants and children throughout the ages,
and archival research on the history of neonaticide, infanticide, and
filicide has become an increasingly well-researched topic in recent
decades (e.g., Brown, 1991; deMause, 1974, 1990, 1994, 2002; Jackson,
1996, 2002; Kahr, 1993, 1994; Koskenniemi, 2009; Radbill, 1968; Turner,
2013).[4] Indeed, one need not struggle to find copious amounts of
evidence about the actual, forensic killing of babies and young children; such data appears not only in the psychiatric and historical liter-
atures but also in paintings, in music, in folklore, in drama, and
elsewhere. Whether Cronos, of ancient Greek mythology, swallowing
his children; whether Aedon murdering her child Itylus, recorded in
Homer's The Odyssey; whether Agave ripping the body of her son
Pentheus to pieces, described so chillingly in Ovid's Metamorphoseon;
whether Francisco Goya's painting of Saturn devouring his son;
whether the eponymous protagonist of Modest Mussorgsky's opera
Boris Godunóv arranging for the murder of the young "Prince Dimitri";
whether the character of "Abbie Putnam" smothering her baby in
Eugene O'Neill's play Desire Under the Elms, evidence of child murder
appears with all too chilling regularity in every corner of our culture.

However, the nature of unconscious death wishes towards infants
and children remains a much more murky terrain, in large measure
owing to its invisible and unquantifiable, yet none the less profound,
nature. Fortunately, the ground-breaking work of Sigmund Freud and
others on unconscious processes in family life (e.g., Flügel, 1935;
Freud, 1900, 1917), the contributions of Ferenczi and Winnicott on
unconscious hatred towards babies and children, and the more recent

empirical researches about aggressive and sadistic erotic fantasy life referred to earlier, all contribute to provide contemporary investigators with a rich platform upon which to explore further the nature of death wishes towards infants as well as the consequences of such wishes.

Section 2: Parental death wishes and infanticidal fears: a day in the consulting room

Death wishes, including neonaticidal wishes towards newborns, infanticidal wishes towards babies, and filicidal wishes towards young children, certainly exist. But what impact do such urges— sometimes conscious, yet often unconscious—have upon us as we progress through the life cycle?

Most psychosocially orientated psychopathological research has focused upon the impact of disrupted attachment relationships, early loss and bereavement, childhood physical abuse, childhood sexual abuse, and childhood emotional abuse as aetiological factors in the development of mental distress or mental illness in later years (e.g., Bowlby, 1980; Brown & Harris, 1978; Herman et al., 1986; Kahr, 2012).[5] But few clinicians have endeavoured to explore the potentially psychopathogenic impact of something much more amorphous, and much less tangible: the death wish itself.

While undertaking clinical work with psychotic patients, more than thirty years ago, I first became aware that many institutionalised people suffer profound psychological anguish simply from being hated, often completely, by a parental figure. As a young psychology trainee, based on a psychogeriatric ward for long-stay patients, virtually all diagnosed as suffering from schizophrenia or from affective psychosis, I spoke regularly to men and women who would describe overtly infanticidal experiences to me, which, I suspected, might have contributed to their great sense of unsafety in the world.

In a very early publication, I identified three individuals in particular who had experienced what I came to refer to as "psychological infanticide" (Kahr, 1993, p. 269), the sense of being "killed off", and yet of remaining alive at the same time in order to suffer on behalf of one's carers, carrying their rage for them. The first patient, "Mr A", a man with a very long-standing history of schizophrenia, grew up in the presence of a cold, distant mother, whom Mr A had described as an "Ice Queen". Apparently, the mother would, on occasion, grasp a carving knife from the kitchen, and chase her son around the house shouting, "I will kill him. I will kill him" (quoted in Kahr, 1993, p. 269). Although one might be tempted to dismiss Mr A's memory of such an incident as a psychotic distortion of reality, tinged with persecutory ideation, I discovered to my surprise that the psychiatrist who had first paid a domiciliary visit to Mr A's home, years previously, had observed such a scene directly, and had subsequently recorded his impressions, complete with direct quotations of the mother's threatening language, in Mr A's bulky case file, buried in the hospital archives (cf. Kahr, 2012).

I also reported on the case of Miss B, a severely schizophrenic woman, born exactly nine months after the death of an elder sister, who had succumbed to diphtheria while still a young child. After the elder sister died, Miss B's parents conceived another baby immediately, and then dared to call the new child—my schizophrenic patient—by the very same name as their dead daughter. Thus, Miss B grew up in the shadow of "deadliness", sensing that she could never compete with the beloved and much-missed elder sibling. Like Mr A, she knew that her parents had wanted her dead, and had wished that the other Miss B (her predecessor) could be brought back to life (Kahr, 1993, 2012).

Finally, I presented the case of Mrs C, yet another schizophrenic person, whose mother had revealed that she had planned to abort Mrs C during pregnancy, but that the rural gynaecologist—a staunch Roman Catholic—would not permit the mother to undergo such a procedure. Thus, Mrs C grew up with the unbearable knowledge that she should really be dead (Kahr, 1993).

In this early paper of 1993, I hypothesised that all three of these deeply psychotic patients suffered from psychological infanticide, which might be a necessary precursor to the development of psychosis in later life. No one had murdered the bodies of these patients, as would be the case in actual, forensic infanticide, but, in all three instances, one or both parents had murdered the patients' minds. Ultimately, all three came to suffer from psychotic symptoms that devolved, at least in part, from the experience of being wished dead by their primary attachment figures.

I then elaborated upon these ideas in a subsequent work, published fourteen years later, after having spent a considerable time

collecting further clinical data, and after having synthesised my observations more systematically. In 2007, I hypothesised that parents who
harbour conscious or unconscious death wishes towards children not
only transmit a sense of psychological infanticide, but also create a
style of interaction—which I termed the "infanticidal attachment"
(Kahr, 2007b, p. 119; cf. Kahr, 2007c)—that might also be described as
a type of disorganised attachment. This form of attachment provides
no sense of safety for the child, and promulgates paranoid ideation,
suicidal ideation, and ongoing fears of assault and deadliness so characteristic of the psychotic.

In that essay, I developed a typology of five varieties of psychological infanticide, or five ways in which an infanticidal attachment
might come to be structured between a parent and a young child.
First, I elaborated upon the phenomenon of actual death attempts and
death threats, wherein a mother or father will endeavour to kill a
child, or express a wish to do so, but fail to succeed. This might be
typified by the aforementioned case of Mr A's mother, who chased her
pre-schizophrenic son round the house with a carving knife, shouting
death threats. Second, I underlined further the painful reality of the
replacement child syndrome, exemplified by Miss B, born exactly nine
months after the death of her elder, cherished sister. Miss B, named
after this favoured sibling, could not compete, and, consequently, she
wished herself dead in a desperate attempt to *become* the deceased
sister. Third, I wrote at greater length about a category of psychological infanticide that I referred to as "aborted abortions" (Kahr, 2007b,
p. 121), emblematised by the case of Mrs C, whose mother would have
aborted her but for the intervention of a fervent Catholic physician
who strongly disapproved of this act.

In addition to these subtypes of psychological infanticide, I also
identified several other variants that had come to my attention
through multiple case examples encountered in my work with psychotic individuals during the 1990s and 2000s. As a fourth type, I
considered the impact of what occurs when a parent murders a child's
pet. For instance, Mr D left home at the age of eighteen in order to
enter the army. Upon his return to the family house some six months
later, he enquired about the whereabouts of his dog, a long-standing
and much cherished childhood companion. Mr D's father confessed
that he killed the dog with a shotgun on the very day that Mr D left
for basic training, explaining that Mr D would no longer have need of

a pet. Shortly after discovering that his father had murdered his dog, Mr D began to hear voices and then he shot himself in the jaw, sensing that his father had actually killed the dog as a symbolic attempt to murder Mr D, his own son (Kahr, 2007b, 2012).

Finally, I theorised about a fifth category of psychological infanticide, comprising those cases in which a schizophrenic patient had begun life as a twin, *in utero*, but had suffered the loss of the co-twin either before birth, during birth, or shortly thereafter. The death of a twin brother or sister—one's first object relation—has, in my clinical experience, proved to be devastating to patients, and has often made them identify with the dead twin. Several of my schizophrenic patients whose twins had died young would adopt classical catatonic postures in emulation of the dead brother or sister (Kahr, 2007b, 2012), and they would, in their minds, blame their parents for the death of the twin brother or sister, harbouring an unconscious belief that mother or father had killed the co-twin deliberately (cf. Piontelli, 1987, 1992).

One could also add a sixth category to this list, namely, the transmission of ordinary, unconscious death wishes, which do not necessarily result in a verbalisation or in an enactment towards the child but which, nevertheless, leave the young person believing that his or her parents crave the child's death or non-existence (cf. Kahr, 2012). For instance, I have encountered several psychotic individuals who cannot remember any direct death threats from parents but who can recall certain looks or glances that the patients experienced as sinister, if not morbid, in quality.

The preceding clinical material provides some indication, I trust, of the many ways in which psychotic men and women have experienced an all too close relationship with deadliness in early life, often caused or exacerbated by a perception of infanticidal cruelty in the mind of a mother or father. Even those patients whose co-twin had died *in utero* or shortly thereafter had blamed their mothers for having killed off their baby brother or sister, and gradually began to regard their parents as deadly objects.

Not all men and women who experience psychological infanticidal moments in early life will become overtly schizophrenic, but many will become more prone to psychotic states.

As the psychotherapist or psychoanalyst becomes more vigilant to the reality of parental death wishes, and to the possibility of the transmission of psychological infanticidal messages, one becomes increasingly sensitive to their appearance in the clinical material. Indeed, some time ago, I saw four patients back-to-back on a certain morning—one at 7.00 a.m., the next at 8.00 a.m., another at 9.00 a.m., and the last at 10.00 a.m.—all of whom reminisced about infanticidal experiences from their growing-up years, or who displayed overtly infanticidal wishes towards their own children.

Mr E, my 7.00 a.m. patient, struggled with depression and with anger, and he would often become embroiled in pub brawls with other men. At the start of this particular session, Mr E told me that he had recently found himself fantasising about smothering his newborn baby daughter. In reality, he had never harmed his daughter physically, and promised me that he would never consider actually doing so, but, none the less, he had become plagued by these troubling infanticidal thoughts. Naturally, we explored his resentments at having to interrupt his life in order to care for a dependent, needy child. I also underlined that his death wishes towards his daughter seemed to have emerged almost immediately after I had announced that I would be raising my sessional fee by a small amount—the first time that I had done so in several years. Although Mr E could readily afford the tiny increase in cost, he became so furious with me that he began to have fantasies about killing me. After many sessions of further work, we came to appreciate that at least part of his deadliness towards his daughter represented a displacement of his transferential deadliness towards me.

Gradually, Mr E's morbid wishes about his daughter abated, as did his death wishes towards me, and he felt extremely relieved that he could verbalise these thoughts in my presence, secure in the knowledge that I would not retaliate by killing him. However, some months later, the infanticidal imagery began to recur, and Mr E reported to his horror that on the previous evening, while holding his beautiful daughter in his arms, fantasies of breaking the baby's neck kept popping into his mind. Once again, we explored the "day residue" which might have contributed to the recurrence of these thoughts; further investigation revealed that shortly before holding his child, Mr E had had a vicious argument with his wife. He gradually confessed that the best way to seek revenge on his spouse would be to kill their daughter. Thankfully, Mr E, a dedicated psychoanalytical patient, had a well-developed capacity to transform murderous thoughts into murderous words in the context of the session, and eventually these deadly fantasies became transmuted, and ultimately he emerged as a truly dedicated, committed, and loving parent.

At 8.00 a.m., I greeted Miss F, a talented, accomplished woman who would often undermine her successes by taking drugs. While free-associating, Miss F recalled that during her early childhood the house of her next door neighbour had caught fire and burned down. Clearly rendered distraught by this tragedy, Miss F asked her mother what would happen if *their* house should ever catch fire. One of five siblings, Miss F wanted to know, particularly, which of the sisters and brothers would be the first to be rescued by the mother. Shockingly, Miss F's mother explained, in a calm and sober voice, that if their home should ever become thus endangered, she would save her husband first, and *not* her children. When Miss F asked why, the mother replied, "Well, if I saved your father, then he and I could have more children. But if I saved you first, and your father died, then I would be in trouble." Miss F burst into tears as she recalled this truly horrifying conversation of years previously, a perfect example of the transmission of psychologically infanticidal wishes from parent to child.

My next patient, Mr G, who came to see me at 9.00 a.m., had recently impregnated his wife after many years of trying to conceive. To his great disquiet, he told me that he found himself plagued by thoughts of plunging a large knife into his wife's tummy, killing both his spouse and their foetus at the same time. I reminded Mr G that during his adolescence he had often experienced suicidal fantasies, and had feared that he might one day take a knife to his own throat. "Oh yeah . . . well done for remembering that," he exclaimed, adding, "I had forgotten about that." After extensive analytical work on his fantasy of stabbing his wife and his unborn child, we came to appreciate more fully that Mr G's rage could be turned either inwards, on himself, or outwards, upon his loved ones. The knowledge that he could just as easily fantasise about cutting his own throat or skewering his family allowed us to focus with increasing care and vigilance upon his deep-seated sadistic urges, which stemmed in part from his own experiences of childhood when he felt that his mother and father never loved him but had, instead, idolised his elder sister.

At 10.00 a.m., Mr H entered the consulting room, and he reminisced about a truly horrible experience. Shortly after his sixth birthday, the family cat had become grievously ill, and Mr H's mother took the ailing animal to the veterinarian. Apparently, the cat's illness had progressed so substantially that nothing more could be done, and the mother agreed that the family pet should be put down. Chillingly, she forced Mr H to watch the "execution" and, extraordinarily, the veterinarian actually permitted the child to observe as he injected the pet with a lethal cocktail of drugs. It will be no surprise to learn that Mr H had first consulted me because of a long-standing addiction to various "recreational" drugs which he injected into his bloodstream, and which had almost killed him on several occasions.

These four vignettes—all back-to-back clinical encounters from just one morning in the consulting room—can in no way be described as unusual. As one becomes increasingly aware of the possibility of death wishes as real phenomena, one's patients sense this and, thus, become more willing to share these truly painful aspects of psychological life.

In each of the aforementioned clinical examples, my patients provided evidence either of death wishes directed towards their own children, or of death wishes directed at themselves many years previously. Mr E experienced infanticidal fantasies of breaking his baby daughter's neck, and Mr G indulged in similar infanticidal wishes. Fortunately, both men had the opportunity to undertake psychoanalytical treatment—Mr E at a frequency of three sessions weekly and Mr G at a frequency of five sessions weekly—and, consequently, each managed to transform these expressions of psychological infanticide into language and thought that could be articulated in the consulting room.

Miss F, by contrast, had found herself the recipient of psychological infanticide, knowing that her mother would have saved the life of her husband from a fire before that of her children. Consequently, she internalised the experience of being wished dead, and in later years Miss F managed to become romantically intertwined with one man after another, each of whom tossed her aside—"killed her off", so to speak—after a short time. Unwittingly, Miss F had become caught in the grip of an infanticidal attachment. And Mr H, the man who had to watch his pet being euthanised, also developed a similar infanticidal attachment and could never manage to stay with one woman for more than a month at a time. Although his parents did not threaten his life directly, his mother did so symbolically by forcing him to watch the death of the cat with whom he had a strong identification; unsurprisingly, Mr H spent much of his adult life sticking deadly needles containing toxic substances into the veins of his arms, just as the veterinarian had done to Mr H's dying pet.

Section 3: Towards a model of the infanticidal attachment: from deathly impulses to extreme psychopathology

Of course, a number of psychoanalytically orientated mental health clinicians have long known about the role of death wishes in the genesis of human psychopathology (e.g., Bloch, 1978, 1985; Chapman, 1959; Kahr, 2001, 2007b, 2012; Lidz, 1973; Minne, 2008, 2009; Motz, 2008, 2009, cp. Motz, 2014; Piers, 1978; Steele, 1978; Welldon, 1988, 1991, 1996, 2001, 2002, 2009, 2011). For instance, the Austrian émigré psychoanalyst Professor Bruno Bettelheim survived the Nazi concentration camps and understood only too chillingly about the experience of being wished dead. In his essay, "Schizophrenia as a reaction to extreme situations", based on work with psychotic children, Bettelheim presented no fewer than three cases in which death wishes towards a youngster will have contributed to the development of extremely severe symptomatology. In his first case, Bettelheim described a schizophrenic boy whose parents thought him feebleminded. They withheld food from him, threatened to send him away, and even told him that he should not have been born. According to Bettelheim (1956, p. 513), "this added to his conviction that his parents wished to kill him through starvation".

Bettelheim also discussed a second case, that of a lad with persecutory delusions, who at the age of two years played a hanging game, involving a noose, with his brother and some friends. The little boy began to choke, and he had to be revived artificially. Bettelheim suggested that this boy sensed the close proximity to death, and the knowledge that his brother—an intimate family member—might have wished him dead. Unsurprisingly, the boy developed psychotic traits in later years.

Finally, Bettelheim wrote about a third youngster who revealed that his mother had had an extramarital affair. The mother urged the boy to remain silent about this sexual secret, and she threatened to kill him if he spoke about it. Once again, Bettelheim linked the maternal death threat to the ultimate development of the boy's schizophrenia in adolescence.

In fact, once the clinician becomes sensitised to the possibility of psychological infanticide, one need not search very strenuously to find copious examples both in the clinical literature and in one's own practice. Of course, one must treat such examples with care and caution, recognising that not all people who have experienced deadly feelings will become psychotic; some will develop other forms of psychopathology. Much will depend upon the nature of one's character structure, the age at which one experiences such deathly feelings, and on the protective, buffering factors (a kindly grandparent, for example), which might militate against the impact of deathly parental wishes.

In an effort to provide a schematisation of the mechanism of the death wish, I propose a working model that could serve as a point of reference to fellow mental health professionals who might wish to contribute their own experiences. Based on more than thirty years of work with death wishes in various forms and contexts, I have arrived at the following conceptualisation.

Most parents, as Winnicott suggested, will experience ambivalence towards their babies. Happily, mentally healthy parents will manage to contain these infanticidal fantasies, impulses, and wishes, and metabolise them sufficiently so that they do not project them on to or into their babies. However, those parents with a more fragile ego structure have a decreased capacity to shield their infants from these toxic thoughts and wishes. Hence, those who cannot contain their infanticidal impulses will transmit them powerfully to their sons and daughters. In certain cases, the infanticidal parents will do so unconsciously—for example, by conveying a look of hatred; in other instances, infanticidal parents will do so quite consciously, verbalising a wish that they had never given birth to the child in the first place. Only in the most extreme instances will such infanticidal wishes and impulses become enacted in the form of forensic neonaticide, infanticide, or filicide, resulting in the child's actual death.

When murderous impulsive parents project their infanticidal wishes on to or into their children, the offspring will respond by internalising those deadly affects and such infants and children will experience what I have come to call psychological infanticide. When young people absorb the infanticidal projection, they become host to an "infanticidal introject" (Kahr, 2007b, p. 124)—an internal representation of being wished dead—which will colour their psychological life.

In particular, the infanticidal introject results in two very specific consequences.

First, the child will come to develop an "infanticidal attachment" pattern—a type of disorganised attachment—in which relationships become killed off with rapidity and with regularity. In other words, the person in question will have no capacity to develop or to sustain a living, reliable, dependable set of interpersonal relationships.

Second, the person in question will display one or more of the approximately fourteen "infanticidal psychopathologies" that I have identified. These are:

1. Schizophrenia and other psychoses.
2. Borderline personality disorder.
3. Suicidality.
4. Autism.
5. Dissociative identity disorder.
6. Somatisation.
7. Anorexia nervosa and other eating disorders.
8. Alcoholism.
9. Drug addiction.
10. Self-mutilation.
11. Attacks on one's own child, e.g., infanticide, abuse, traumatisation, Munchhausen's syndrome by proxy.
12. Forensic enactments, including murder.
13. Philobatism (i.e., thrill-seeking that might result in dangerous, deadly situations; see Balint, 1959).
14. Road traffic accidents and other types of accidents.

When one knows that a parental figure wishes one dead, one will then be at great risk of going "mad" as a result. The list of fourteen infanticidal psychopathologies—by no means a complete catalogue—provides some indication of the ways in which people might develop symptoms that express and enact the wish to be dead. In cases of anorexia nervosa, for instance, the sufferer will gradually starve herself or himself, often as an unconscious enactment of the parental wish that one should simply not be alive.

When those patients who have experienced early death wishes and who have also developed an infanticidal attachment style first embark upon psychotherapy, they will often re-create the early experience of psychological infanticide in the consulting room. Indeed, I would even suggest that an "infanticidal transference" (Kahr, 2007b, p. 125) might manifest itself in the more extreme cases.

I once worked with a young man called "Ira" who suffered from profound brain damage at birth, and who developed with the burden of profound learning disabilities and severe physical handicaps. His parents admitted only too bluntly that they wished that he had died at birth, guilt-ridden and pained that they had subjected him to such a challenging existence. Although the parents also conveyed much loving feeling towards this young man, Ira knew that they would have preferred a "normal", healthy child, like his younger brother, who joined the family one year later. When this patient first entered my consulting room on a hot summer's day, he ran straight into the centre of the room, looked at the open window, and before I could even say hello, jumped on the ledge and catapulted himself out, landing on the adjoining rooftop! During the whole of my psychotherapeutic career, I never encountered such a dramatic entrance (and exit). But I suspect that this young gentleman harboured a terror at meeting me, wondering whether I would also wish him dead; thus, in the grips of an infanticidal transference, he threw himself out of my window as a means of controlling his fear that I might actually throw him away, as he feared that his parents had done by replacing him with a "normal", non-disabled son.

Eventually, Ira and I managed to establish a more calm approach to the use of the room; gradually he came to trust me and he never again jumped out of the window of my consulting room. Some seven months into treatment, he entered the office and announced proudly, "Today is my birthday!" I wished him a very happy birthday. The young man then began singing to himself, "Happy *birthdeath* to me. Happy *birthdeath* to me. Happy *birthdeath* dear Ira. Happy *birthdeath* to me."

To my astonishment, the patient had wished himself a "birthdeath" rather than a "birthday". In spite of his multiple handicaps, he knew, perhaps quite accurately, that his birthday represented a day of death, rather than a day of life. Ira's experience of the birthdeath has informed my thinking tremendously, and I have enshrined his chilling phrase in the title of this chapter.

A topic of immense challenge and deep complexity, the death wish—both the ordinary variety and the more toxic version—appears with great regularity in the parent–child relationship. Most healthy parents manage to process and digest their death wishes quite successfully and protect their beloved children from undue hatred. But for certain parents, the death wish has impacts on the child, sometimes with great profundity and, often, with devastating clinical consequences.

During the past quarter of a century, mental health workers have made enormous strides in the recognition of child sexual abuse and child physical abuse. As a consequence, professionals have become more sensitised to the causes and treatments of such acts of cruelty, and, thus, we have become much better at supporting parents who might be at risk of harming their children's bodies (e.g., Acquarone, 2004; Bar-On, 1996; Barron & Topping, 2011; Clark & Clark, 1989; Cohn, 1986; Crewdson, 1988; Parent & Demers, 2011; Renvoize, 1974; Willis, 1993; Wurtele et al., 1992). Yet, we have devoted far less attention to the problem of the death wish, and now, fortunately, we have an opportunity to begin to explore this relatively neglected aspect of psychological life in an increasingly serious manner.

With the many medical advances of the past hundred years, most babies survive infancy with great ease, at least from a bodily point of view. However, no laboratory-manufactured antibiotics will protect newborns from psychological death wishes. As yet, high-quality parenting and parent–infant psychotherapy remain the primary tools for supplying newborn infants with a "psychological antibiotic" that allows them to survive the potential landmines of the early months and years. Fortunately, parent–infant mental health professionals, and colleagues from related fields, now have an opportunity to devote increased attention to the psychology of the death wish, and, by doing so, we may be better able to transmogrify a child's *birthdeath* into a much more unambivalent *birthday*.

Notes

1.   Professor Buss's book teems with a large selection of personal testimonies from various research participants. For instance, Case #P86, that of an eighteen-year-old female, reported the following fantasy of killing her stepmother: "She was always saying rude things and then she began hitting me, and throwing me down the stairs . . . One day, after throwing me down the flight of stairs into the basement, I told

my dad. He didn't believe me and that was when I started thinking about killing her" (quoted in Buss, 2005, p. 181). The young woman further confessed, "I thought about slitting her throat with a kitchen knife" (quoted in Buss, 2005, p. 181). This case typifies the death wishes and death fantasies reported in the study.

2.   In my book *Sex and the Psyche*, I reported a wide range of violent sexual fantasies offered by research participants. The sexual fantasy shared by "Yannis" (a pseudonym) strikes me as representative of the way in which eroticism and sadism become deeply intermingled. Yannis revealed his favourite sexual fantasy: "Taking all my enemies, anyone who's ever been cruel to me, and fucking them until they bleed to death" (quoted in Kahr, 2007a, p. 336).

3.   Professor Sigmund Freud (1917) made a notable contribution to the contribution of death wishes among siblings, most particularly in his essay on the childhood of Johann Wolfgang von Goethe. He wrote far less about the murderousness of parents towards children.

4.   The historiography of infanticide and child murder has become increasingly broad and impressive during the past half-century, a fact which in itself provides certain testimony to the overwhelming number of cases of adults killing children throughout the centuries. Further notable contributions to this literature include: Baumgarten, 2004; Behlmer, 1979; Bellamy, 2005; Carter, 2007; Finucane, 1997; Golden, 1988; Harrington, 2009; Harris, 1982; Helmholz, 1975; Johnstone, 2006; Kellum, 1974; Langer, 1974; Lefkowitz & Fant, 1977; Martin, 2008; McDonagh, 2003; McLaughlin, 1974; Newton, 2012; Pernick, 1996; Rose, 1986; Roth, 1977; Sauer, 1978; Schulte, 1984; Tierney, 1989; Trexler, 1973; Tucker, 1974.

5.   Other notable works on the psychogenesis of "mental illness", from a variety of psychosocial perspectives, include: Bebbington et al., 2011; Brill and Liston, 1966; Bryer et al., 1987; Chen et al., 2010; Read and Gumley, 2008; Read and Hammersley, 2005; Read et al., 2005; Schetky, 1990.

References

Acquarone, S. (2004). *Infant–Parent Psychotherapy: A Handbook*. London: Karnac.

Asch, S. S., & Rubin, L. J. (1974). Postpartum reactions: some unrecognized variations. *American Journal of Psychiatry, 131*: 870–874.

Ashby, H. T. (1915). *Infant Mortality*. Cambridge: Cambridge University Press.

Balint, M. (1959). *Thrills and Regressions*. London: Hogarth Press.

Bar-On, D. (1996). Attempting to overcome the intergenerational transmission of trauma: Dialogue between descendants of victims and of perpetrators. In: R. J. Apfel & B. Simon (Eds.), *Minefields in Their Hearts: The Mental Health of Children in War and Communal Violence* (pp. 165–188). New Haven, CT: Yale University Press.

Barron, I. G., & Topping, K. J. (2011). Sexual abuse prevention programme fidelity: video analysis of interactions. *Child Abuse Review, 20*: 134–151.

Baumgarten, E. (2004). *Mothers and Children: Jewish Family Life in Medieval Europe*. Princeton, NJ: Princeton University Press.

Bebbington, P., Jonas, S., Kuipers, E., King, M., Cooper, C., Brugha, T., Meltzer, H., McManus, S., & Jenkins, R. (2011). Childhood sexual abuse and psychosis: data from a cross-sectional national psychiatric survey in England. *British Journal of Psychiatry, 199*: 29–37.

Behlmer, G. K. (1979). Deadly motherhood: Infanticide and medical opinion in mid-Victorian England. *Journal of the History of Medicine and Allied Sciences, 34*: 403–427.

Bellamy, J. (2005). *Strange, Inhuman Deaths: Murder in Tudor England*. Thrupp, nr Stroud: Sutton.

Bender, L. (1934). Psychiatric mechanism in child murderers. *Journal of Nervous and Mental Disease, 80*: 32–47.

Bettelheim, B. (1956). Schizophrenia as a reaction to extreme situations. *American Journal of Orthopsychiatry, 26*: 507–518.

Bloch, D. (1978). *"So The Witch Won't Eat Me": Fantasy and the Child's Fear of Infanticide*. Boston, MA: Houghton Mifflin.

Bloch, D. (1985). The child's fear of infanticide and the primary motive force of defense. *Psychoanalytic Review, 72*: 573–588.

Bowlby, J. (1980). *Attachment and Loss: Volume III. Loss. Sadness and Depression*. London: Hogarth Press and the Institute of Psycho-Analysis.

Bowley, A. H. (1947). *The Psychology of the Unwanted Child*. Edinburgh: E. and S. Livingstone.

Brill, N. Q., & Liston, E. H., Jr. (1966). Parental loss in adults with emotional disorders. *Archives of General Psychiatry, 14*: 307–314.

Brouardel, P. (1897). *L'Infanticide*. Paris: Librairie J.-B. Baillière et Fils.

Brouardel, P. (1909). *Les Attentats aux moeurs*. Paris: Librairie J.-B. Baillière et Fils.

Brown, G. W., & Harris, T. (1978). *Social Origins of Depression: A Study of Psychiatric Disorder in Women*. London: Tavistock.

Brown, S. (1991). *Late Carthaginian Child Sacrifice and Sacrificial Monuments in Their Mediterranean Context*. Sheffield: JSOT Press/Sheffield Academic Press.

Bryer, J. B., Nelson, B. A., Miller, J. B., & Krol, P. A. (1987). Childhood sexual and physical abuse as factors in adult psychiatric illness. *American Journal of Psychiatry, 144*: 1426–1430.

Bud, R. (2007). *Penicillin: Triumph and Tragedy*. Oxford: Oxford University Press.

Buss, D. M. (2005). *The Murderer Next Door: Why the Mind is Designed to Kill*. New York: Penguin.

Campion, J. F., Cravens, J. M., & Covan, F. (1988). A study of filicidal men. *American Journal of Psychiatry, 145*: 1141–1144.

Carter, J. (2007). Infanticide: a woman's crime? An investigation into the nineteenth century experience of gender and its effects on perceptions of child murder. BSc Dissertation. Wellcome Trust Centre for the History of Medicine, University College London, University of London, London.

Chapman, A. H. (1959). Obsessions of infanticide. *Archives of General Psychiatry, 1*: 12–16.

Chen, L. P., Murad, M. H., Paras, M. L., Colbenson, K. M., Sattler, A. L., Goranson, E. N., Elamin, M. B., Seime, R. J., Shinozaki, G., Prokop, L. J., & Zirahzadeh, A. (2010). Sexual abuse and lifetime diagnosis of psychiatric disorders: systematic review and meta-analysis. *Mayo Clinic Proceedings, 85*: 618–629.

Chesser, E. (n.d., *ca* 1945). *Unwanted Child*. London: Rich and Cowan.

Clark, R. E., & Clark, J. F. (1989). *The Encyclopedia of Child Abuse*. New York: Facts on File.

Cohn, A. H. (1986). Preventing adults from becoming sexual molesters. *Child Abuse and Neglect, 10*: 559–562.

Crewdson, J. (1988). *By Silence Betrayed: Sexual Abuse of Children in America*. Boston, MA: Little, Brown.

deMause, L. (1974). The evolution of childhood. In: L. deMause (Ed.), *The History of Childhood* (pp. 1–73). New York: Psychohistory Press.

deMause, L. (1990). The history of child assault. *Journal of Psychohistory, 18*: 1–29.

deMause, L. (1994). Why cults terrorize and kill children. *Journal of Psychohistory, 21*: 505–518.

deMause, L. (2002). *The Emotional Life of Nations*. New York: Karnac.

DiMaio, V. J. M., & Bernstein, C. G. (1974). A case of infanticide. *Journal of Forensic Sciences, 19*: 744–754.

d'Orbán, P. T. (1979). Women who kill their children. *British Journal of Psychiatry, 134*: 560–571.

d'Orbán, P. T. (1990). A commentary on consecutive filicide. *Journal of Forensic Psychiatry, 1*: 259–264.

Emery, J. L., Gilbert, E. F., & Zugibe, F. (1988). Three crib deaths, a babyminder and probable infanticide. *Medicine, Science and the Law, 28*: 205–211.

Engels, D. (1984). The use of historical demography in ancient history. *Classical Quarterly, New Series, 34*: 386–393.

Ferenczi, S. (1929). The unwelcome child and his death-instinct. *International Journal of Psycho-Analysis, 10*: 125–129.

Finley, M. I. (1981). The elderly in classical antiquity. *Greece and Rome, 28*: 156–171.

Finucane, R. C. (1997). *The Rescue of the Innocents: Endangered Children in Medieval Minds.* Basingstoke: Macmillan.

Flügel, J. C. (1935). Psychological aspects of marriage and the family. In: J. A. Hadfield (Ed.), *Psychology and Modern Problems* (pp. 159–186). London: University of London Press.

Freud, S. (1900). *Die Traumdeutung.* Vienna: Franz Deuticke.

Freud, S. (1917). Eine Kindheitserinnerungen aus "Dichtung und Wahrheit". *Imago, 5*: 49–57. London: Hogarth.

Frier, B. (1982). Roman life expectancy: Ulpian's evidence. *Harvard Studies in Classical Philology, 86*: 213–251.

Funayama, M., & Sagisaka, K. (1988). Consecutive infanticides in Japan. *American Journal of Forensic Medicine and Pathology, 9*: 9–11.

Golden, M. (1988). Did the ancients care when their children died? *Greece and Rome, 35*: 152–163.

Green, C. M., & Manohar, S. V. (1990). Neonaticide and hysterical denial of pregnancy. *British Journal of Psychiatry, 156*: 121–123.

Harder, T. (1967). The psychopathology of infanticide. *Acta Psychiatrica Scandinavica, 43*: 196–245.

Hare, R. (1970). *The Birth of Penicillin and the Disarming of Microbes.* London: George Allen and Unwin.

Harrington, J. F. (2009). *The Unwanted Child: The Fate of Foundlings, Orphans, and Juvenile Criminals in Early Modern Germany.* Chicago, IL: University of Chicago Press.

Harris, W. V. (1982). The theoretical possibility of extensive infanticide in the Graeco-Roman world. *Classical Quarterly, New Series, 32*: 114–116.

Helmholz, R. H. (1975). Infanticide in the province of Canterbury during the fifteenth century. *History of Childhood Quarterly, 2*: 379–390.

Herman, J. L., Russell, D., & Trocki, K. (1986). Long-term effects of inces-
tuous abuse in childhood. *American Journal of Psychiatry, 143*: 1293–
1296.

Hrdy, S. B. (1999). *Mother Nature: A History of Mothers, Infants, and Natural
Selection*. New York: Pantheon Books.

Jackson, M. (1996). *New-Born Child Murder: Women, Illegitimacy and the Courts
in Eighteenth-Century England*. Manchester: Manchester University Press.

Jackson, M. (2002). The trial of Harriet Vooght: continuity and change in the
history of infanticide. In: M. Jackson (Ed.), *Infanticide: Historical Perspectives on Child Murder and Concealment, 1550–2000* (pp. 1–17). Aldershot:
Ashgate.

Johnstone, N. (2006). *The Devil and Demonism in Early Modern England*.
Cambridge: Cambridge University Press.

Kahr, B. (1993). Ancient infanticide and modern schizophrenia: the clinical uses of psychohistorical research. *Journal of Psychohistory, 20*:
267–273.

Kahr, B. (1994). The historical foundations of ritual abuse: an excavation
of ancient infanticide. In: V. Sinason (Ed.), *Treating Survivors of Satanist
Abuse* (pp. 45–56). London: Routledge.

Kahr, B. (2001). The legacy of infanticide. *Journal of Psychohistory, 29*: 40–44.

Kahr, B. (2003). Masud Khan's analysis with Donald Winnicott: on the
hazards of befriending a patient. *Free Associations, 10*: 190–222.

Kahr, B. (2007a). *Sex and the Psyche*. London: Allen Lane/Penguin Books.

Kahr, B. (2007b). The infanticidal attachment. *Attachment: New Directions
in Psychotherapy and Relational Psychoanalysis, 1*: 117–132.

Kahr, B. (2007c). The infanticidal attachment in schizophrenia and dissociative identity disorder. *Attachment: New Directions in Psychotherapy
and Relational Psychoanalysis, 1*: 305–309.

Kahr, B. (2008). *Who's Been Sleeping in Your Head? The Secret World of Sexual
Fantasies*. New York: Basic Books.

Kahr, B. (2011). Winnicott's *Anni Horribiles*: the biographical roots of "hate
in the counter-transference". *American Imago, 68*: 173–211.

Kahr, B. (2012). The infanticidal origins of psychosis: the role of trauma in
schizophrenia. In: J. Yellin & K. White (Eds.), *Shattered States: Disorganised Attachment and its Repair. The John Bowlby Memorial Conference
Monograph 2007* (pp. 7–126). London: Karnac.

Kahr, B. (2016). *Winnicott's Anni Horribiles: The Creation of 'Hate in the
Counter-Transference'*. London: Karnac (in press).

Kaplun, D., & Reich, R. (1976). The murdered child and his killers. *American
Journal of Psychiatry, 133*: 809-813.

Kellum, B. A. (1974). Infanticide in England in the later middle ages. *History of Childhood Quarterly, 1*: 367–388.

Kirk, R. (1887). Notes on a case of infanticide. *Edinburgh Medical Journal, 33*: 15–17.

Koskenniemi, E. (2009). *The Exposure of Infants Among Jews and Christians in Antiquity*. Sheffield: Sheffield Phoenix Press.

Langer, W. L. (1974). Infanticide: a historical survey. *History of Childhood Quarterly, 1*: 353–365.

Lefkowitz, M. R., & Fant, M. B. (1977). *Women in Greece and Rome*. Toronto: Samuel-Stevens.

Lidz, T. (1973). *The Origin and Treatment of Schizophrenic Disorders*. New York: Basic Books.

Ludovici, L. J. (1952). *Fleming: Discoverer of Penicillin*. London: Andrew Dakers.

Macfarlane, G. (1979). *Howard Florey: The Making of a Great Scientist*. Oxford: Oxford University Press.

Macfarlane, G. (1984). *Alexander Fleming: The Man and the Myth*. London: Chatto and Windus.

Martin, R. (2008). *Women, Murder, and Equity in Early Modern England*. New York: Routledge.

Masters, A. L. (1990). Infanticide: the primate data. *Journal of Psychohistory, 18*: 99–108.

McDonagh, J. (2003). *Child Murder and British Culture: 1720–1900*. Cambridge: Cambridge University Press.

McKee, G. R. (2006). *Why Mothers Kill: A Forensic Psychologist's Casebook*. Oxford: Oxford University Press.

McLaughlin, M. M. (1974). Survivors and surrogates: children and parents from the ninth to the thirteenth centuries. In: L. deMause (Ed.), *The History of Childhood* (pp. 101–181). New York: Psychohistory Press.

Meyer, E. C. (1921). *Infant Mortality in New York City: A Study of the Results Accomplished by Infant-Life-Saving Agencies. 1885–1920*. New York: Rockefeller Foundation/International Health Board.

Minne, C. (2008). The dreaded and dreading patient and therapist. In: J. Gordon & G. Kirtchuk (Eds.), *Psychic Assaults and Frightened Clinicians: Countertransference in Forensic Settings* (pp. 27–40). London: Karnac.

Minne, C. (2009). Infanticide, matricide or suicide. *British Journal of Psychotherapy, 25*: 194–202.

Motz, A. (2008). Women who kill: when fantasy becomes reality. In: R. Doctor (Ed.), *Murder: A Psychotherapeutic Investigation* (pp. 51–64). London: Karnac.

Motz, A. (2009). Thinking the unthinkable: facing maternal abuse. *British Journal of Psychotherapy*, 25: 203–213.

Motz, A. (2014). *Toxic Couples: The Psychology of Domestic Violence*. London: Routledge/Taylor and Francis.

Newman, G. (1906). *Infant Mortality: A Social Problem*. London: Methuen.

Newton, H. (2012). *The Sick Child in Early Modern England, 1580–1720*. Oxford: Oxford University Press.

Overpeck, M. (2003). Epidemiology of infanticide. In: M. G. Spinelli (Ed.), *Infanticide: Psychosocial and Legal Perspectives on Mothers Who Kill* (pp. 19–31). Washington, DC: American Psychiatric Publishing.

Parent, S., & Demers, G. (2011). Sexual abuse in sport: a model to prevent and protect athletes. *Child Abuse Review*, 20: 120–133.

Pernick, M. S. (1996). *The Black Stork: Eugenics and the Death of "Defective" Babies in American Medicine and Motion Pictures Since 1915*. New York: Oxford University Press.

Piers, M. W. (1978). *Infanticide*. New York: W.W. Norton.

Piontelli, A. (1987). Infant observation from before birth. *International Journal of Psycho-Analysis*, 68: 453–463.

Piontelli, A. (1992). *From Fetus to Child: An Observational and Psychoanalytic Study*. London: Tavistock/Routledge.

Radbill, S. X. (1968). A history of child abuse and infanticide. In: R. E. Helfer & C. H. Kempe (Eds.), *The Battered Child* (pp. 3–17). Chicago, IL: University of Chicago Press.

Read, J., & Gumley, A. (2008). Can attachment theory help explain the relationship between childhood adversity and psychosis? *Attachment: New Directions in Psychotherapy and Relational Psychoanalysis*, 2: 1–35.

Read, J., & Hammersley, P. (2005). Child sexual abuse and schizophrenia. *British Journal of Psychiatry*, 186: 76.

Read, J., van Os, J., Morrison, A. P., & Ross, C. A. (2005). Childhood trauma, psychosis and schizophrenia: a literature review with theoretical and clinical implications. *Acta Psychiatrica Scandinavica*, 112: 330–350.

Renvoize, J. (1974). *Children in Danger: The Causes and Prevention of Baby Battering*. London: Routledge and Kegan Paul.

Resnick, P. J. (1969). Child murder by parents: a psychiatric review of filicide. *American Journal of Psychiatry*, 126: 325–334.

Resnick, P. J. (1970). Murder of the newborn: a psychiatric review of neonaticide. *American Journal of Psychiatry*, 126: 1414–1426.

Rose, L. (1986). *The Massacre of the Innocents: Infanticide in Britain. 1800–1939*. London: Routledge and Kegan Paul.

Roth, R. (1977). Juges et médecins face à l'infanticide à Genève au XIXe siècle. *Gesnerus, 34*: 113–128.

Sauer, R. (1978). Infanticide and abortion in nineteenth-century Britain. *Population Studies, 32*: 81–93.

Schetky, D. H. (1990). A review of the literature on the long-term effects of childhood sexual abuse. In: R. P. Kluft (Ed.), *Incest-Related Syndromes of Adult Psychopathology* (pp. 35–54). Washington, DC: American Psychiatric Press.

Schulte, R. (1984). Infanticide in rural Bavaria in the nineteenth century. In: H. Medick & D. W. Sabean (Eds.), *Interest and Emotion: Essays on the Study of Family and Kinship* (pp. 77–102). Cambridge: Cambridge University Press, and Paris: Éditions de la Maison des Sciences de l'Homme.

Scott, P. D. (1973). Parents who kill their children. *Medicine Science and the Law, 13*: 120–126.

Scrimshaw, S. C. M. (1984). Infanticide in human populations: societal and individual concerns. In: G. Hausfater & S. B. Hrdy (Eds.), *Infanticide: Comparative and Evolutionary Perspectives* (pp. 439–462). Hawthorne, NY: Aldine.

Spinelli, M. G. (2001). A systematic investigation of 16 cases of neonaticide. *American Journal of Psychiatry, 158*: 811–813.

Spinelli, M. G. (2003). Neonaticide: a systematic investigation of 17 cases. In: M. G. Spinelli (Ed.), *Infanticide: Psychosocial and Legal Perspectives on Mothers Who Kill* (pp. 105–118). Washington, DC: American Psychiatric Publishing.

Steele, B. F. (1978). Psychology of infanticide resulting from maltreatment. In: M. Kohl (Ed.), *Infanticide and the Value of Life* (pp. 76–85). Buffalo, NY: Prometheus Books.

Strean, H. S., & Freeman, L. (1991). *Our Wish to Kill: The Murder in All Our Hearts*. New York: St Martin's Press.

Tardieu, A. (1868). *Étude médico-légale sur l'infanticide*. Paris: J.-B. Baillière et Fils/Libraires de l'Académie Impériale de Médecine.

Tierney, P. (1989). *The Highest Altar: The Story of Human Sacrifice*. New York: Viking/Penguin Books.

Titmuss, R. M. (1943). *Birth, Poverty and Wealth: A Study of Infant Mortality*. London: Hamish Hamilton Medical Books.

Trexler, R. C. (1973). The foundlings of Florence, 1395–1455. *History of Childhood Quarterly, 1*: 259–284.

Tucker, M. J. (1974). The child as beginning and end: fifteenth and sixteenth century English childhood. In: L. deMause (Ed.), *The History of Childhood* (pp. 229–257). New York: Psychohistory Press.

Turner, W. J. (2013). Defining mental afflictions in medieval English administrative records. In: C. R. Rushton (Ed.), *Disability and Medieval Law: History, Literature, Society* (pp. 134–156). Newcastle upon Tyne, Tyne and Wear: Cambridge Scholars Publishing.

Welldon, E. V. (1988). *Mother, Madonna, Whore: The Idealization and Denigration of Motherhood.* London: Free Association Books.

Welldon, E. V. (1991). Psychology and psychopathology in women: a psychoanalytic perspective. *British Journal of Psychiatry, 158,* Supplement *10*: 85–92.

Welldon, E. V. (1996). Contrasts in male and female sexual perversions. In: C. Cordess & M. Cox (Eds.), *Forensic Psychotherapy: Crime, Psychodynamics and the Offender Patient. Volume II: Mainly Practice* (pp. 273–289). London: Jessica Kingsley.

Welldon, E. V. (2001). Babies as transitional objects. In: B. Kahr (Ed.), *Forensic Psychotherapy and Psychopathology: Winnicottian Perspectives* (pp. 19–25). London: Karnac.

Welldon, E. V. (2002). *Sadomasochism.* Duxford, Cambridge: Icon Books.

Welldon, E. V. (2009). Dancing with death. *British Journal of Psychotherapy,* 25: 149–182.

Welldon, E. V. (2011). *Playing with Dynamite: A Personal Approach to the Psychoanalytic Understanding of Perversions, Violence, and Criminality.* London: Karnac.

Wilczynski, A. (1997). *Child Homicide.* London: Greenwich Medical Media.

Wilkins, A. J. (1985). Attempted infanticide. *British Journal of Psychiatry, 146*: 206–208.

Willis, G. C. (1993). *Unspeakable Crimes: Prevention Work with Perpetrators of Child Sexual Abuse.* London: Children's Society.

Winnicott, D. W. (1949a). *The Ordinary Devoted Mother and Her Baby: Nine Broadcast Talks. (Autumn 1949).* London: C. A. Brock.

Winnicott, D. W. (1949b). Hate in the counter-transference. *International Journal of Psycho-Analysis, 30*: 69–74.

Winnicott, D. W. (1958). Letter to M. Masud R. Khan. 28 November. Box 1. File 11. Donald W. Winnicott Papers. Archives of Psychiatry, The Oskar Diethelm Library, The DeWitt Wallace Institute for the History of Psychiatry, Department of Psychiatry, Joan and Sanford I. Weill Medical College, Cornell University, The New York Presbyterian Hospital, New York, New York.

Winnicott, D. W. (1966). The ordinary devoted mother. In: D. W. Winnicott (1987). *Babies and Their Mothers.* C. Winnicott, R. Shepherd & M. Davis (Eds.) (pp. 3–14). Reading, MA: Addison-Wesley.

Woods, R. (2009). *Death Before Birth: Fetal Health and Mortality in Historical Perspective*. Oxford: Oxford University Press.

Wurtele, S. K., Kvaternick, M., & Franklin, C. F. (1992). Sexual abuse prevention for preschoolers: a survey of parents' behaviors, attitudes, and beliefs. *Journal of Child Sexual Abuse, 1*: 113–128.

PART II

REACHING THE VULNERABLE AT RISK FROM "EXTERNAL" CIRCUMSTANCES

Chapters Four–Nine discuss the mothers who have become vulnerable due to "external" circumstances, such as external trauma. For the mothers to be able to become reflective and insightful about their babies and themselves, they need to overcome the trauma, and here we look at different models used to help this process and develop a helpful relationship with therapists, which allows the essential provision for babies to develop in a healthier way.

CHAPTER FOUR

Creating a safe space: psychotherapeutic support for refugee parents and babies

Zack Eleftheriadou

Introduction

In 2013, the number of refugee people exceeded 50 million for the first time since the Second World War. An estimated 6.3 million have been refugees for years, if not decades (United Nations High Commissioner for Refugees, 2014). In addition to their traumatic losses and cultural dislocation, a significant number of these are women who have experienced a form of torture or sexual violation/rape. It is now urgent to consider how psychotherapy can support the parents, with the hope that it can interrupt and prevent the transmission of intergenerational trauma for future generations.

Many refugees experience multiple traumata, such as loss of family, friends, religion, and culture. Additionally, their political status is often uncertain, and, as a consequence, there is a persistent risk of deportation or, at best, relocation. We know from research that the parents' loss and trauma has an impact on the whole family (Losi, 2006) and that the experience of exile is profound and has lasting consequences. As stated by Von Overbeck Ottino:

> Exile also separates an individual from his or her own cultural representation of the world—life, death, illness and so forth. These

representations, which until that time belonged to the other world and were in line with the representations of the inner world on the basis of a culturally codified grid, now lack points of reference and lose their own coherence and efficiency because of the discrepancy between the inner and the outer worlds . . . [T]hese cultural representations make up an important therapeutic resource. (2006, pp. 132–133)

Taking into account the client's racial and cultural context and how these inform their beliefs is essential throughout the therapeutic work (Meurs, 2014; Paris & Bronson, 2006). Additionally, just as our clients bring their cultural contexts, as clinicians, we bring our own cultural value systems and biases. We strive to work within this system, especially at a time when our refugee clients have lost their cultural references. It is "vital that loss and mourning are allowed to take place" (Eleftheriadou, 2010, p. 175). Furthermore, it is crucial that clinicians are familiar with the theoretical and clinical debates of cross-cultural therapeutic work. These complex debates are beyond the scope of this chapter but can be accessed through other sources (Eleftheriadou, 1994, 2010; Losi, 2006).

The therapeutic work described in this chapter follows a psychodynamic framework, drawing predominantly from the work of Winnicott (1965, 1971, 1987), Bion (1962), and Stern (1995). First, the psychoanalyst Donald Winnicott (1965) introduced the concept of the "holding environment", which is helpful in parent–infant psychotherapy because it encapsulates the experience of being physically and emotionally supported by the carer. This enables the child to feel safe, develop trust, and slowly learn to understand his own feelings, which eventually leads to the capacity to think, symbolise, and play. The psychotherapist provides this holding environment for each member and for the parent–infant pair/triad (Aquarone, 2004)..

The second useful concept in psychotherapy is that of "containment", introduced by the psychoanalyst Wilfred Bion (1962). This is the notion that the infant projects their unmanageable feelings to the primary carer. This is a continual process of absorbing a baby's emotional states (for example, fear) or physical states (such as hunger) and responding appropriately. These states are then reflected back to the baby in a "digested" way, and are, thus, experienced as being less overwhelming. Similarly, the psychotherapist provides containment for the mother and baby, with the primary focus of enabling the parent to think and consequently help their baby cope with her emotional and physical states. In the long term, this provides the building blocks for self-regulation.

Third, other indispensable therapeutic ideas are drawn from the work of the researcher and clinician Daniel Stern (1995). He proposes that there are different points of entry in psychotherapeutic work: the parent's mental state, the infant's mental state, and the parent–infant interaction. Stern also believes that it is impossible to support the family without allowing oneself to get involved; that is, to experience the unconscious communications, or the countertransference feelings. This is a balanced stance of deep emotional engagement as well as retaining enough distance for thinking space.

Clinical case material

The following case material is used to demonstrate the process of parent–infant psychotherapy. I have intentionally focused on the aspects of the clinical vignettes where the parent–infant relationship was facilitated. However, it is important for the reader to appreciate that the therapeutic process would not have been possible without in-depth thinking and understanding of the mothers' psychic processing of their traumatic experiences. It is also paramount to stress that, in mother and baby psychotherapy, one has to work as part of a team of professionals—many of the refugee families need different kinds of legal, medical, and psychosocial support. If there is external coherence, it is more likely to support them to create an internal psychological coherence.

The names of the clients and some cultural and political identifying characteristics in the following cases have been changed or omitted in order to protect their identity.

Amina and Abdi

Amina, a twenty-one-year-old Somalian–Muslim woman, and her baby, Abdi, were referred to me by her (African–Muslim) midwife who knew of my professional interest in, and commitment to, working with refugee people.

Amina had fled Somalia with her male cousin as a result of the political unrest. She had suffered the death of her two brothers, her other male relatives were missing, and she had witnessed wide-ranging suffering in her community. Her husband had been unable to leave with her but was planning to follow Amina to the UK. By the time she went into labour, Amina had been in the UK for seven months. Abdi was her first child and the referral was made due to her concerns that Abdi cried continuously and did not sleep.

When I first saw Amina, Abdi was just over three months old. She arrived late for our first meeting, having got lost. Understandably, she was cautious, as I was different from her—culturally, racially, and professionally—and she was unsure what I could offer her and her child. I reflected to her that despite being cautious about, and unfamiliar with, the therapy, she had attended our meeting. She nodded, saying how she had had to speak to so many strangers, especially to help her with the "medical things", but how grateful she was to her midwife. I then gently enquired about her journey to the UK and about the baby's arrival. She told me tearfully that her pregnancy "should have been a happy time, but it was full of sadness". She cried, saying that Abdi "has no home, like me now".

During this session, I noted that there was some level of maternal "keeping an eye on him" (Winnicott, 1987), but that at times Amina seemed to drift into depression and grief. Abdi remained in the buggy. He looked as if he was getting hot and uncomfortable, and was on the verge of tears. This was a good starting point to begin to look at some of the subtle communications from him. I spoke to him directly, saying, "Oh dear, how uncomfortable you look", and "Perhaps we could find a way together that you can be more comfortable . . . What do you think?" Alongside this communication was an invitation to Amina to observe him with me, opening up questions such as what she had noticed he liked or disliked. My aim was to help her to understand his stress signals and what type or amount of stimulation he required, emphasising to her that every baby has completely different needs (Aquarone, 2004).

In one of the subsequent sessions, Amina arrived at the wrong time and far too early for her session. The muddle with the timing made sense when she broke down and told me that there was a further delay with her husband's departure and in addition they were going to be moved from their accommodation. As she was conveying all this, the baby began to cry. She told me how she did not manage to get anything done or any sleep because the baby had been up the previous night. She put him on her breast but he continued fussing and it took him time to settle (this was a regular event I had witnessed), and she wondered if he was unwell. Amina looked sad as she held him; he responded by opening and closing his eyes. Despite his tiredness and need for gentle holding, he did not know whether he should be awake for his agitated and grieving mother. In fact, I noticed in later sessions that he either cried or looked on the verge of crying a lot of the time. I spoke to Amina quietly, trying to communicate to her what he might need, such as "Look how tired you are Abdi . . . we are keeping you awake with these sad stories". Amina eventually matched my tone, her posture loosened, and Abdi responded by falling asleep. She was anxious that he would wake up if she put him in his buggy. I enquired about his sleeping, and realised that she would always hold Abdi as she feared he would cry if she did not. Of course, holding a baby or co-sleeping in some families or cultures is practised widely. If Amina had not been alone in another culture and had other adult support perhaps it would not have been problematic. However, being alone and in a grieving state we had to explore ways to help her cope, and how the baby could get his necessary rest and sleep time.

In later sessions, Amina was able to share with me how her own mother had suffered a short illness and died when she was five years old. She was raised by her maternal grandmother and her two older sisters. She had very fond memories of her mother and grandmother and wished they were still alive to help her. She felt loved by her father, but she did not see him much as he remarried and lived far from them. Her husband was a much older man, depicted as being "caring and kind" to her. There was a great deal of guilt for those family members that had not survived or were left behind. Nevertheless, her Muslim faith gave her some hope and courage during the bleakest times.

Amina's refugee experience was raw and unconsciously being picked up psychologically by Abdi. The result was that she interrupted her baby's attempts to self-comfort or regulate. Abdi was caught up in tantrums, chaotic sleeping patterns, and crying (especially at night, when Amina felt more isolated and frightened) instead of being in a much-needed restful state. Despite this, I felt hopeful as Amina obviously loved her baby, and Abdi was intentionally communicating and responsive; for example, when I spoke to him, he readily produced sounds or kicked his legs in excitement.

I saw mother and baby for a period of seven months, sometimes on a fortnightly basis and at times with longer gaps. Amina gradually came to feel less isolated and she found it easier to access the support around her; for example, she began visiting her health centre and started making connections with other mothers from a local community centre. She seemed more confident in differentiating between Abdi's different emotional states. I felt she had made use of the support around her and that she had found a calmer place in herself. Abdi appeared less anxious, slept more, and, as a consequence, both mother and baby were more rested.

With Amina's consent, I kept in contact with the medical staff and encouraged her to check her (often highly anxious) concerns about Abdi with her doctor and a community health visitor, which she found very helpful; for example, it proved highly beneficial for Amina to develop more of a routine for Abdi after she learnt about ordinary infant sleep–wake cycles.

Wesesa and Adroa

Wesesa, an Eritrean woman and her son, Adroa, were referred to me from her social worker because there was concern about her depressed mental state and what impact this might have on her mothering capacity.

Wesesa had been captured for ten days (due to religious reasons) and tragically raped by a soldier, resulting in a pregnancy. Soon after, with the help of a fellow Eritrean, she travelled to the UK, where her son was born prematurely at thirty-two weeks (without an apparent medical reason). Adroa was just over six months old when I first met them. In terms of her family history, Wesesa came from an extremely poor family and had lived away from home for a while. Due to financial reasons, their contact had been scarce, and they were not aware that Wesesa had fled the country.

From the outset, this pair was of great concern to the professionals. Adroa was a well-groomed baby who was looked after physically, but he was quite clearly rather neglected psychologically. If Adroa became distressed and his mother noticed, she would describe it as "nothing". It was easier for her to interpret any discomfort or distress as due to physical demands rather than his need for (physical and psychological) holding and containment. Her way of relating seemed to be guided by the "ghost" of her traumatic past (Fraiberg et al., 1980), which distorted her perception of her son. There was little "matching" of his affect, or "joining" of the infant's distress in an attempt to lower it (Beebe, 2003, p. 32).

Wesesa seemed dissociated (van der Kolk, 2007) and had intrusive thoughts about what had happened to her (McFarlane, 1992). It was heartbreaking to witness how unbearable it was for her to look at Adroa. Gaze aversion is strongly linked to a baby's ability to self-comfort. Infants whose mothers are depressed have little (inconsistent) gazing, and they attempt "to manage distress more or less on their own" (Beebe, 2003, p. 32). These babies display more self-comforting behaviours, such as fingering clothes or objects (Tronick, 1989).

Adroa would rarely signal to his mother or look at her directly. When she took him out of his buggy, he was placed on the floor facing away from her while she remained sitting on a chair. I felt concerned that if I did not keep him in mind she simply could not. My overall impression was that Adroa was not psychologically seen in any way. As Acquarone (2007) states, "there is a big difference between being born physically and being born emotionally" (p. 215). Adroa was conceived through a traumatic event and through a mother who was still frozen in fear. Early on, I tried to assess how much he could respond to a stranger. To my great relief, albeit with caution, Adroa seemed to be responsive.

Wesesa and Adroa often left me feeling preoccupied with them after the sessions, and (like the other professionals involved) I had concerns about the baby boy's psychological welfare. With supervision (which is absolutely critical in trauma work and particularly when babies are involved), I was able to process my own feelings and think carefully about what they needed from the different professionals. With Wesesa's consent, I decided it was important to have closer contact with her social worker and GP. In addition, it was urgent to assess early on whether, with the right help, she could create more psychological space for Adroa. I talked to her about ordinary infants, how they explore the world, and how they might express their frustrations. Through modelling and open questions, I tried to activate her curiosity, in order for her to notice how her son communicated.

Adroa's tragic conception circumstances, which had not been mentioned in the first few sessions, were slowly brought into our work. Initially, this took place through bodily communications; for example, about her fears that she had a gynaecological infection or damage and some horrifying images. It was important that if any narrative about the rape and torture were to emerge it should be when she was ready; any direct questions could have been experienced as a further assault on her. Understandably, having one's body violated in such a traumatic way, it takes some time for such a person to trust again, if ever. I tried to provide containment for her feelings of shame and anger, as well as her ambivalence towards motherhood. Sometimes, I provided carefully formulated interpretations about her fears of trusting people around her (including me), but on another level it was just as important to acknowledge her desperate plea for help, and so I facilitated external, supportive connections. For example, we had a discussion about talking to a doctor regarding her own health fears and attending the drop-in clinic regarding her concerns about Adroa.

In one significant session, Wesesa was sitting with Adroa on her lap when she stood up abruptly, put Adroa on the floor, and said she needed to go to the toilet. Adroa sat rather still and after a slightly delayed reaction (compared to other babies of the same age) eventually started to whimper. He could not lock into my eyes to seek comfort. As Wesesa was taking a long time, I felt I had to reach him somehow. First, I sat closer to him on the floor. He noticed me and held my gaze briefly. I felt he was literally collapsing psychologically and needed something to lean on. His distressed state escalated further (noted by his reaching out for the strap of his mother's bag and desperately trying to put it in his mouth). I found a position where I could be on the same eye level as him, and I tried to match his distress, but in a lower tone, as suggested by Beebe (2003). I put my hand around him so he could be supported better. He slowly became slightly calmer and I felt I had connected with him.

When his mother returned, she sat down on the chair instead of picking Adroa up again. I asked her how she was and she said she had felt dizzy. I wondered if she had had a physical reaction to the traumatic material she had disclosed to me earlier. Once I established she was settled again, I felt I had to place him back on her psychological radar, so I gently said how he had looked for her, elaborating that he kept looking in the direction from where she had left. This was an attempt to mobilise their relationship and reinforce the fact that there was no doubt that he recognised (and preferred) his mother's voice.

Once more, I said to him gently, "You know mummy's voice, don't you?" Wesesa laughed, saying, "No, it could be anyone. He is too curious about people." I just said, "Look," being mindful that it was in the same calm tone so that Wesesa would hear it and not feel criticised in any way. I talked to Adroa again, saying, "Shall I return you to mummy?" and I handed him to Wesesa. She made brief eye contact with him and then held him facing sideways. He seemed uneasy and jumpy; she gave him his dummy, but he continued looking uncomfortable, so she gave him a biscuit. At this point once again I matched his tone in order to model to her how to match his distress, with the aim of slowly lowering the volume and calming him. He settled somewhat and he was gently placed back on the floor. I noted that, rather unusually, she continued to look at him. She said, "Babies listen more than we think", and I nodded.

In due course, Wesesa was able to talk about her guilt for not visiting Adroa very much in the special care baby unit after he was born. She felt that the staff had secretly criticised her for it and she felt ashamed. She told me when she saw him that "it was as if he was someone else's child" and she feared he was "damaged" because of how he had come into the world. This is not uncommon with mothers whose babies are moved straight into a special care unit after birth, but with her it was much more complex. Wesesa projected a great deal to this baby, saying "how strong he will be" or how "he gets so angry" when she did not feed him straight away. In her mind, any emotional intimacy with Adroa was equated as being psychologically connected to the abuser. She told me how she had wanted to punish the abuser and disclosed some of her revenge fantasies (via her dreams). In one of the most painful sessions, she told me of her fears of what he might look like as an adult man. It was an extremely slow process of separating her image of Adroa being strong like the soldier who assaulted her with that of a baby who was vulnerable and dependent on her.

Through my capacity to bear to look at him, the very subtle noticing and interpreting of Adroa's states and interactions with his mother, Wesesa began to tolerate thinking about him more and, therefore, she could bear to look at him. She became curious about his communications. I strongly believe that her increased attentiveness also led to his increased vocalisations, as well as greater range of them (Beebe, 2003). It was now safer for him to look at his mother and to be looked at. Her voice softened towards him, and I was delighted when in one session she referred to him in a more endearing manner as "my handsome boy". With time, Wesesa began to talk more frankly and disclosed more of her nightmares of being chased or confined. She was able to cry and she thanked me for helping her to see that Adroa "could not be blamed for what happened".

The last time I saw them was when Adroa was just under two years. Wesesa continued to have individual support after our work was finished and she was managing well. Eventually, she also felt less ashamed, and, therefore, could tolerate being able to attend parent and baby playgroups with the support of her social worker.   .

Discussion

In both the cases I have described, the mothers were offered containment (Bion, 1962). In different ways and in front of a validating witness, they were helped to talk about their painful journeys and create some distance from their psychosocial trauma. The capacity to reflect and create a coherent narrative, or a "reflective self-function", is more likely to prevent the parent's affective content from being transmitted to the next generation (Fonagy et al., 1993). We cannot expect people to "manage" or ever forget their experience, but, through reflection, they are able to acknowledge their impact and keep them at bay so that they can get on with everyday life. As the mothers learnt to trust me, they began to take more interest in their babies and to try to see the real baby rather than their internally held image. In Amina's case, the baby was seen as weak and as if he could not regulate at all without her holding and (unknowingly) over-stimulating him. It was undoubtedly a more complicated process for Wesesa, who could not (physically and psychologically) see the real baby and felt persecuted by his demands.

In both of the cases discussed, the babies were developing normally (as confirmed by the medical staff) but required support, alongside their mothers, to feel more psychologically contained. When babies' emotional states are matched, "but without the full volume or intensity, [it] . . . is often effective in helping the infant to dampen arousal. Matching the rhythm (but not the volume) of the crying, and then gradually slowing down, facilitates infant distress regulation" (Beebe, 2003, p. 32). Throughout, there was an active process of inviting the mother to join in this process, so that I did not become the special one who could calm the baby. It was vital that a mother's feelings of competence are increased.

In all stages of the therapeutic process, I have to allow myself to experience and tolerate the anxieties and despair, especially those experienced by a newborn. A newly born infant needs a great deal of containment, protection, and integration "from the onslaught of sensory and emotional data" (Acquarone, 2007, p. 217). If the mother is somewhat preoccupied or, even worse, traumatised as a result of torture, it can be experienced as raw and overwhelming. This was, of course, especially the case with Wesesa and her baby. It is also imperative to bear in mind that young babies have not separated off the "me" and "not me" aspects of themselves; they absorb communications from their environment, and especially their primary carer, as being part of them (Winnicott, 1971). Babies seem to know when the parent is in a depressed state, and so react in defensive ways, such as sleeping, or demonstrate this physically by being sick (Dowling, 2006). As clinicians, we have to carefully observe the babies and their relating to us in order to separate the impact of trauma and that of experiencing a traumatised carer from what might be the early stages of psychopathology or autism (see Acquarone 2007 for a detailed discussion).

There was a slow process of weaving mothers' inner unconscious worlds, as well as acknowledging that all the communications were in the context of their cultural background and external experiences and not my western training values (Eleftheriadou, 2010). In other words, both internal and external experiences were validated and I believe this is what created the trust with these mothers, allowing them to bring their babies and remain in psychotherapy. It is a careful balance to explore these, but not to underestimate the real, external, trauma of the exile—the cultural shock of and socio-economic dependency on a new country.

Conclusion

In both of the clinical cases presented, the shadow of loss, cultural dislocation, trauma, and torture had had an impact on the mothers at a delicate time of the babies' psychosocial development. This chapter illustrates that it can have a profound effect if someone is interested in your baby and his development; even with the most traumatised mothers, it can be a helpful way to facilitate their bonding process. The observations and decoding of the baby's emotional states and behaviours, alongside other subtle interventions in parent–infant psychotherapy, can provide a good holding environment and containment for a mother and baby. Mindful and culturally respectful therapeutic support at this early stage of development can have a constructive and lasting impact on the mother and baby relationship.

References

Acquarone, S. (2004). *Infant–Parent Psychotherapy: A Handbook.* London: Karnac.

Acquarone, S. (2007). *Signs of Autism in Infants: Recognition and Early Intervention.* London: Karnac.

Beebe, B. (2003). Brief mother–infant psychoanalytically informed video feedback. *Infant Mental Health Journal, 24*(1): 24–52.

Bion, W. R. (1962). *Learning from Experience.* London: Heinemann.

Dowling, D. (2006). 'The capacity to be alone': rediscovering Winnicott and his relevance to parent–infant psychotherapy. In: M. Lanyado & A. Horn (Eds.), *A Question of Technique* (pp. 63–80). London: Routledge.

Eleftheriadou, Z. (1994). *Transcultural Counselling.* London: Central Books.

Eleftheriadou, Z. (2010). *Psychotherapy and Culture: Weaving Inner and Outer Worlds.* London: Karnac.

Fonagy, P., Steele, M., Moran, G., Steele, H., & Higgitt, A. (1993). Measuring the ghost in the nursery: an empirical study of the relationship between parents' mental representations of childhood experiences and their infant's security of attachment. *Journal of the American Psychoanalytic Association, 41*(4): 957–989.

Fraiberg, S., Adelson, E., & Shapiro, V. (1980). Ghosts in the nursery: a psychoanalytic approach to the problems of impaired infant–mother relationships. In: S. Fraiberg (Ed.), *Clinical Studies in Infant Mental Health* (pp. 164–196). London: Tavistock.

Losi, N. (2006). *Lives Elsewhere: Migration and Psychic Malaise.* London: Karnac.

McFarlane, A. C. (1992). Avoidance and intrusion in posttraumatic stress disorder. *Journal of Nervous and Mental Disease, 180*: 258–262.

Meurs, P. (2014). The first steps: a culture-sensitive preventive developmental guidance for immigrant parents and infants. In: R. N. Emde & M. Leuzinger-Bohleber (Eds.), *Early Parenting and Prevention of Disorder* (pp.165–185). London: Karnac.

Paris, R., & Bronson, M. (2006). A home-based intervention for immigrant and refugee trauma survivors: paraprofessionals working with high-risk mothers and infants. *Zero to Three* (www.zerotothree.org).

Stern, D. (1995). *The Motherhood Constellation: A Unified View of Parent–Infant Psychotherapy*. London: Karnac.

Tronick, E. (1989). Emotions and emotional communication in infants. *American Psychologist, 44*(2): 112–119.

United Nations High Commissioner for Refugees (2014). See www.unhcr. org/53a155bc6.html, 1 August 2014.

Van der Kolk, B. (2007). Trauma and memory. In: B. Van der Kolk, A. C. McFarlane, & L. Weisaeth (Eds.), *Traumatic Stress* (pp. 279–302). New York: Guilford Press.

Von Overbeck Ottino, S. (2006). Psychotherapeutic practice with migrant families: the case of a young child traumatized by war. In: N. Losi (Ed.), *Lives Elsewhere: Migration and Psychic Malaise* (pp. 123–155). London: Karnac.

Winnicott, D. W. (1965). *Maturational Processes and the Facilitating Environment*. London: Hogarth Press.

Winnicott, D. W. (1971). *Playing and Reality*. London: Routledge.

Winnicott, D. W. (1987). *Babies and their Mothers*, C. Winnicott, R. Shepherd, & M. Davis (Eds.) Reading, MA: Addison-Wesley.

CHAPTER FIVE

Interventions with mothers and babies in prisons: collision of internal and external worlds

Pamela Windham Stewart

> "Two traits are essential in the criminal: boundless egoism and a strong destructive impulse. Common to both of these, and a necessary condition for their expression is the absence of love, the lack of emotional validation of humans"
>
> (Freud, 1928b, p. 178)

There is no such thing as a baby outside of a social context

Prison provides an opportunity to work with people who, in ordinary life, are often beyond the reach of psychotherapy. Working in prisons with mothers and babies provides the additional opportunity for thinking about the impact of early experience in the development not only of the baby before us, but also of the mother.

Forensic psychotherapy requires sensitivity to the internal world of patients and therapists. Of equal importance is the therapist's connection to the external worlds of politics, the legal system, and society at large. Psychotherapy with mothers and babies demands attunement to the mother–baby dyad, while also keeping in mind the

101

very concrete external reality of prison life. The external social reality is a key component in working with prisoners. Almost without exception, in nearly twenty years of forensic work, the mothers in my groups come from deprived and depriving social backgrounds where thinking, as much as material wellbeing, was in short supply.

Statistical context

Statistics can be helpful in giving a picture of the lives and backgrounds of imprisoned women. One of the most up-to-date sources comes from the Prison Reform Trust (www.prisonreformtrust.org.uk). In autumn 2014, it published the Bromley Briefings Prison Factfile, in which it states that the female prison population in England and Wales doubled between 1995 and 2010. Other statistics include the following:

- more than six out of ten female prisoners (66%) have dependent children under the age of eighteen;
- approximately 17,000 children a year are separated from their mothers due to her incarceration, eight out of ten of which have never been separated for more than a few days prior to their mother's conviction;
- 2000,000 children in England and Wales have a parent in prison— more than the number of children affected by divorce each year;
- 40% of women prisoners surveyed reported having attempted suicide at some point in their lives, compared with 7% of the general population;
- 49% of women in prison suffer from anxiety and depression, while 25% report symptoms of psychosis; 30% of the women have previous psychiatric admissions before entering prison.

In December 2013, the ten-place mother and baby unit closed at HMP Holloway in London, which has reduced the number of places on mother and baby units from one hundred to ninety. In a guide for mothers in prison, "Mum's the Word", the five other mother and baby units available in 2014 are listed as: Bronzefield in Ashford, Surrey, Eastwood Park in Gloucestershire, Styal in Cheshire, New Hall in West Yorkshire, and Peterborough in Cambridgeshire. These locations mean that many women will be in prisons very far from their families.

Although the number of women in prison is falling—3,893 at the time of writing (Howard League for Penal Reform, 12 December 2014)—the impact on the lives of prisoners and their children is enormous. Not only are the children separated from their mother, who is often the sole carer, but most children are unable to stay in their own home, leading to broken attachments and school disruption, which is damaging for educational success. Many children go into care when their mother is sent to prison. Being in the care system increases a child's chance of going to prison by thirteen times. One mother I worked with, who was convicted of murder, experienced fifty-seven foster placements before the age of sixteen.

Loss is central to incarceration—loss of freedom, home, family ties. Locking up women has many serious implications. Many of the female prisoners have suffered huge losses as children. Unresolved mourning brings with it high incidents of self-harm. Ironies and difficulties abound. Recently, I was working with a young woman who kept trying to burn herself to death as well as put a plastic bag over her head. As I arrived on the unit, the officers were desperate to find a match so they could go for a cigarette break. Difficult not to despair—what to do, laugh or cry?

The original idea behind my interest in working in a prison with mothers came from my curiosity about the interplay between internal and external worlds. I was very keen to see what impact an institution could have on a mother and baby. Taking prison as a place of high anxiety, I wanted to see how well, or otherwise, mothers could cope in such a setting. As you will see, my discoveries surprised me.

While accepting the importance of statistics, the stories of the women carry emotional power. From the beginning of time, stories have provided a way of giving form to feelings and illuminating human experience. Two stories from prison are described in the following sections.

Marie and her nine-month-old daughter, Teri

As I arrived on the unit to start the weekly group, the mothers were eating their lunch in a windowless room; many were facing the wall. In came Marie with her daughter, Teri. Wearing a soiled T-shirt, worn cotton slippers, and a pair of torn sweat pants, Marie appeared dirty and dishevelled. Equally, Teri's pink shorts and shirt were crusty with old food. Teri was wearing only one slipper that looked too small, as her foot appeared red and puffy. In the past, I had noticed that Marie made the other mothers tense. They stiffened when she spoke in her harsh voice and they avoided her wild eyes. Marie told me that she had been born while her mother was in prison many years ago.

Teri watched her mother carefully. Sitting well back in her buggy, the nine-month-old baby at first appeared relaxed. One leg was dangled, slipperless, the other was pulled up into her body, as if for protection. In contrast to her grubby clothes, her fingernails and toenails appeared cared for and clean.

Marie said she was going to make Teri's lunch. Teri watched her mother leave the room and then switched her gaze to me. Teri started making little kicking motions with her dangling leg, as if marking time until her mother returned. Gathering momentum, she started kicking harder and smiled at me. This time she touched my knee and looked contentedly into my face as if happy to make contact—or to hit dry land.

When Marie came back into the room, I noticed how small she looked in contrast to her huge daughter. Teri looked from me to her mother, and then at the plastic bowl that held her lunch. Pulling her eyebrows down, she seemed to frown briefly. There did not seem to be a drink for her, only the bowl. Without putting a bib on Teri, Marie quickly started feeling Teri with huge, dripping spoonfuls, saying, "This is Weetabix, this has lots of lovely sugar in it, just the way you like it."

Obediently, Teri opened her smooth, pink mouth. In a way that is hard to describe, her mouth seemed to stay open, as if the food was not being fed to her but funnelled straight down into her stomach. Images of suffragettes being force-fed in prison drifted across my mind. The food looked like dirty hay, hot and lumpy. Would it be hard to swallow without a drink?

Teri's eyes widened and stayed glued to her mother's face—all the focus on her mother, not the spoon coming towards her. Her mouth looked like a target, a bull's eye. As Marie fed the baby, she poured her own story into me.

In a tired voice she said that there were four children in her family when she was growing up. Her little sister died of leukaemia. Her name was Erica and she died when she was thirteen. I said that I remembered that Marie had a son named Eric and she smiled at me as she continued feeding and talking. "Yeah, I named him after me sister . . . My family fell apart when Erica died. My parents blamed each other. We was all round the bed in the hospital when she died. Me mum and dad never spoke to each other again. We all fell apart after that." Marie said she started working on the streets soon after. "No one was home. No one looked after me. I was fifteen."

I was thinking about Marie's other three children at home while she and her husband, her co-defendant, were away in prison. Earlier, Marie had revealed to me that Eric had already run away from home, desperately trying to find his mother. Like many inmates, Marie had not told the children that she was in prison. She just told them that she was "in hospital to have the baby". Marie's fifteen-year-old daughter has also run away from home and was working for her aunt's escort agency, which is an easier way of saying she was an underage sex worker.

Marie said it was too painful to keep in touch with her family. Her eyes filled with tears. It was at this point that Teri suddenly started to vomit in a strange way, as if her head were haemorrhaging. With what looked like no effort at all, no wrenching or heaving, all the straw-coloured food came streaming out of her little mouth, as if a tap had been turned on by someone else. Weetabix shot out like lava, settling in the creases of her neck, moving down into her collar and into her shorts. Food fell on the seat of the chair and slid down her legs. Food fell between her toes and into the edges of her one slipper.

As if shaking herself awake, Marie startled. Looking around frantically, she saw a roll of toilet paper. Vainly, she started to mop up the mess. The small amount of paper was inadequate to the task. Weetabix was everywhere. Teri stared out with her mouth still open, like a door gaping off its hinges. Unblinking, Teri's eyes looked out unfocused, glassy as marbles, as if she had seen a ghost.

Marie yanked Teri from her soiled seat, smearing her own clothes with the residue of lunch, and rushed from the room saying that she had to change her daughter.

Sadly for our work together, Marie and Teri were transferred to another prison. All Marie's undigested sense of grief and loss seemed to be spooned, undigested, into her daughter. There was the sense of history repeating itself, a broken record, stuck in a groove with no hope of remedy or repair. Absence of understanding guarantees endless repetition. With no other mind to hold her, Marie seemed to be passing on her own suffering to her daughter, who, like her own mother, was born in prison. The image of the Russian doll came to my mind, the doll seeming to get larger with each generation.

Ashton and her son, Kayne (from six to nine months), December–June

I am calling this nineteen-year-old white British mother Ashton because, in the beginning, she reminded me of the character in Harold Pinter's play *The Caretaker* who had suffered electric shock therapy. Initially, Ashton appeared lonely, afraid, and toneless. I came to wonder who was the carer in the relationship: mother or baby?

Ashton's skin appeared engraved; she was covered with elaborate tattoos. Serving a sentence for violent assault, this was her first time in prison. Ashton is gay and her baby, Kayne, is the product of a very abusive relationship with a much older man.

Working with both men and women in prison always makes me so regret that Freud's radical courage did not stretch to staying with his formulation (1890s) of the seduction theory. In my clinical experience, all the women I have worked with have been the victim of early sexual abuse, either by their men (usually the fathers) or other women. As Estella Welldon makes clear in *Mother, Madonna, Whore* (1988), the stark reality of this abuse is far from a fantasy and has implications across the generations. Men are not the only perpetrators of sexual abuse, as we see from the ongoing rise in female sexual offending. As women's social roles change, so, too, does the nature of their offending.

Due to funding difficulties for my work, there was an eight-month gap running the weekly mother and baby group. (This reminded me of the broken ties and relationships the prisoners experience.) I first met Ashton in the run-up to Christmas. It was during the nativity play, when Kayne (six months old) was dressed up as Joseph. At the end of the play, an officer dressed as Father Christmas came in to give the babies Christmas presents. One look at Father Christmas and Ashton started to sob and shake uncontrollably. Later, she told me of the long sexual abuse she suffered at the hands of a neighbour when she was little. This neighbour often dressed up as Father Christmas for the holidays.

Gradually, as the weekly group got back on its feet, Ashton became more keen, always ready and waiting for me. She would sit very close to me on the sofa and together we would look at Kayne. I would ask her what she thought he was thinking as we gazed at him, and he would smile back.

As we sat together, I would think about providing a perspective from which to observe Kayne, the two compass points as the mother and I experience the child together. I was reminded of Andre Green's suggestion in *On Private Madness: "The Dead Mother Complex"* (1986), where he asserts that the child needs a father to protect it from the mother's madness. As much as a mother might need another mind to protect the child from her own madness, it is also vital for there to be a mind to protect the child from the physical advances of another—not always the father. The increase in paedophilia is noticeable in the current prison population.

The other mothers in the group chatted and gradually seemed to become more interested in their babies, although a lot of time could be taken up with discussions about their clothes. Increasingly, the mothers took their babies out of the buggies that imprisoned them and either held them or let them play freely on the floor.

One of the many paradoxes in prison is the way in which the babies are also incarcerated in their buggies. The buggies stand for the great pride and value the mothers feel they are showing for their children. The elaborate buggies, often far beyond the comfortable financial reach of the mothers, are a concrete representation to the mothers, and often the staff, of how much the mothers value their babies. It is a measure of how difficult it is to express and explore with these young women how much it is that they have to offer their children without ostentatious displays of consumerism. Obviously, conveying this requires a great deal of sensitivity, as the women are highly vigilant and quick to pounce on any comment that sounds judgemental. In a forensic setting, the therapist struggles not to repeat the adversarial experience of the courtroom and police station. Questions must be kept to a minimum while still encouraging curiosity and reflection.

As Kayne became more mobile, Ashton would put him on the floor. If he began to cry, she would take toys to show him and we would talk in the group about crying, whether babies could be "naughty", and wonder about what they were thinking. The mothers would talk about their children at home, any feelings of sadness, or simply engage in ordinary chitchat. Something was happening with Kayne and Ashton. I had the feeling he was pulling his mother to him. Wide-eyed and with an engaging grin, Kayne worked hard to keep his mother's attention. He was richly rewarded.

Who was the mother here? Why do we think that "mothering" is gendered? Can mothering not be a relationship open to all?

In the spring, a mother duck and her ducklings appeared in the prison garden. Together, the group would watch this mother and her babies from the window. Ashton became very concerned that they be "given" enough to eat: "We have to give them some bread. They will starve," she would say, anxiously. She had no sense that Mother Nature, in the way of worms and insects, would provide. To myself, I wondered what this said about her sense of a reliable, ready mother with a breast and a mind ready for feeding. Also, I am ashamed to recall that my initial feelings were of shock at her lack of education and general knowledge. But why would Ashton know about ducks or baby animals? Perhaps her parents had never explained to her or taken her to the zoo.

As is so often the case, as the release date approached, Ashton became more anxious and worried. Unlike many of the other mothers, she did have a home to return to and was able to talk about plans on her release. By now, Kayne was trying to walk and was even more charming than ever. Smiling with his eyes as well as his mouth, he teetered around the room, looking back and beaming at this mother. He was flirtatious and beguiling. While his development was a pleasure to see, I could not help also wondering about the need to charm and keep his mother on the line. He was delighted with himself and his developing prowess—and, fortunately, so was she.

Within the group, Ashton was able to think and plan ahead. She was also able to talk in the group about what the loss of the prison, and her son's second home (the first being her body–mind), would mean to them both. She wondered how Kayne would feel when he no longer saw the other mothers and babies. It is also important to remember what impact the loss of the mothers and babies have on the prison staff. These young women work with them so closely during their sentences and then are banned from having any contact with them after they are released.

Evidence of Ashton's emotional growth was seen in her ability to say goodbye to the prison staff, the other mothers, and to me. Through this process of ending, she was acknowledging what it meant to say goodbye to the loss of her and her son's home by making goodbye cards for her friends. She also made one for me, thanking me for the group (and saying that "My Friday afternoons will never be the same again"). Ashton acknowledged, rather than fudged, the loss and sadness of leaving prison—as paradoxical as that might sound.

Contrary to some psychoanalytic rulebook, for a time Ashton stayed in touch. For several weeks she would send me a letter that arrived on a Saturday morning. I wondered if perhaps she wrote the letter on Friday when the group took place.

Her first letter after release said,

> Leaving prison has been weird. I cried as I left. I got home and had time to chill before I went to probation. My parents have two dogs. Kayne was petrified of them but he is warming to them now. He calls the little one "cat". He has settled in really well and sleeps all night in his travel cot. He is still doing steps—not really walking yet. I have bought him a whole new wardrobe of clothes. I haven't ventured out anywhere on my own yet. I have no social life . . . it will take time. I keep forgetting that I can actually go out. I feel paranoid and afraid I will get sent back to prison.

Then, in June, she wrote that she was doing very well. Kayne had a new word—"shoe". She was going to a parent–toddler group, and Kayne loved it.

> He enjoyed watching the older kids play but it was a bit upsetting because they did not take any notice of him and you could tell he wanted to play. The other mums were all a lot older than me and didn't really talk to me but I will be going again next week and I am sure in time it will be all right.

After a while, the letters stopped. How to see this? Was it a good sign that Ashton was on her way and could let go of contacting me by letter? I hoped that thinking was now something that could take place between the people in her life and in her own mind.

Ashton was able to express her fears and disappointment not only for herself but also for Kayne. There they were back in the world and facing up to difficult feelings. Ashton was able to contain her anxiety enough to make realistic and helpful plans for the future. She had made the very difficult transition from prison to the world outside.

Her once immaculate prison cell is now inhabited by another young woman with her baby. Despite the surface tidiness of the cell, the new mother, when moving in, found piles of dust and rubbish hidden under the bed. No doubt there are still many pockets of darkness for Ashton and Kayne; however, they were able to make the most out of prison and to take home with them the strong relationship they developed while there.

Kayne was learning to think and be in the world because he had a mother who could do this for him. I had the sense that Ashton would not be passing on her own undiluted trauma, but would remain steadfast in her relationship with her son. Returning to Freud's comment on the essential traits in the criminals concerning the absence of love and the lack of human validation, I witnessed Ashton's developing love and respect for ("emotional validation") Kayne's experience. He will learn to think as a result of having been thought about by a very young mother who, in turn, is now being cared for, and loved, by her parents: "My Dad taught me how to make a shepherd's pie the other day. Slowly but surely things are starting to fall into place."

Conclusion

Prison presents the unique opportunity of working with women who might not come within a million miles of psychotherapy in the community. The huge impact of their experiences of early maternal deprivation, and emotional and physical neglect and abuse comes out in their stories. Through the therapeutic relationship, at times these destructive patterns can be held long enough to be transformed, producing statements like the following from a young mother named Claire: "I have been better off in prison—I never would have had this help in the community." This is an indictment not of the prison service, but of society itself.

Unloved themselves, many prison mothers struggle to love their children as independent beings and not, as Welldon says, as "fetishes, extensions of themselves" (1992). In *Why Love Matters: How Affection Shapes a Baby's Brain* (2004), Sue Gerhardt quotes from neuroscience research that supports earlier psychoanalytic observations that serious maternal deprivation has catastrophic consequences for individual brain development and, ultimately, for society. Without love's regulation, children grow up impulsive and wild. Writing seventy years ago, John Bowlby describes children who suffered maternal deprivation and rejection in *Forty-four Juvenile Thieves: Their Characters and Home-life* (1946). In *The Mark of Cain: Psychoanalytic Insight and the Psychopath* (2001), J. Reid Meloy quotes recent research showing the relationship between high levels of cortisol and criminal activity that can be predicted at the age of fifteen.

Working with the prison staff, and not in isolation, it becomes possible to encourage and model thoughtfulness and curiosity in the mothers and the staff. Given enough time, such interactions can have positive outcomes, as I hope the work with Ashton illustrates. The weekly group makes it possible to help the mothers think about, rather than feel persecuted by, their babies, providing them with a better start in life than their mothers experienced; this is not only beneficial for them but also for society at large—and that means you and me.

History does not have to repeat itself.

References

Bowlby, J. (1946). *Forty-four Juvenile Thieves: Their Characters and Home-life*. London: Bailliere, Tindall & Cox.

Freud, S. (1928b). Dostoevsky and parricide. *S. E.*, 21: 177–196. London: Hogarth.

Gerhardt, S. (2004). *Why Love Matters: How Affection Shapes a Baby's Brain*. London: Routledge.

Green, A. (1986). *On Private Madness "The Dead Mother Complex"*. London: Hogarth Press.

Howard League for Penal Reform (2014). Weekly prison watch. Week ending 12 December 2014 (www.howardleague.org/weekly-prison-watch-archive).

Meloy, J. R. (Ed.) (2001). *The Mark of Cain: Psychoanalytic Insight and the Psychopath*. Hillsdale, NJ: Analytic Press.

Prison Reform Trust (2014). Bromley Briefings Prison Factfile. Autumn 2014.

Welldon, E. V. (1992). *Mother, Madonna, Whore: The Idealization and Denigration of Motherhood*. London: Karnac.

CHAPTER SIX

Talking to, and being with, babies: the importance of relationship in the neonatal intensive care unit*

Lucie Zwimpfer

Introduction

Talking to, and being with, infants are key aspects of the parent–infant relationship and also of the analyst–infant relationship in some parent–infant psychotherapies (Acquarone, 2004; Norman, 2001, 2004). This chapter discusses the importance of relationships for infant development and suggest that knowledge gained from the exploration of psychoanalytic treatment for infants might be useful for the nurse–infant relationship in the neonatal intensive care unit (NICU). A model of vocal soothing is presented, which is underpinned by the psychoanalytic concept of containment. Ideas for supporting NICU parents to be able to talk to, and be with, their infants are suggested.

Infant exposure to pain and stress is associated with adverse physical and emotional outcomes (Anand, 1998; Anand & Scalzo, 2000; Grunau, 2002; Ozawa et al., 2011; Winberg, 1998) and later behavioural and emotional problems (Anand & Scalzo, 2000). Researchers and clinicians have sought to develop effective pharmacological and non-pharmacological methods to manage pain and stress for preterm infants (Winberg, 1998).

There is good evidence available that relationships with adults are critical to facilitate the growth of healthy infant brains that are able to manage stress (Schore, 1996). It is in moments of stress that the infant most needs the support of an adult carer to help them regulate their emotional state. When infants are attended to and soothed by an adult carer, their ability to do this for themselves is facilitated through development of the neural pathways for emotional regulation. When this does not happen, the infant is at risk of adverse mental health sequelae later in life (Schore, 1996). Emotional regulation, thus, depends on having an emotionally available adult who can tune in and communicate with the infant.

The primary carer for preterm infants in a NICU changes daily. When parents are unable to be with their babies, for whatever reason, nurses step in as the temporary keepers of the infant's emotional health. The NICU is increasingly being seen as a place not just for the physical care of the infant, but also their emotional and developmental care, meaning that NICU staff members are taking on the job of helping infants manage their stress. Further, NICU staff members are in a unique position of being able to screen for, and intervene in, relationship difficulties between infants and their parents.

Talking to, and being with, infants as part of their neonatal care has been identified as an important aspect of pain management (Anand & Hall, 2008; Bellieni et al., 2012). Some relationship-based care practices have been developed and are now a routine component of neonatal care in many units (Legendre et al., 2011).

Relationship-based care in the neonatal intensive care unit

Relationship-based care practices in NICU include the neonatal individualised care and assessment programme (NIDCAP), infant-led singing, and sensorial saturation. The unifying philosophy of these approaches is that the infant is regarded as an individual with emotional as well as physical needs.

The NIDCAP approach focuses on planning individualised care based on observations of the infant's behaviour, thereby recognising the infant as a person with goals and facilitating the development of a carer relationship with the infant (Als & Gilkerson, 1997). Numerous studies have now been published reporting favourable outcomes for infants using this approach (Als et al., 1996, 2004; Westrup et al., 2007). It is, however, an expensive programme to implement fully (Westrup et al., 2007).

Infant-led singing, within an attuned relationship, is an approach aimed at facilitating self and mutual regulation (Shoemark, 2006). The spontaneous nature of the singing means that the therapist is led by the infant's immediate responses and aims to connect with the infant's emotional experience (Shoemark, 2006). This is seen to be particularly important, given the hospital experience being largely non-contingent with the infant's psychological needs (Shoemark, 2006).

Sensorial saturation has also been shown to be effective in managing pain and stress (Bellieni et al., 2012). The aim is to distract the infant's senses so that pain has less chance of being perceived centrally (Bellieni et al., 2001). Bellieni and colleagues have studied the effectiveness of sensorial saturation extensively and have refined the technique in the "Triple T intervention" using touch, taste, and talk as the distractor. Bellieni and colleagues suggest that an important aspect of sensorial saturation is that the baby should feel accompanied by a human presence during the painful procedure (Bellieni, 2002; Bellieni et al., 2003). The importance is stressed of the carer being caring and attentive, and it is argued that effective treatment of neonatal pain can only be realised when the infant is seen as a person and, as such, treated with both dignity and empathy (Bellieni et al., 2003, 2012).

These aspects of the nurse–infant relationship—"talk" and "human presence"—have, therefore, been identified in the medical literature as being relevant to medical care. But does it matter what sort of "talk" is used with preterm infants? Also, what kind of human presence might be required for the effective soothing of neonatal pain and stress?

Talk and emotional presence are key elements of the psychoanalytic approach to managing psychic pain. The field of psychoanalysis has long been interested in the impact of relationships on mental health, and theories have been proposed that describe how relationships with primary carers (external environment) meet an infant's experience (internal environment) to co-create the infant's emerging sense of self. Parent–infant psychotherapeutic approaches are generally aimed at recognising and soothing the emotional expressions of the infant. While some therapists may do this by focusing on helping the parents to "talk to", and "be with", their infant (Baradon et al.,

2005; Cohen, 1999; Fraiberg, 1975), others "talk to", and "are with", the infant directly (Acquarone, 2007; Norman, 2001; Thomson-Salo, 2007). In the following section, some of the tools of the analyst–infant relationship that might be helpful to use with infants during painful and stressful procedures in NICU are described. A model of vocal soothing that could be an effective non-pharmacological pain management technique in NICU is also proposed.

Talking to, and being with: nurse–infant relationships in NICU

The approach of psychoanalyst Johan Norman was to focus on the help the therapist could offer directly to the infant (Norman, 2001). Three important features of his technique are discussed in turn to consider how they can be applied to nurse–infant relationships in NICU.

The analyst seeks to establish a therapeutic relationship with the baby

In seeking to establish a relationship with a baby, the therapist is required to attune to the infant and be open to wondering about how the baby might be feeling. This requires focus and attention, and the adult needs to be calm and unpreoccupied. Typically, analytic therapy occurs in a quiet room, and the therapist focuses on one baby for a significant period of time. Contrast this with a busy NICU where there are constant demands on staff time. Neonatal nurses have multiple babies to attend to, sometimes all at once, and they do not have the luxury of time. However, they do have moments of engagement with individual infants and there will always be a nurse who is with the baby during stressful procedures and caring activities. This nurse can choose to enter into a relationship with the infant at this moment in time.

The analyst assumes the infant will use their primary intersubjectivity to obtain containment

Preterm infants seek communication and comfort from carers: that is, anyone who offers them care. Even preterm infants are born with an innate primary intersubjectivity, ready to relate to other human beings and expecting a response to their bids for communication (Aitken & Trevarthen, 1997; Trevarthen, 2001). Infant researcher Colwyn Trevarthen suggests that it does not necessarily have to be the biological mother that meets the needs of the infant as infants are born ready to have their needs met by any sympathetic adult willing and able to enter their emotional world (Trevarthen, 2001).

Within psychoanalysis, the school of object relations is particularly concerned with the relationships, real and imagined, between infants and their primary carers. Theorists within this school of thought stress the importance of primary carers for helping infants manage "big feelings", both joyful and painful (Bion, 1962; Ogden, 1992; Winnicott, 1990). This process is often described as containment (Bion, 1962).

Psychoanalyst Wilfred Bion suggested that in infancy we have many raw feelings and experiences, but they cannot be made sense of without a container, without someone else who can metabolise them for us and give them back in a digested form (Bion, 1962). It is a bit like the albatross that chews the fish for their babies then regurgitates it in a way that is digestible to the chicks. Bion said that in this way, through the receiving of thought about thoughts, we develop the capacity to think ourselves (1962). The infant has the emotional experience, the parent recognises it, accepts it, and reassures the infant that it is a valid feeling to have and they are not alone.

When Bellieni and colleagues suggested the importance of human presence alongside the infant during painful procedures, an empathetic presence was presumed (Bellieni, 2002; Bellieni et al., 2003). In order for a mother to be able to offer containment to her infant, Bion suggested that she needed to be in a state of reverie, a sort of daydream state, where she is emotionally open to receiving the infant's communications, both good and bad (1962). He postulated that this state of attunement allows the mother to more accurately understand the infant. It would not be practical for nurses to enter a state of reverie with every infant in their care; however, tuning into the infant during a painful experience would be achievable. Studies have demonstrated that interventions can be more effective when the clinician focuses their attention on the infant (Ventegodt & Merrick, 2004). Anand and colleagues stress the importance of clinicians working in the NICU expressing empathy and love for their patients and suggest that this is crucial in order to "maximize the benefits" of evidence-based medical interventions to reduce stress (Anand & Hall, 2008). Clinicians are urged to be like secure mothers who are sensitive and responsive to the infant's needs (Anand & Hall, 2008).

The analyst assumes that the baby processes the non-lexical aspect of interactions

The assumption here is that although infants do not understand the actual words spoken to them, they do understand the emotional intention behind the words. If this is the case, then there might be therapeutic value in offering vocal soothing to infants under stress. This vocal soothing would need to be truthful, that is, recognise and name the infant experience, in order to be meaningful to the infant and help them feel understood and reassured and, therefore, contained. A soothing voice might be particularly important for premature infants who are unable to be cuddled often or touched freely.

Infants prefer infant-directed speech to adult-directed speech (Cooper & Aslin, 1990). Infant-directed speech, also known as "motherese" (although it can be offered by anyone), is characterised by longer sounds in the words, higher pitch, more variation in the pitch, and repetition (Trainor, 1996). The falling and rising pitch contours depend on whether the infant is being soothed (falling) or whether their attention is been attracted (rising) (Fernald, 1991). Because of these cadences in the speech, infants can sense the emotions being conveyed (Caron et al., 1988).

If a nurse offers their voice and emotional presence to an infant during a procedure, they need to be in an attuned state, thinking about the infant and "being with" the infant emotionally. Nurses who speak to their colleagues while carrying out a painful procedure on an infant are physically present with the infant during the procedure but not emotionally present. When nurses say to infants in their care "It doesn't hurt", or "Nothing is happening", the infant's experience is, in fact, being minimised or denied and the nurse is clearly neither emotionally present with the infant nor attuned to what they are experiencing. Containment is only possible if the nurse is open to receiving and accepting the infant's communications, and, in particular, their level of stress. The psychotherapeutic viewpoint is that the human presence is about being with, and thinking about, the infant emotionally and not just physically.

In a recent observational study, we found that despite speaking regularly to their colleagues, nurses did not often offer vocal soothing to infants during a heel prick procedure (Zwimpfer et al., 2012). Also, despite being recommended as a standard of care in the NICU, there was limited use of other non-pharmacological interventions to relieve pain during the procedure (Zwimpfer et al., 2012). Others have reported that despite much research demonstrating the effectiveness of these techniques, general implementation of pain management programmes appears to be limited internationally (Spence & Henderson-Smart, 2011).

It is not likely that nursing staff deliberately withhold pain relief from their patients. However, to be available to talk to infants during a painful procedure, a nurse needs to be attuned to the reality of the painful experience. This, in itself, can be an emotionally taxing thing to do. It is possible that psychological protective mechanisms, of which the nurse is not likely to be fully conscious, minimise the perceived effect of the painful procedure on the infant and, therefore, in turn lead to the underuse of pain management techniques in the nursery. More research is required to establish whether this is, in reality, a barrier to the use of these techniques.

A model of vocal soothing

Bringing together these elements of talking to, and being with, an infant, a model of vocal soothing during painful procedures is proposed. If a nurse is emotionally available to the infant's communications and conveys this to the infant through an attuned, empathic voice, similar to "motherese", it is hypothesised that the infant could achieve containment. In this way, the nurse is responsive to the infant's communications in the moment, leaving the infant feeling that they are accompanied in their pain and, therefore, soothed.

The words used are a critical component of this communication. They must be truthful and used in context in order to help the infant feel that their experience has been well understood. The nurse can accompany an infant through their painful experience from the start to the finish: see it from their point of view, offer warning or preparation about what is to come, be aware of how the infant is feeling during the procedure, and then have a verbal review of what has happened before moving on to the next task. During this process, the nurse must be attuned to the experience of the infant. They need to feel both empathic and confident that the infant will tolerate the procedure and recover well from any temporary stress that they experience. The essence of the theory of containment is that when an infant feels that a stronger other person understands how they are feeling and remains calm and supportive, it will be reassuring and soothing for the infant.

We are undertaking research to determine whether non-parental vocal soothing and emotional availability can be experienced as soothing by infants during painful procedures. If attuned, empathic vocal soothing is found to be an effective mitigator of preterm infant stress, then this will provide evidence for a relationship-based, non-pharmacological, cost-effective intervention that might mean that the infant's emotional needs are met more effectively in the NICU.

Talking to, and being with: supporting parent–infant relationships in NICU

Parents of NICU babies are not always able to be emotionally available to their infants. This can be for a variety of reasons. Each family has their own trauma to work through and some parents will be more emotionally equipped and socially supported to manage this than others. How a baby is held in the mind of their parents is a result of complex psychological factors, some conscious and some not. The early weeks of a baby's life are an important part of setting the stage for the kind of relationship they will have with their primary carers. What does having this baby in NICU mean for these parents? How is this baby viewed by their parents? Are they allowing themselves to connect with their baby?

It is becoming more common to see allied health clinicians working alongside medical staff in the service of the premature infant and his or her family. Multi-disciplinary psychosocial meetings provide an opportunity to plan care for families that need extra help. Input from social workers, occupational therapists, speech and language therapists, physiotherapists, lactation consultants, and psychotherapists ensure that families have access to a wide range of support.

As a psychotherapist and infant researcher in an NICU, I have spent many hours working alongside neonatal nurses. I have come to know the detail of their work and, over time, have come to be trusted in this environment. While I am still considered to be in a "fluffy" profession, they see me using equipment that they know—heart rate and respiratory rate monitors—and that has, in a way, served as a bridge between the worlds of psychology and medicine. It means that when I am asked to teach seminars on infant mental health to the nurses, we already have a shared understanding and respect for each other's work. One of the most important aspects of the field of infant mental health is that it is multi-disciplinary. All disciplines that have input into the wellbeing of infants and young children have a responsibility to learn about brain development and the importance of attuned relationships for emotional health. Neonatal nurses can and do promote the principles of infant mental health, whether they realise it or not.

Neonatal nurses are in a unique position to be able to support parent–infant relationships by helping parents to get to know and psychologically claim their baby. They encourage parents to actively participate in the routine physical care of their baby, and kangaroo cuddles are offered when possible. Nurses provide guidance to parents around how to touch and hold their babies. They tell parents about how their baby has been during the shift, as often parents are hungry for as much feedback as possible, perhaps looking for proof that their absence has not been damaging to their child.

Neonatal nurses delight in their infant patients, showing parents that their babies are lovable and unique and special. Many parents will never have had a baby to care for and so take their lead from staff in how to interact with this little person who might seem quite alien to them. All of these things promote the relationship between parents and their babies. It keeps them wondering and interested in their infant's experience.

In our NICU, parent–infant psychotherapy takes place cotside. The work of the psychotherapist is to be alongside the parents in their experience of their baby, to help them process and understand the thoughts and feelings that arise in the presence of their baby. The psychological containment that is offered to parents by the psychotherapist allows the parents then to feel strong enough to be able to wonder about, and be open to, their infant's feelings and experiences.

While privacy can be an issue in a busy NICU ward, the nature of the therapy being cotside means that any discomfort that parents may have about being "in therapy" might be reduced. The therapy is facilitative: it allows the parents to have the experience of being psychologically supported to be in tune with their infant in the way that is optimal for infant mental health and brain development.

The nurses are taught how to be psychologically minded in their interactions with families. There are five key messages for parents that I teach nurses to use to support and strengthen parent–infant relationships in the neonatal intensive care unit. These messages are designed to be shared as much or as little as the family can tolerate, and their simplicity makes them straightforward for nurses to administer. Some of them could also serve as screening tools for possible relationship difficulties that would warrant a referral to local parent infant mental health services.

Message one: your baby is ready to relate to you.

It is still not common knowledge that babies are born ready to relate, that their emotional and physical development is dependent on relationships with people who care deeply for them. Parents need to be told that their premature or sick baby has the capacity to interact with them and that they are ready to get to know them.

Message two: let your baby hear you and see you.

Parents need to know the importance of their baby being able to hear them, that it is comforting for a newborn baby to hear the voices they knew *in utero*.

Psychoanalyst and paediatrician Donald Winnicott suggested that so much could be understood by an infant in a gaze. He described how, in looking at the mother's face, the infant does not see the mother, but instead sees a reflection of what the mother thinks of him (Winnicott, 1971). He was postulating that babies learn about themselves and how lovable they are through the gaze of another person.

Message three: be with and notice your baby.

Neonatal nurses can help parents to observe their baby and find pleasure and pride in them. At cotside, the parent can be invited to watch and wonder about their baby. What is this baby doing? What is this baby's experience in this moment? Nurses can alert parents to their baby's abilities and needs. They can identify and enhance a parent's ability to respond positively to their baby.

Message four: how do you feel about this baby?

Nurses are in a key position to be able to sound out a parent's feelings in relation to their baby. What is the parent's experience in this moment? How they are feeling about this baby? What is it like for them having a baby in hospital? What had they hoped for this baby? Did they know their child would be admitted to NICU? The nurse can get a sense of what it is like to be the parent of this baby at this particular time. It is important to listen well to the parent, who might or might not share their own history of abandonment, separation, unresolved loss—all very difficult experiences that could further compound their ability to tolerate having a baby in hospital.

Message five: this is your baby.

Nurses can help parents claim their baby. Statements such as "She's your baby", or "He's really listening to you" can be incredibly powerful to parents who are not sure they believe it. To bring their attention back to their baby, a nurse might ask, "How did you choose his or her name?" After they have been with their baby, they might ask, "What was that like for you?" These statements or questions are inherently relational in nature. They serve the purpose of bringing the baby into the parents' mind and helping them claim their baby. Where risk is detected in the relationship, a referral to local parent–infant mental health services might be indicated.

Conclusion

This chapter has made a case for offering attuned, empathic vocal soothing for preterm infant stress. It has been proposed that some of the elements of the parent–infant and analyst–infant relationship are useful to consider in a neonatal intensive care unit setting with nurses, and that this might be of benefit to the emotional development of the preterm infant. Parents need to be supported to be able to offer containment to their babies, and five key messages for parents can be shared by nursing staff to encourage parents to connect emotionally with their infants.

References

Acquarone, S. (2004). *Infant–Parent Psychotherapy: A Handbook*. London: Karnac.

Acquarone, S. (2007). *Signs of Autism in Infants: Recognition and Early Intervention*. London: Karnac.

Aitken, K. J., & Trevarthen, C. (1997). Self/other organization in human psychological development. *Development and Psychopathology, 9*(4): 653–677.

Als, H., & Gilkerson, L. (1997). The role of relationship-based developmentally supportive newborn intensive care in strengthening outcome of preterm infants. *Seminars in Perinatology, 21*(3): 178–189.

Als, H., Duffy, F. H., &. McAnulty, G. B. (1996). Effectiveness of individualized neurodevelopmental care in the newborn intensive care unit (NICU). *Acta Pædiatrica, 85*: 21–30.

Als, H., McAnulty, G. B., Rivkin, M. J., Vajapeyam, S., Mulkern, R. V., Warfield, S. K., Huppi, P. S., Butler, S. C., Conneman, N., Fischer, C., & Eichenwald, E. C. (2004). Early experience alters brain function and structure. *Pediatrics, 113*(4): 846–857.

Anand, K. J. S. (1998). Clinical importance of pain and stress in preterm neonates. *Neonatology, 73*(1): 1–9.

Anand, K. J. S., & Hall, R. W. (2008). Love, pain, and intensive care. *Pediatrics, 121*(4): 825–827.

Anand, K. J. S., & Scalzo, F. M. (2000). Can adverse neonatal experiences alter brain development and subsequent behaviour? *Neonatology, 77*(2): 69–82.

Baradon, T., Broughton, C., Gibbs, I., Joyce, A., & Woodhead, J. (2005). *The Practice of Psychoanalytic Parent–Infant Psychotherapy—Claiming the Baby*. London: Routledge.

Bellieni, C. V. C. (2002). Effect of multisensory stimulation on analgesia in term neonates: a randomized controlled trial. *Pediatric Research, 51*(4): 460–463.

Bellieni, C. V. C., Bagnoli, F. F., & Buonocore, G. G. (2003). Alone no more: pain in premature children. *Ethics & Medicine, 19*(1): 5–9.

Bellieni, C. V. C., Buonocore, G., Nenci, A., Franci, N., Cordelli, D. M., & Bagnoli, F. (2001). Sensorial saturation: an effective analgesic tool for heel-prick in preterm infants. A prospective randomized trial. *Biology of the Neonate, 80*(1): 15–18.

Bellieni, C. V., Tei, M., Coccina, F., & Buonocore, G. (2012). Sensorial saturation for infants' pain. *Journal of Maternal–Fetal & Neonatal Medicine, 25*(Suppl. 1): 79–81.

Bion, W. R. (1962). *Learning From Experience*. London: Karnac.

Caron, A. J., Caron, R. F., & MacLean, D. J. (1988). Infant discrimination of naturalistic emotional expressions: the role of face and voice. *Child Development, 59*(3): 604–616.

Cohen, N. J. (1999). Watch, wait, and wonder: testing the effectiveness of a new approach to mother–infant psychotherapy. *Infant Mental Health Journal, 20*(4): 429–451.

Cooper, R. P., & Aslin, R. N. (1990). Preference for infant-directed speech in the first month after birth. *Child Development, 61*(5): 1584–1595.

Fernald, A. (1991). Prosody in speech to children: prelinguistic and linguistic functions. *Annals of Child Development, 8*: 43–80.

Fraiberg, S. (1975). Ghosts in the nursery: a psychoanalytic approach to the problems of impaired infant–mother relationships. *Journal of the American Academy of Child Psychiatry, 14*(3): 387–421.

Grunau, R. (2002). *Early Pain in Preterm Infants: A Model of Long-Term Effects*. New York: Elsevier.

Legendre, V., Burtner, P. A., Martinez, K. L., & Crowe, T. K. (2011). The evolving practice of developmental care in the neonatal unit: a systematic review. *Physical & Occupational Therapy in Pediatrics, 31*(3): 315–338.

Norman, J. (2001). The psychoanalyst and the baby: a new look at work with infants. *International Journal of Psychoanalysis, 82*(1): 83–100.

Norman, J. (2004). Transformations of early infantile experiences: a 6-month-old in psychoanalysis. *International Journal of Psychoanalysis, 85*(5): 1103–1122.

Ogden, T. (1992). *The Matrix of the Mind. Object Relations and the Psychoanalytic Dialogue*. London: Karnac.

Ozawa, M., Kanda, K., Hirata, M., Kusakawa, I., & Suzuki, C. (2011). Influence of repeated painful procedures on prefrontal cortical pain responses in newborns. *Acta Paediatrica, 100*(2): 198–203.

Schore, A. N. (1996). The experience-dependent maturation of a regulatory system in the orbital prefrontal cortex and the origin of developmental psychopathology. *Development and Psychopathology, 8*: 59–87.

Shoemark, H. (2006). Infant-directed singing as a vehicle for regulation rehearsal in the medically fragile full-term infant. *Australian Journal of Music Therapy, 17*: 54–63.

Spence, K., & Henderson-Smart, D. (2011). Closing the evidence-practice gap for newborn pain using clinical networks. *Journal of Paediatrics and Child Health, 47*(3): 92–98.

Thomson-Salo, F. (2007). Recognizing the infant as subject in infant–parent psychotherapy. *International Journal of Psychoanalysis, 88*(4): 961–979.

Trainor, L. J. (1996). Infant preferences for infant-directed versus noninfant-directed playsongs and lullabies. *Infant Behavior and Development, 19*(1): 83–92.

Trevarthen, C. (2001). Intrinsic motives for companionship in understanding: their origin, development, and significance for infant mental health. *Infant Mental Health Journal, 22*(1–2): 95–131.

Ventegodt, S., & Merrick, J. (2004). Clinical holistic medicine: applied consciousness-based medicine. *Scientific World Journal, 4*: 96–99.

Westrup, B., Sizun, J., & Lagercrantz, H. (2007). Family-centered developmental supportive care: a holistic and humane approach to reduce stress and pain in neonates. *Journal of Perinatology, 27*(S1): S12–S18.

Winberg, J. (1998). Do neonatal pain and stress program the brain's response to future stimuli? *Acta Pædiatrica, 87*(7): 723–725.

Winnicott, D. W. (1971). The mirror-role of mother and family in child development. In: D. W. Winnicott, *Playing and Reality* (pp. 111–118). London: Tavistock [reprinted New York: Routledge, 1989.

Winnicott, D. (1990). *The Maturational Processes and the Facilitating Environment: Studies in the Theory of Emotional Development.* London: Karnac.

Zwimpfer, L., Wiltshire, E., & Elder, D. (2012). Talking to babies: a baseline study of vocal soothing by neonatal nurses during painful procedures. *Journal of Paediatrics and Child Health, 48*(Suppl. 1): 8–81.

CHAPTER SEVEN

"Toward the baby": first steps in supporting parents in early encounters with their infants. A reflection from Poland

Magdalena Stawicka and
Magdalena Polaszewska-Nicke

Introduction

I n this chapter, we would like to share some reflections on the supportive work offered for families with infants in the programme "Toward the baby", which is being implemented by ZERO-FIVE, the Foundation for Infant Mental Health in Poznań, Poland. The idea, along with theoretical background and sources of inspiration, as well as the clinical practice for the benefit of families with infants, is elaborated below. The major elements of the project are described: for example, the workshops for parents-to-be and the psychological consultations for families with infants. Discussing the method used during the workshops and consultations, we highlight aspects of the work that are specific to countries like Poland with a history of recurring war traumas, as it might be of some importance for those who work in societies with a similar burden.

Background

In the opening chapter of his book on treating parent–infant relationship problems, Sameroff and colleagues (2005) write that it is ridiculous for some people to think in infant mental health categories and to believe that infants may have mental health problems. Their statement echoes the attitude still found throughout Polish society, and even among professionals working in the field of health and social welfare. The idea that supporting an early parent–infant relationship could serve to promote healthy child development—and to a great degree shield the families from many adverse phenomena, such as emotional and conduct disorders in children—is alien to many. Such attitudes are reflected in the very poor response of the state[1] to demands for support from parents: demands that are being voiced more and more often.[2]

A young pregnant woman anxious about her ability to take care of her baby, or parents struggling with excessive crying in their newborn, most often have nowhere to turn for professional support. At best, they are offered advice on the physical aspects of handling the baby, or psychiatric support for serious problems, such as postpartum depression or the appearance of psychotic symptoms. However, in such help, the idea of supporting the adult patient as the infant's parent sinks into complete oblivion. Infant mental health is not what is recognised as being at stake, even in such serious cases.

This kind of attitude is even more surprising when one looks at the somewhat forgotten history of Polish psychology and health services. After the Second World War, many families found themselves on the verge of extreme deprivation. At that time, a paediatrician named Izabela Bielicka was able to create a hospital department that treated severely emotionally and physically deprived young children. Her work, as well as that of Hanna Olechnowicz, drew on the observations of René Spitz and John Bowlby, and was translated into therapeutic efforts in order to improve the lives of the young patients. These efforts—presented in several papers written by Bielicka and Olechnowicz (see, for example, Bielicka & Olechnowicz, 1967)—are documents of incredible dedication, insight, attentiveness, and creativity, and continue to serve as a model of professional accuracy and resourcefulness, deeply rooted in sound theoretical knowledge.

Being aware of this tradition, and having studied the English language literature on infant mental health, attachment, and psychoanalysis, in addition to learning about early intervention and prevention programmes, we became fascinated with the idea of setting up a centre that offered early intervention programmes. In order to set out working with families, we created the ZERO–FIVE Foundation and a centre where—regardless of their social, cultural, or economic backgrounds[3]—parents can come for help when faced with a wide spectrum of problems in relating to their babies.

Toward the Baby: a programme of workshops and consultations

One of our projects is the special preventive programme called Toward the Baby. The programme was designed to be interdisciplinary, so as to offer as much comprehensive help as possible (covering the aspects that were lacking in the system), and to encourage parents wanting more than just psychological help. As a result, it also includes physiotherapy and first-aid classes. Moreover, participants are invited to take advantage of psychological, physiotherapeutic, and lactation and feeding consultations after the birth of their baby. For the past several years, the curriculum has been constantly evolving, and, at present, we have settled on a twelve-hour course of psychological workshops accompanied by psychological, and lactation and feeding consultations after the baby is born. These consultations are optional for the workshop participants, but most parents use them.

It must be added that despite the idea of prevention that underlies the programme, it is not meant to focus on reaching multi-risk families, and, thus, is not specifically targeted at this group. It is addressed to all mothers and fathers-to-be who feel they need support in entering their new role as parents. Everyone is invited, and we do not exclude single mothers or very young parents from participating in a group where the majority are couples, since our experience shows that such mixed groups work very well. Meeting with parents from various backgrounds and with different experiences becomes the value-added for all who take part. Parents usually enrol personally (as the programme is advertised in the local press and in local clinics), but more and more often participants are being referred to us by other professionals (such as social services centres and midwives).

Workshops: the inspiration and the idea

The direct and indirect sources of inspiration for the programme were many, and came from such fields as psychoanalysis and psychodynamic psychotherapy (e.g., Fraiberg, Stern, Raphel-Leff), attachment theory (e.g., Bowlby, Ainsworth, Sroufe), neuroscience (e.g., Schore, Panksepp), developmental psychology (e.g., Trevarthen), and other domains of scientific and practical work with infants (e.g., Papousek, Brazelton, Tronick). Inspiration also came from personal encounters with such specialists as Dr Stella Acquarone, founder and head of the School of Infant Mental Health in London, and Dr Karl Heinz Brisch from the University of Munich, who introduced us to his programme called SAFE (Safe Attachment Family Education).

The idea of the workshops is based on the assumption that scaffolding parents' mentalizing competence, described also as "reflective function" (Fonagy et al., 2002) and "mind-mindness" (Meins, 1997), could help them in sensitive caring. Peter Fonagy and colleagues (Fonagy & Target, 1997; Fonagy et al., 2002) developed the concept of mentalization, referring to attachment theory, infant research, and psychodynamic theory. The authors define it as an individual's competence to envision mental states (thoughts, feelings, desires, beliefs, and intentions) in one's self and in others, and to understand behaviour in terms of mental states. Mentalization, thus, implies a competence to identify mental states and to interpret one's own as well as others' inner states. This capacity is of crucial importance when it comes to building and maintaining a relationship with a baby.

Mentalization is proposed to be the main building block of secure attachment, and, when well developed, makes it possible for a mother to accurately read her child's intentions and feelings and to respond sensitively to them (Slade, 2005). Similarly, the construct of mind-mindedness allows one to distinguish a general sensitivity to a child's physical and emotional needs (suggested by Ainsworth et al., 1978) from a more specific sensitivity to the child's mental states and their ongoing activity. This skill requires the ability to use information drawn from the child's outward behaviour for the purpose of making accurate inferences about mental states governing this behaviour, by constructing (or co-constructing) the meaning behind them (Meins, 1997).

The method

With the above ideas in mind, throughout the course of the workshops for parents-to-be, we are first and foremost trying—by means of the various activities described below—to focus on "discovering" the internal life of a newborn and his inferred mental processes (feelings, needs, and intentions). The first meeting with the parents starts with a discussion on the main facts about foetus development and pregnancy (feelings, fantasies, changes). Encouraging parents to reflect on their ideal baby as a person growing into an ideal adult, and asking them to voice their fantasies and feelings are, for us, the base from which they will, we hope, become able to work towards encountering their real babies at the moment of delivery.

We then follow this with a discussion of birth as experienced by the baby and the parents, which leads us to the part of the workshop dedicated to the newborn and her functioning, usually beginning with a description of the baby's competence. As it is vital, in our view, constantly to draw the parents' attention to the mental condition of their new baby, we try to present the whole repertoire of the infant's competence in pursuing close physical and emotional contact, and mutual communication with the carer. The illustrations and examples we use come from the work of Brazelton, Trevarthen, and Murray.

Next, the parents are introduced to the concept of attachment, with particular emphasis on its evolutionary aspect with reference to knowledge about brain development and its implication for the infant's wellbeing. Focus is placed on the vitality of self-regulatory mechanisms, and the carer's role as the external supporter in co-regulating the infant's functioning, as well as in shaping the developing child's self-regulatory capacity. On the other hand, the use of Brazelton's idea of systems (autonomic, motor, state, social interaction, and attention), and terms such as "competence", "the level of maturity", or "signalling", are particularly helpful in enabling the parents to understand how rich the contact with their baby can become, and how informative the infant's behaviour and the changes in their functioning can be. At the same time, parents set out to determine what kind of response would be most adequate at a particular moment.

To help parents enter the world of the baby, we invite them to become involved in some practical exercises: for example, encouraging the group to closely observe babies filmed in normal everyday situations, and then trying to share their impressions with reference to the already discussed information about the mechanisms of infantile functioning. In one such exercise, we analyse a short video clip presenting a little baby boy filmed in his cot as he quietly absorbs the sounds of normal family life from another room. The scale of the baby's reactions observed in this way, shows the intensity of the response to the world around him, evident, for example, in his bodily movements, facial expressions, and changes in levels of activity. All these tiny behaviours inspire the participants to reflect upon the intensity of the infant's reactions to received stimulation, and on the ongoing hard work a baby has to undertake in order to process what we think of as banal and routine everyday experiences.

Exercises of this kind are a powerful tool for capturing the attention and emotional response of the audience, virtually enabling them to "be in the shoes" of the little boy. It is also particularly helpful in "studying" the cues that reflect the baby's states, allowing parents to better understand their needs.

A substantial part of the workshop discussion is dedicated to the dynamics of the antenatal and post natal period (Raphael-Leff, 2004), with reference to the concept of "ghosts in the nursery" (Fraiberg et al., 1994). By encouraging parents to reflect on the changes in their couple relationship, their reconstructed identities as mother (Stern, 1995) and father, and discussing the changing lifestyle or their image of life with their baby, we aim to look at the reality of parenthood from many different angles. The concept of "ghosts in the nursery" is especially useful in this respect. It helps bring to light the inevitable, and often very powerful, factors that enter the scene when a baby is born, playing their part silently below the surface of our consciousness. These are the unspoken expectations, traumas, or emotions that determine, in large part, the quality of the environment of the new person in the family. On the other hand, by using an exercise in which parents are encouraged to evoke memories of a good relationship they once had with another adult[4]—not necessarily their parents or relatives— we also introduce the idea of "angels in the nursery". This is a way of expressing our belief that these good memories of a safe haven could serve as a kind of anchor whenever they feel helpless or lost in their caring.

The general goal of the workshops is to provide knowledge and promote reflection, rather than enforce ready solutions to concrete problems. Nevertheless, the last part of the workshops is usually dedicated to discussing the more practical aspects of childcare. Here, parents may ask questions concerning, for example, crying, feeding, sleeping, separation, or play, and try to find their own answers to them, based on our previous work. As each of these issues is presented with reference to knowledge about attachment, regulation processes, and brain development, parents are encouraged to look for the best solutions, keeping the ideas and facts learnt during the workshops in mind. What we wish they will carry with them into parenthood is the awareness that each and every behaviour and cue enacted by their baby has some meaning, and that the best way to read their meaning is to observe, contain, and think for the baby. Doing this is what will probably help the baby settle into this world and come to terms with it.

Psychological considerations

Inspired by the programmes mentioned above, as well as some others (such as "Minding the baby" by A. Slade, or the "Nurse–family partnership" by D. Olds, or the Colombian FANA project), we have supplemented the programme with individual consultations for families with small children.

Inspirations and aims

During the individual consultations,[5] we offer psychodynamically informed support and brief therapy (Acquarone, 2004). In this kind of work, a variety of interventions and techniques may be used, as well as flexibly chosen by the therapist, according to the particular problems of the family (see also Maldonado-Duran & Latrigue, 2002: multimodal parent–infant psychotherapy). These techniques include:

- practical help (modelling): for example, showing how to feed the baby without using force;
- giving advice and information: for example, on effective communication with the child;
- emotional support (as in the case of anxious parents);
- behavioural and cognitive interventions;
- psychodynamic interpretation.

We also use the concept of psychotherapeutic consultation (Lebovici et al., 2002) as a form of short-term intervention and stress the development of a mentalizing stance in parents as a crucial aspect in changing their attitude and interaction with their child (Slade, 2005).

In the attempt to describe the goals of the intervention, the concept of "intuitive parenting" (Papoušek et al., 2008) comes as another useful point of reference. It is defined as the innate, instinctual behavioural competence of parents (adults in general), allowing for intuitive, spontaneous communication with the baby, and the ability to adapt one's own reactions to the infant's signals in several spheres, such as eye contact, dialogue, handling, and play. When parent and baby are well synchronised, the relationship between them has the characteristics that Papoušek describes as "angel's circles". However, if something goes wrong, a "vicious circle" forms and gains power, as it is self-enhancing in nature.

One of the questions that arises here is how much do we need to tackle the "ghosts from the nursery" when intervening in a short-term way. To answer this, we have to look at what Bowlby (1988) stated: that therapeutic attention to the past is useful only to the extent that it helps an individual make sense of the present feelings and behaviours in order to answer the question of why he/she behaves in this particular way. We try to combine this view with what Selma Fraiberg has proposed: that the experience of remembering and discussing with a supportive "other" a painful childhood event might help increase the mother's empathy for her own infant and his feelings. When the impact of a difficult past needs extra attention, we try to encourage parents to follow up with their own therapy.

Method: using NBAS as a port of entry

While planning the consultations in the form of home visits, we had to take into account Polish cultural and historical reality, such as the history of invigilation, mistrust of any social institutions, and a generally negative attitude towards mental health services. Being aware that most families might be reluctant to invite a specialist from the field of mental health into their home, we had to address the possible difficulties in reaching them. Thus, we thought it might be easier for parents to accept support when it was presented as part of the Neonatal Behaviour Assessment Scale (NBAS),[6] developed by Brazelton in the 1970s (Brazelton & Nugent, 1995). As Stern (1995) states, when problems of early relationships arise, "the client is the relationship", but most often the infant is the "delegate". In our observations, we have seen that, for many parents, it is much more natural to invite someone in to check on the baby, and then to start talking about themselves and their mutual relationship. According to Stern, the NBAS could serve as a "port of entry"—a powerful tool opening the door to early intervention and prevention.

With this idea in mind, we use NBAS in a very flexible way. Depending on the situation and problems presented by the family, we would choose to proceed with the full version of NBAS or just use some elements of the scale—an "informal NBAS".[7] Sometimes, we decide not to use it at all, despite the fact that the initial wish of the parents was to have us visit them and administer the scale (for example, when the mother is in crisis). Usually, however, NBAS serves as a starting point for counselling, as it provides an opportunity to talk about important issues surrounding the baby (the level of stimulation tolerance, maturity, need of contact, attachment, etc.), as well as the parents' concerns (anxieties, perceptions, family situation, "ghosts from the past").[8]

During the consultation with the use of NBAS, we work to keep mothers and fathers aware of their baby's physical and mental states, and continuously model the reflective stance in relation to everyday caring and nurturing. It is particularly helpful in situations where there are problems with the transition from the relationship with an "imagined baby" to the one with a real newborn, with his or her unique characteristics. It seems effectively to diminish the initial possible feeling of strangeness of one's own baby, while helping to adapt to a new being in the home and in the family. Putting a name to the infant's behaviour, and understanding it as a way of signalling things, as well as a way of communicating, with underlying intention, might also help the mother cope with the raw emotions and "contagious arousal" (see Raphel-Leff, 2004) that is transmitted by the infant. In this way, it is useful in promoting observation and enhancing mentalization and reflective function (see Fonagy et al., 2002; Slade, 2005). We also find NBAS effective as a means of modelling adequate handling of the baby and, what is most important, adequate attitude towards the baby.

Case examples and discussion

The described programme—preventative in its nature—is our Foundation's initial step in supporting parents in their early encounters with their baby. For the time being, we are not able to present any long-term results and we cannot say anything about the programme's effectiveness in bringing about stable changes. We can, however, observe the immediate improvements in the knowledge and beliefs expressed by the parents who attend the workshops. We measure these factors each time in the process of the project evaluation. Positive changes are found in every survey carried out so far, and when asked about their reflections after the workshops, parents always report how much their thinking with regard to their baby has changed, which is one of the important goals of the programme.[9]

Most valuable and significant are the histories of families that have benefited from the programme. The cases reported below are just vignettes to present the nature of the help we offer, and show only some aspects of this work.

The first case concerns Jolanta, a young, pregnant woman, twenty years of age, who had lost contact with the father. She was referred to the programme by a social worker, who was concerned for Jolanta and her alcoholic, aggressive mother, who lived with her in very poor conditions (in a little summer house). Jolanta joined the workshops after a diagnostic consultation (during which she confessed that she was deeply worried about whether she would be able to accept the baby), and, after some initial reluctance, she managed to develop a long-term relationship with one of the psychologists leading the group. As she was in great need of prolonged support, she had several consultations before the birth of her child, and then contacted us straight after her son was delivered. There were several home visits made, during which she often referred back to what she had learnt during the workshops, stressing that they had helped her become stronger in her very difficult situation. The psychologist could observe how she managed to develop strong mentalizing skills in relation to her baby, as well as a tender attitude towards him. Not only had she kept the baby, but had become a loving mother who only contacted the Foundation later when she faced some other problems in parenting. We also organised some "practical" help for her—for example, we moved her to a mother–baby shelter for the winter period.

Another example of long-term support is the story of Anna. She enrolled in our workshops but, for health reasons, could not participate. However, after her daughter was born, she called the Foundation specialist to make an appointment for a home visit, declaring that she was curious about the Neonatal Behaviour Assessment Scale, and would like someone to examine her baby. During the first and second home visits, it became obvious that the baby girl exhibited several problems, including having difficulty in calming down and sleeping only for short periods. Anna was struggling with serious worries about her own ability to properly care for, feed, and support her baby. She was tormented by the question, "What am I to her if she needs me only to feed her?"

During the meetings, the history of her traumatic childhood and her depression (as well as that of the father) were unveiled and discussed in the context of her own mothering capabilities. Her positive and warm interactions with her baby were strongly supported, which helped Anna believe that she was the one her daughter looked up to as the attachment figure and point of reference in all aspects of her existence at this stage.

Regular contact with the specialist was then planned—sometimes as home visits, sometimes in the consulting room—and we used to meet for a couple of sessions every few months, whenever Anna felt she needed support. Throughout this period, Anna's daughter was able to develop a healthy and secure attachment relationship with her mother, and become an empathic and well-regulated pre-schooler. However, the mental state of the father had probably been deteriorating for some time, and the girl is now experiencing some suffering related to the fact that he is not able to fully accept and respond to his daughter's needs and emotional expectations. This has become a source of serious concern for Anna. As a result, we are at the point of planning a new chapter of our co-operation, aimed at improving the father's relationship with the girl. Many attempts at this task have been made, including supporting the father's own therapy, but so far with limited results. We hope that this problem will be solved in the near future.

At the time of writing, we believe we are at a point where first steps and attempts at implementing our project aimed at supporting babies and their families have allowed us to gather enough experience, awareness, and courage to realise the directions our future activities should follow. There are, however, areas that still need inten-sive work. One of them is to develop a reliable and methodologically valid tool for evaluating the programme, as this would help us refine our working methods and plan future projects.

Notes

1.   This situation has resulted in the creation of non-governmental organisations that work towards creating a better quality of life for the infants and their parents in the broadest sense. The most distin-guished among them is probably the Childbirth with Dignity Foundation, whose major goal is to empower women so that they may experience childbirth and motherhood with due respect and with dignity. Thanks to the powerful social campaigns and pressure on the state health system, this Foundation has successfully intro-duced many positive changes in Polish obstetric hospitals, as well as in the law, which now permits, for example, prolonged mother–baby intimate contact following delivery.

2.   For example, in a survey conducted for the Foundation by a group of students in obstetric hospitals and paediatric outpatient units, a majority of eighty-one parents (51.9%) expressed their need for infor-mation during pregnancy and in the first weeks after childbirth. When asked whether they had been informed about the infant's psychological needs (e.g., attachment, security, bodily contact) by the medical staff in the hospital (their paediatrician or a midwife), 68.6% of them replied "no".

3.   Usually, services in the form of prevention or intervention pro-grammes are addressed to specific groups—teenage mothers or poor families, for example—that correspond to easily recognised risk factors, such as age groups, socio-economic status, etc. What is miss-ing, we believe, are services for families with more disguised prob-lems—of a relational nature—that may occur in any social setting. Our experience shows that among those who seek help or who are referred to us are various kinds of families at risk: foster or adoptive families, single or teenage mothers, parents with psychiatric prob-lems, parents of preterm babies, families with infants showing diffi-culties in emotional, social, or behavioural functioning. What is common among them is the distorted nature of their parent–child relationships, and their difficulties in fulfilling their parental roles.

Our Centre, and the programmes we run, aim to address these issues and help these families.

4.   This exercise is directly borrowed from the SAFE programme by K. H. Brisch (mentioned above).

5.   Bakermans-Kranenburg and colleagues (2003), discussing the results of the meta-analysis of the research on the effects of early intervention, designed to affect parental sensitivity or infant/child attachment, conclude that "interventions with a clear focus and modest number of sessions are preferable". Yet, according to Egeland and colleagues (2000), interventions that start as early as possible and provide the most comprehensive support, are longer and have more sessions, are most effective, especially when it comes to high-risk families. Due to the fact that the programme "Toward the Baby" is financed from various sources, we have the opportunity to offer one, two, or up to five consultations for parents. Thus, within the debate on "less is more" *vs.* "more is better", in considering the early intervention aimed at supporting early parent–child interactions, we are currently "forced" to choose the first option, hoping that, at least in some cases, it might be enough to bring about a change and, what might be even more important, encourage parents to return in the future, when new problems arise.

6.   We also found that participation in the workshops was one of the ways of building trust. Another was to start a close co-operation with home-visiting midwives that we had established by training a group of them from Poznan. The community midwives play an important role in spotting the families that, in their opinion, are struggling with some problem, and thanks to them we can reach families with difficulties. They also act as someone "opening the door" for the psychological support we offer.

7.   Hanne Munck proposes that a clinician trained in using NBAS in a clinical setting is able to focus flexibly on whatever aspect of it, in order to adapt to a particular setting and characteristics of parent–infant interactions. It is even possible to make very accurate observations of infant behaviour in ordinary settings with the parents (see Munck, 1995).

8.   It is clear that one consultation with NBAS is not sufficient to achieve significant and long-term changes, but may only be the starting point for building a collaborative relationship with parents, using the baby's behaviour as a language of communication, as Nugent (1985) proposed. While planning early intervention and early prevention measures, it is essential to take into account the level of involvement

and the extent to which we are going to affect the family. It is of particular importance when we think about individual consultations. The goal of these consultations is to help early relationships to develop properly, in order to make it possible for the child to build safe attachment. They are also quite often meant to lessen the suffering of the baby or of the parent (usually the mother).

9.   In one of the questionnaires, we ask the participants about their personal impressions of the change the workshops brought about. Below are the statements presented to the parents in the last two groups (thirty-four people), together with the results (in percentage). *I feel that participating in the workshops "Toward the Baby" has made me think about my unborn baby* (more often—86%; less often—1%; no difference—13%); *I think that participating in the workshops "Toward the Baby" has enabled me to understand newborn and infant functioning* (much better—50%; better—50%; worse—0%; did not influence my understanding—0%); *I feel that now, having attended the workshops "Toward the Baby", I am better prepared for the first encounter* (yes—98%; no—1%; no opinion—1%); *I have an impression that participating in these workshops will make me feel more competent in taking care of my baby* (yes—88%; no—0%; difficult to say—12%); *I have an impression that participating in the workshops made me think about my parenthood* (in a more positive way—55%; in a more negative way—0 %; in a more realistic way—40%; did not influence it—5%).

References

Acquarone, S. (2004). *Infant–Parent Psychotherapy: A Handbook.* London: Karnac.

Ainsworth, M. D. S., Blehar, M. C., Waters, E., & Wall, S. (1978). *Patterns of Attachment: A Psychological Study of the Strange Situation.* Hillsdale, NJ: Lawrence Erlbaum.

Bakermans-Kranenburg, M. J., van IJzendoorn, M. H., & Juffer, F. (2003). Less is more: meta-analyses of sensitivity and attachment interventions in early childhood. *Psychological Bulletin, 129:* 195–215.

Bielicka, I., & Olechnowicz, H. (1967). A note on the rehabilitation of the family in the treatment of the orphan syndrome in infants. *Journal of Child Psychology and Psychiatry, 8(2):* 139–142.

Bowlby, J. (1988). *A Secure Base.* New York: Basic Books.

Brazelton, T. B., & Nugent, J. K. (1995). *The Neonatal Behavioural Assessment Scale* (3rd edn). London: MacKeith Press.

Egeland, B., Weinfield, N. S., Bosquet, M., & Cheng, V. K. (2000). Remembering, repeating and working through: lessons from attachment-based interventions. In: J. D. Osofsky & H. E. Fitzgerald (Eds.), *Handbook of Infant Mental Health (Volume 4). Infant Mental Health in Groups at High Risk* (pp. 35–89). New York: Wiley.

Fonagy, P., & Target, M. (1997). Attachment and reflective function: their role in self-organization. *Development and Psychopathology, 9*: 679–700.

Fonagy, P., Gergely, G., Jurist, E. J., & Target, M. (2002). *Affect Regulation, Mentalization and the Development of the Self.* New York: Other Press.

Fraiberg, S., Adelson, E., & Shapiro, V. (1974). Ghosts in the nursery: a psychoanalytic approach to the problems of impaired infant–mother relationships. *Journal of the American Academy of Child Psychiatry, 13*: 387–421.

Lebovici, S., Latrigue, J. A., & Salinas, J. L. (2002). The therapeutic consultation. In: J. M. Maldonado-Duran (Ed.), *Infant and Toddler Mental Health: Models of Clinical Intervention with Infants and Their Families* (pp. 161–185). Washington, DC: American Psychiatric Publishing.

Maldonado-Duran, J. M., & Latrigue, T. (2002). Mulitimodal parent–infant psychotherapy. In: J. M. Maldonado-Duran (Ed.), *Infant and Toddler Mental Health: Models of Clinical Intervention with Infants and Their Families* (pp. 129–159). Washington, DC: American Psychiatric Publishing.

Meins, E. (1997). Security of attachment and maternal tutoring strategies: interaction within the zone of proximal development. *British Journal of Developmental Psychology, 15*: 129–144.

Munck, H. (1995). Using the NBAS with families: a psychotherapeutic approach. In: T. B. Brazelton & J. K. Nugent, *The Neonatal Behavioural Assessment Scale* (3rd edn) (pp. 108–110). London: MacKeith Press.

Nugent, K. J. (1985) *Using the NBAS with Infants and Families.* White Plains, NY: March of Dimes.

Papoušek, M., Schieche, M., & Wurmser, H. (2008). *Disorders of Behavioral and Emotional Regulation in the First Years of Life.* Washington, DC: Zero to Three Press.

Raphael-Leff, J. (2004). *Psychological Processes of Child Bearing.* London: Anna Freud Centre.

Sameroff, A. J., McDonough, S. C., & Rosenblum, K. L. (Eds.) (2005). *Treating Parent–Infant Relationship Problems: Strategies for Intervention.* New York: Guilford Press.

Slade, A. (2005). Parental reflective functioning: an introduction. *Attachment and Human Development, 7*: 269–281.

Stern, D. N. (1995). *The Motherhood Constellation: A Unified View of Parent–Infant Psychotherapy.* New York: Basic Books.

CHAPTER EIGHT

Adoption and fostering: facilitating healthy new attachments between infant and adoptive parent

Maeja Raicar, with contributions by
Colette Salkeld and Franca Brenninkmeyer

Introduction

In this chapter, I explore the emotional and developmental risks inherent in fostering and adoption through separating infants (from birth to five-year-olds) from their mothers, whether due to voluntary relinquishment for adoption or removal from the birth family because of neglect and/or abuse. While acknowledging the life-long hurt for the growing child and adult of such profound losses, long-term foster carers and adoptive parents can be helped to attune to the infant and create positive new attachments to promote optimal emotional development.

Three early intervention programmes that focus on such support are described: the CcAT programme, Sing & Grow, and the PAC model of Intensive Therapeutic Work with Families.

The impact of adoption

Loss is the bedrock on which the social and legal edifices of adoption are built. And on which they can crumble if this stark reality is not honoured by all those involved in their construction. Far from the romantic myth of "a new forever family living happily ever after together", the living experience of adoption is imbued with the colours of ambivalence for all the parties to adoption: the hoped-for gains by child and parents in constructing a new family balanced by the ongoing losses and pain of the adoptee, their birth relatives and the adoptive family. (Raicar, 2010, p. 6)

This might seem a bleak description of the impact of adoption, which is intended to provide new families for children. However, as John Simmonds writes (2008, p. 28), ". . . adoption, as social engineering, is one of the most radical interventions that can be made. It totally and irrevocably changes lives—for better or worse—not just for the child but for the adoptive and birth families too."

Nancy Verrier, an adoptive parent herself as well as a therapist and researcher, states,

The severing of that connection between the adopted child and his birthmother causes a primal or narcissistic wound, which affects the adoptee's sense of self and often manifests in a sense of loss, basic mistrust, anxiety and depression, emotional and/or behavioural problems and difficulties in relationships. (1994, p. 21)

Verrier goes on to suggest that such primal wounding affects the child in every aspect of their development: emotional, psychological, mental, physical, and spiritual:

This wound, occurring before an infant has begun to separate its own identity from that of its mother, may result in a feeling that part of oneself has disappeared, leaving the infant with a feeling of incompleteness or lack of wholeness. That incompleteness is often experienced, not only in the genealogical sense of being cut off from one's roots, but in a felt sense of bodily incompleteness. (1994, p. 38).

Verrier's thinking, informed by her own experience of having an adopted daughter from three days old, was substantiated by ten years of research carried out with adult adoptees, adoptive parents, and birth parents in the USA. Betty Jean Lifton, an adoptee who also became a therapist and a researcher, had previously come to similar conclusions. She described the painful lifelong sense of loss and identity confusion even more poignantly in her two books, *Lost and Found*

(2009) and *Journey of the Adopted Self* (2002). Lifton explained that the latter title "came out of my musing about why many adoptees say they feel alienated, unreal, unborn, and that they have no self".

These writers describe *not* the reactions of very hurt children who have been removed from their parents because of severe neglect and/or abuse, but the felt experience of adoptees relinquished by their mothers soon after birth, usually because of social stigma and lack of financial support for "unmarried mothers" at that time. These might sound like extreme reactions to separation by babies who are then placed with caring adoptive families. However, there is evidence of such trauma in the deeply disturbing films *John* and *A Two-Year-Old Goes to Hospital*, which were made in the 1950s by James and Joyce Robertson, research collaborators of John Bowlby. These films show the devastating effects of even a few days' separation, with no consistent substitute carer, on two previously securely attached toddlers who then return to their own families.

So why does continuity in care matter so much? John Bowlby, the father of attachment theory, suggested over sixty years ago (1953, p. 11),

> . . . what is believed to be essential for mental health is that the infant and young child should experience a warm, intimate, and continuous relationship with his mother (or permanent mother-substitute—one person who steadily "mothers" him) *in which both find satisfaction and enjoyment*. (my italics)

The basic bonding cycle (Figure 8.1) shows how consistent loving care by an attuned parent helps baby and carer to form secure attachments. Louis Cozolino explains almost lyrically that the right hemispheres of a child and carer's brains are linked "through eye contact, facial expressions, soothing vocalisations, caresses, and exciting exchanges". Interestingly, Cozolino also notes the plasticity of the mother's brain after giving birth, so that she too grows "emotional synapses" to help her become more attuned to her child's needs (2006, p. 83).

Neuroscience and attachment research over the past several decades confirms that loss of, or damage to, the baby's primary attachments through abuse or neglect can distort or inhibit the normal development of neural connections in the baby's brain (Wassell, 2008, p. 50).

The Basic Bonding Cycle

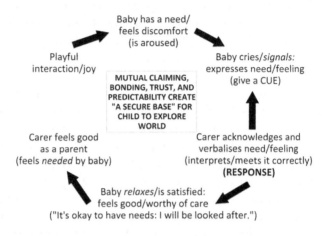

Figure 8.1. The basic bonding cycle (© A. M. Raicar, 2009).

Constant interruptions to the basic bonding cycle at any point, or repeated failure to complete it, will adversely affect the baby's capacity to develop trust that his needs will be met or, indeed, that it is *safe* to have needs and express them (CUES). So, as in Figure 8.2 below, the baby is more likely to give confusing misCUES to bewildered carers.

Wassell describes how a child can get stuck in learnt survival responses of fight, flight, or freeze:

> In circumstances of stress or danger which characterise abusive experiences, the child's brain accommodates by becoming hyper-aroused and ultimately dissociated, cutting off from the intolerable stress. The more severe the maltreatment, the more likely it will be that the infant's brain will be "wired" for these experiences of threat. (2008, p. 49)

After repeated abuse, rejection, and abandonment, the child might project all his feelings of rage, hurt, and disappointment to new foster or adoptive parents. Kate Cairns (2008, chapter 5) warns that the carers themselves might then experience secondary traumatisation, while being expected to provide "therapeutic parenting". If left unsupported, the parents could unwittingly react to reinforce their child's low self-view and lack of trust in others. This will make further

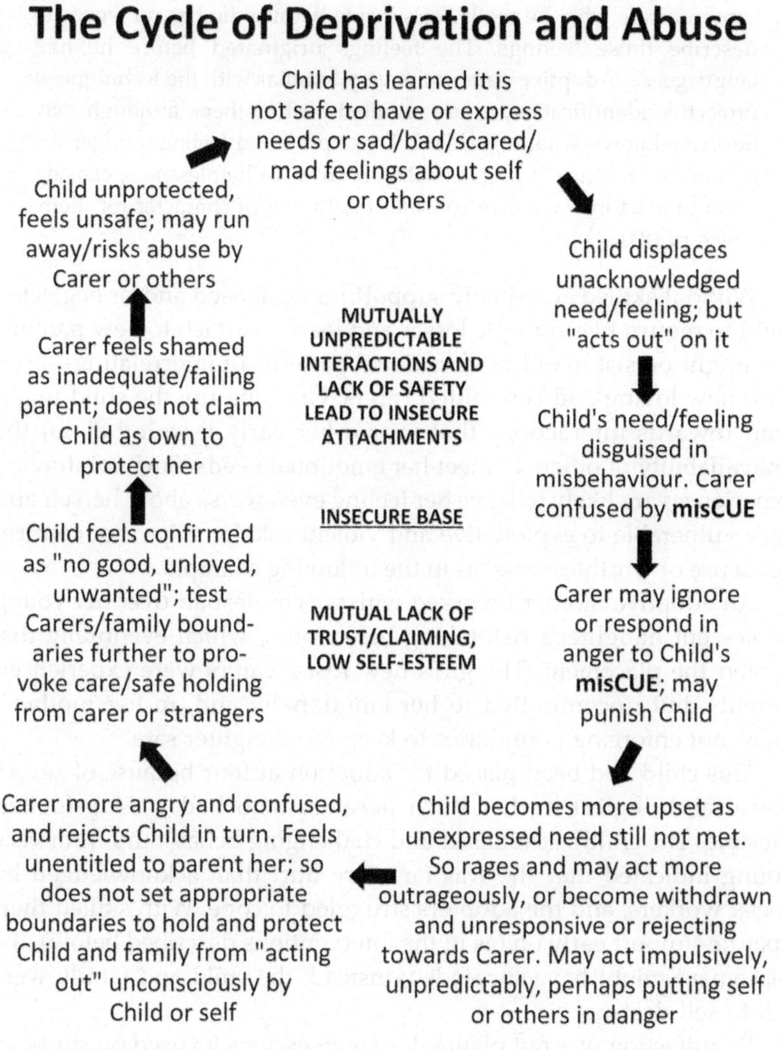

The Cycle of Deprivation and Abuse

Child has learned it is
not safe to have or express
needs or sad/bad/scared/
mad feelings about self
or others

Child unprotected,
feels unsafe; may run
away/risks abuse by
Carer or others

Child displaces
unacknowledged
need/feeling; but
"acts out" on it

Carer feels shamed
as inadequate/failing
parent; does not claim
Child as own to
protect her

**MUTUALLY
UNPREDICTABLE
INTERACTIONS AND
LACK OF SAFETY
LEAD TO INSECURE
ATTACHMENTS**

Child's need/feeling
disguised in
misbehaviour. Carer
confused by **misCUE**

INSECURE BASE

Child feels confirmed
as "no good, unloved,
unwanted"; test
Carers/family bound-
aries further to pro-
voke care/safe holding
from carer or strangers

**MUTUAL LACK OF
TRUST/CLAIMING,
LOW SELF-ESTEEM**

Carer may ignore
or respond in
anger to Child's
misCUE; may
punish Child

Carer more angry and confused,
and rejects Child in turn. Feels
unentitled to parent her; so
does not set appropriate
boundaries to hold and protect
Child and family from "acting
out" unconsciously by
Child or self

Child becomes more upset as
unexpressed need still not met.
So rages and may act more
outrageously, or become withdrawn
and unresponsive or rejecting
towards Carer. May act impulsively,
unpredictably, perhaps putting self
or others in danger

Figure 8.2. The cycle of deprivation and abuse (© A. M. Raicar, 2009).

moves, separations, and losses more likely, keeping him stuck in a
cycle of deprivation and abuse (see Figure 8.2).

Nancy Verrier describes the power of such unconscious communications:

 . . . anyone in a relationship with him will begin to experience his feelings and react to them. The adoptee uses projective identification to

communicate what he really feels inside because he has no words to describe those feelings. The feelings originated before he had language. . . . Adoptive parents are very familiar with the technique of projective identification, as are reunited birthmothers, although may not have known what it is called. Those projected feelings trigger the parents' own sense of rage, hostility, sorrow, or helplessness, causing them to react in ways they consider totally out of character for them. (1994, p. 184)

Without skilled and timely support for an abused and/or neglected child to mourn her multiple losses and learn to attach to new parents, she might persist in old dysfunctional patterns of interrelating—even with new loving and committed carers. Growing up, the child might tend towards interactions that mirror her early learning about the unavailability of others to meet her emotional needs. Such reinforcing experiences are likely to leave her feeling even worse about herself and very vulnerable to exploitative and violent relationships that confirm her sense of worthlessness, as in the following example.

An adoptive mother I worked with was in despair over her young adolescent daughter's risk-taking behaviours, which eventually disrupted the placement. The girl's new foster carers were experienced parents, but uncommitted to her emotionally and, in her mother's view, not enforcing boundaries to keep the daughter safe.

This child had been placed for adoption at four because of severe abuse and neglect by her birth parents, who had a drug-fuelled lifestyle. The child's sexualised and challenging behaviours from very young indicated that she was far more hurt than acknowledged by social workers, and the adopters struggled to cope. With skilled therapeutic support early on (as in the interventions described below), the placement might have succeeded; instead, the child and family were left to self-destruct.

Reunifaction was not planned, so our sessions focused on supporting the adoptive mother, who was near breakdown. I encouraged self-care, to empower her to continue being an advocate for her daughter and slowly heal their relationship for the future.

Why are children adopted?

For social, economic, and political reasons, adoption has been favoured in the UK for infants and children who need new carers because of possible further damage if they remain in their birth families through:

- severe abuse—physical, sexual, emotional, psychological;
- intergenerational abuse; lack of protection from sexual or other exploitation;
- parental rejection/abandonment; scapegoating of child;
- gross neglect when parents are incapable of providing safe and consistent care because of chronic mental or physical illness, severe learning difficulties, alcohol and/or substance abuse, domestic violence, social isolation, or chaotic/criminal lifestyles;
- imprisonment or death of the primary carer;
- living in extreme poverty; homelessness; environmental dangers.

Vulnerabilities and losses

Foetal vulnerabilities

Well before birth, an infant might have had unfavourable experiences, which can lead to long-term neurological, emotional, mental, and/or physical damage. These may include:

- where the pregnancy is unwanted, with possible attempts at abortion;
- threats to survival in the womb because of mother's alcohol and/or substance abuse;
- violence by partner or others to mother while pregnant; foetus constantly alarmed;
- environmental stressors for mother increasing stress hormones and cortisol flooding;
- foetal failure to thrive because of toxicity in the womb;
- foetal abnormalities; risk of genetic defects.

Birth mother vulnerabilities

There might be additional maternal stressors because of complications in pregnancy or previous miscarriages, stillbirths, deficiencies in the womb, pre-eclampsia, physical or mental illness, or lack of family or social support. Where a mother has already had a child placed for adoption, the real possibility of also then losing her next baby can leave her so traumatised that this can affect the development of the foetus and her bonding with him.

Adoptive parents' vulnerabilities

These may arise from the fact that:

- they, too, had child losses through miscarriages and/or stillbirths, or failed to "make" a child through any means;
- they had little or no time or support to grieve for their own child losses before a strange child, with his own traumatic history of hurt and multiple losses, is placed with them for adoption;
- they suffered recent bereavements of a parent or other close family member and have had insufficient time to mourn;
- they are immature and/or insecure and expect the child to meet their emotional needs and reflect well on them as parents;
- because childless, one partner might have been infantilised by the other, and is then unwilling to give up that role, so competing with the child to have his/her emotional needs still prioritised in the family;
- one parent might develop an overly close relationship with the child, perhaps repeating her previous history, so excluding the other parent and any other children;
- the birth children of the adopters might be negatively affected by the placement.

A crucial task in adoption, therefore, is griefwork, to acknowledge the ongoing losses for both adoptive parents and the child:

Adoptive parents' losses

- The child placed is not related by "blood" and might never be fully accepted by themselves and/or their extended family as their own, as if born to them.
- The adoptee might not feel like a true emotional replacement for their birth child(ren) lost through miscarriages, stillbirths, fatal illness, or accidents, or for the dream child the adopters fantasised they would have.

- The child still has a birth family, peopling his and the adopters' emotional and fantasy worlds like ghosts waiting in the wings to reclaim their child when he or she reaches eighteen—or, these days, much earlier through Facebook and other social networking sites.
- The child might have bonded with his previous foster carers, who might have wanted to adopt him themselves, thus inhibiting his new parents' sense of entitlement to claim and treat him as their own.
- Extended family and friends reject the adoptive placement because of religious or cultural prejudices against adoption, homophobia, etc., so that there is no public acknowledgement of the child as a full family member.
- The child's disturbed behaviours, including extreme aggression, inhibit extended family members and friends from offering much-needed respite care for the beleaguered adoptive parents, who become exhausted and even depressed, unable to cope with the considerable and ongoing challenges of adoptive parenting.
- The new family might become increasingly isolated, their sense of failure and shame and being negatively different reflecting exactly how the adopted child feels.

Ongoing losses for the adopted child.

- Permanent loss of the child's birthright: his or her birth identity, relationships, and history.
- Lasting identity confusion—"Who am I?"—symbolised by different birth and adoptive names.
- Inherent sense of difference from adoptive family, reinforced by any others: appearance, race, class, ethnicity, culture, language, religion, sexual orientation.
- No sense of belonging to either birth or adoptive family, remaining on the outside of both, but left with divided loyalties even as adults.
- Permanent legacy of parental hurt—abuse, neglect, rejection, abandonment.
- Loss of birth family throughout childhood, and often for life. Adoption leads to ongoing intergenerational losses for the

extended birth family and for the adoptee and their children in turn.

- Fearing further rejection, the adopted child might adapt to the expectations of the adoptive family, becoming a "people-pleaser" to survive and losing touch with who she/he really is. Typically, adoptees try to suppress their true feelings of anger, hurt, sadness, yearning for their birth family, etc., in order to avoid upsetting their adoptive parents.

- Operating habitually in "false self" mode, adoptees might find it difficult when growing up to connect spontaneously with others and identify and express their own feelings and needs, so that making and sustaining intimate relationships can become problematic for them

- Deep psychological and emotional wounding that never heals for many adopted adults, scarring them for life.

Table 8.1 shows some of the things that help or hinder adoptive parents' bonding with their child.

Taleb (2012) has developed an intriguing and controversial concept of "anti-fragility", which, he argues, is the true opposite of fragility and much more than robustness or resilience. If applied to adoption, anti-fragility—or post traumatic growth—can positively connote a process whereby the losses and stressors inherent in this artificially created relationship are acknowledged, and both child and parent supported in building healthy new attachments *without* denial of the child's birth family and history.

Table 8.1. Hindrances and help for bonding between adoptive parents and the child.

What hinders adoptive parents	What helps them bond with the child
Ungrieved losses and hurt	Post-traumatic growth
Denial of feelings of loss, sadness, anger	Acknowledgement, validation, and support
Ignorance of child's pre-placement history	Knowledge and understanding of impact
Lack of skilled therapeutic support	Ongoing support as needed by family

Early intervention programmes

Described below are three early intervention programmes that are attachment based, psychoanalytically informed, and integrate talking and arts therapies with psycho-education. The CcAT (Child-Centred Attachment Therapy) programme and PAC (formerly the Post-Adoption Centre) incorporate energy therapies like EFT (emotional freedom technique) and EMDR (eye movement desensitisation and reprocessing), while Sing & Grow uses music to access and connect with deep unconscious parts of parent and child.

The CcAt programme

This has a three-pronged approach with intertwining strands (Raicar, 2009, pp. 74–75):

1. The parent needs to attune to the child's true feelings and needs (CUES), naming and meeting them appropriately (RESPONSES). CcAT helps carer and child to match their CUES and RESPONSES in order to improve their communication and strengthen their attachment.

2. Playwork with child and carer to build their "fun time" together and promote bonding through mutual enjoyment.

3. Sensitive support for griefwork with both child (Life Story Work) and adoptive parent ("Inner Child" and adult losses), as needed.

The main principles of the American parenting programme, The Nurtured Heart Approach (Glasser & Easley, 1999), can usefully be incorporated in CcAT to foster a mutually respectful relationship and lead to a win–win situation for parent and child through its encouragement of carers to:

- carefully attune to the child to notice anything he or she does right and give them immediate and specific positive feedback to reinforce desired behaviours and honour their inherent "greatness";
- reserve high-intensity parental responses—previously sought by the child for negative behaviours—for positive behaviours or even tiny steps taken by her towards a desired outcome;

- be clear and consistent when enforcing, in a neutral manner, pre-determined essential rules with agreed brief consequences for non-compliance.

This helps the child learn to make better behaviour choices, and the approach can usefully be applied to parental relationships, too.

I increasingly encourage self-care by parents, who often become angry and depressed martyrs to their persecutory child. I also share a simple and effective self-help technique to acknowledge the parents' and the child's feelings, while tapping on acupressure points: EFT (Ortner, 2013) (Figure 8.3).

For safe griefwork (Figure 8.4) (mourning and detachment from real or "fantasy" losses in the past), support and safe therapeutic holding/containment of difficult feelings are needed for life story work with children, and inner child work with carers who may have "ghosts in the nursery" (Fraiberg et al., 1975).

For re-attachment to new carers to occur, both child and carer will need to grieve and release emotional energy invested in the child's wish to return to their own family, or the carer's wish to have a different kind of child.

Detachment and re-attachment work

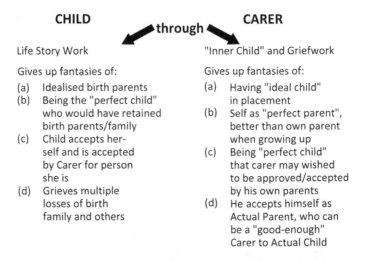

CHILD	CARER
through	
Life Story Work	"Inner Child" and Griefwork
Gives up fantasies of:	Gives up fantasies of:
(a) Idealised birth parents	(a) Having "ideal child" in placement
(b) Being the "perfect child" who would have retained birth parents/family	(b) Self as "perfect parent", better than own parent when growing up
(c) Child accepts herself and is accepted by Carer for person she is	(c) Being "perfect child" that carer may wished to be approved/accepted by his own parents
(d) Grieves multiple losses of birth family and others	(d) He accepts himself as Actual Parent, who can be a "good-enough" Carer to Actual Child

Figure 8.3. Detachment and re-attachment work © A. M. Raicar, 2009.

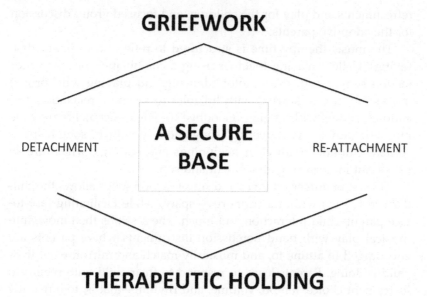

Figure 8.4.   Griefwork: detachment and re-attachment work
© A. M. Raicar, 2009.

"Sing & Grow": music therapy as preventative work with infants and their adoptive parents (Colette Salkeld, Regional Director, Chroma, and Senior Music Therapist at The Portland Hospital for Women and Children, London)

Sing & Grow originated in Australia in 2001 and was introduced to the UK in 2010 as an evidence-based, ten-week structured music therapy programme for children up to four years of age in birth families with complex needs. Sing & Grow is being used in Essex specifically to support the developing attachments between adoptive parents and their newly placed children. It aims to enhance parent–child interactions, build parent confidence, increase social connectedness, and improve child development outcomes.

The sessions have a simple structure to help adoptive parents and children feel safe and anticipate the activities. Cairns (2002, p. 75) considers that structured time is vital for insecurely attached children to enable them to understand the routine of sleeping, waking, stimulation, and soothing. Each Sing & Grow session begins with music therapy for adoptive parents and children together, followed by refreshments and play for the children, and focused group discussion for the adoptive parents.

The music therapy time is structured to reflect an ordinary day: saying "Hello"; playing together using a combination of fine motor (action songs) and gross motor (dancing and playing with props) movement, use of scarves with lullabies to promote relaxation and cuddles, ending with singing "Goodbye" (going to sleep). Framing the music therapy with a "greeting" song and a "goodbye" song helps to contain emotions with clear beginnings and endings, which are so important in mirroring attachment and separation.

The use of nursery rhymes and simple action songs allows the children to regress within a supportive space, while facilitating face-to-face parent–child interaction and touch. The sessions then move into musical play with hand percussion instruments where parents are encouraged to attune to, and musically match and mirror, what their child is doing. Parents learn to respond to their child with regard to instrument choice, tempo, volume, and rhythm—that is, to musically match the mood of their child and to encourage her, musically, to participate. This same responsiveness can then be applied in other situations (Fuller, 2011).

Music is a perfect medium through which children can learn to share, take turns, and be with others in a safe contained space (Salkeld, 2008, p. 154). Sing & Grow therapists share their knowledge of musical play with parents, through modelling, explanation and conversation, so developing parent confidence in using music to play and bond with their adopted child. As Casement (1985, p. 22) comments, "If the mother feels adequately held, then she is much more likely to be able to learn from her baby how best to be the mother which, at that moment, her baby most needs her to be".

Parents are given a CD to try out at home the musical play ideas they used in the group. Parents report that the music does calm their child, the songs defusing potentially difficult situations in a fun or playful manner (Hayward & Salkeld, 2013).

Group discussion, co-facilitated by a music therapist and social worker, rounds off each music therapy session. Parents talk about their own adoption issues, and are supported in understanding their child's behaviour and responding with empathy. Themes include the impact of trauma on family dynamics, regression and re-parenting, the importance of boundaries and routine, as well as using music for co-regulation.

As the weeks progress, the music-making helps parents to relax and share experiences more openly. Peer support also increases. Having Sing & Grow groups in Essex specifically for adopters is valued: "... when my child was really disturbed I felt that I could handle her behaviour without having to justify it, whereas I feel far more anxious in an environment with birth parents and their children so maybe I don't deal with it quite so well."

While parents chat together, the children have play time. Here, it is possible to observe their social skills and if they are starting to use their adoptive parents as a secure base, returning to them for emotional refuelling and sharing of their new discoveries (Raicar, 2009).

The following cameo illustrates the process of change an adoptive family can experience over ten weeks. The music therapy space enables a child to regress and be re-parented by her adoptive mother in a nurturing, holding environment where they can experience one another anew, bonding together.

A four-year-old girl sits facing the music therapist with her adoptive parent sitting behind her, mirroring her posture. Both seem cautious, perhaps anxious, as they embark on the ten-week Sing & Grow programme. Eight sessions later, the same child sits cradled in her mother's lap, a colourful scarf draped over them both. In the background the music therapist is singing "Twinkle Twinkle Little Star". As the mother sings to her child and they gaze into one another's eyes, the little girl reaches up to stroke her mother's face.

A parent who attended the programme thirteen months after placement commented, "We struggled for so long because adoption is not a natural attachment ... Sing & Grow is so beneficial as it can be early on and it gives your child that recognition that you are their mum and dad and it strengthens that bond better."

PAC's intensive therapeutic support for adoptive families and families with permanently placed children (Franca Brenninkmeyer, Head of Child and Family Service, PAC, London)

PAC's Child and Family Service offers a specialist consultation, assessment, and therapeutic service for families with adopted or permanently placed children and young persons.

The children referred have typically experienced developmental trauma (van der Kolk, 2005)—that is, chronic and pervasive neglect and abuse in early life—as well as several disrupted attachments through being moved from carer to carer before their adoptive/ permanent placement. The aims of PAC's intensive therapeutic family work are, therefore, to help

- the child develop a more secure attachment to their parents and thrive;
- the child process and integrate their traumatic life stories and adoption;
- strengthen the child's adoptive, cultural, and ethnic identity;
- support parents in providing therapeutic parenting and, thus, a secure base for their traumatised child.

PAC's model incorporates the ARC (attachment, regulation, and competence) framework developed at the Trauma Center in Boston (van der Kolk, 2005; Blaustein & Kinniburgh, 2010). These three core domains, being greatly affected by chronic trauma, need to be addressed to strengthen future resilience in a child.

ARC contains ten "building blocks" for therapeutic intervention. *Attachment*

1. Carer affect management.
2. Attunement.
3. Consistent response.
4. Routines and rituals.

(Self-)regulation

5. Affect identification.
6. Affect modulation.
7. Affect expression.

Competence

8. Developmental tasks.
9. Executive functions.
10. Self-development.

ARC provides a flexible framework that allows various integrative ways of using different interventions: for example, SI (sensory integration), SE (somatic experiencing), Theraplay, DDP (dyadic developmental psychotherapy), EMDR (eye movement desensitization and reprocessing), attachment focused family therapy, VIG (video interaction guidance), ACT (attachment communication training), and therapeutic parenting support. Other movement, music, and art-based therapies can all be offered under the ARC model; the key is that the therapists using these interventions need to be "(developmental) trauma informed".

PAC's work with under-fives typically addresses the three main domains of the ARC model and the ten building blocks.

An initial parent consultation is followed by a family assessment, which includes questionnaires and psycho-diagnostic measures that the parents complete, as well as the MIM (Marshak interaction method)—a Theraplay assessment (Booth & Jernberg, 2009). The MIM involves each parent having an individual session with their child during which they are asked to engage in a number of short games/ activities: for example, playing with squeaky animals, combing each other's hair, singing together, teaching the child something new.

The therapist observes each child–parent dyad via video-link or a one-way screen, and begins to assess their functioning with regard to the four Theraplay dimensions of "structure", "nurture", "engagement", and "challenge". The ARC building blocks are included, especially each parent's capacity for "affect management", "attunement", "affect modulation", and "affect expression". At the start and end of the assessment, the therapist engages with the family in some play, music, and movement activities; these allow observation of the child's reactions to each and how they interact with a "stranger" (the therapist).

The therapy starts with parent sessions, where their own histories of attachment, loss, and trauma are explored, since these can affect their capacity to guide and support their child in the ARC building blocks, especially those in the attachment and regulation domains.

Parts of the parents' histories can be processed, drawing on the therapists' repertoire of techniques such as EMDR, SE, and ACT. Such intervention seems most effective when the parents have enough current "attachment security" between them (i.e., they are able to be a secure base for each other) or, in the case of a single parent, with friends or family members. Sometimes, individual or couples therapy is recommended.

Family sessions involve the parent(s) and just *one* child at any time to allow total concentration on, and attunement to, the child by the therapist and parents. With very young children, the family sessions are initially mainly Theraplay based, with some sensory integration activities to help regulate the child.

The Theraplay intervention consists of the therapist guiding the parent and child through interactive, playful, fun activities—including some "routines and rituals"—that are developmentally appropriate for the child. These include the four Theraplay dimensions of engagement, nurture, structure, and challenge. The interactive and multi-sensory activities are sequenced by the therapist to allow delight between child and parent as well as shared enjoyment of the child's mastery. To facilitate this, the therapist actively supports the parent in *attuning to*, *regulating*, and *containing* the child's emotions and behaviours.

Thus, the child experiences and "learns" that their parents are available and interested, that they delight in them, and that they can emotionally hold them and keep them safe, with consistent and empathic boundaries. All this helps the child to become more regulated, feel more valued and attached, and frees him or her to invest in the development of age-appropriate competence.

Basic emotional literacy work is included with very young children and their parents to specifically address "affect identification" and "affect expression" (two ARC building blocks). Bear Cards® (a set of cards for young children with bears depicting feelings) and other creative ways may be used, such as musical instruments, mime and movement, painting and drawing, etc.

When using the Bear Cards®, feelings are simply named, given a context, located "in the body", expressed non-verbally, and validated. The therapist and parents model such expression of feelings and those of the child, especially acceptance and containment of "negative" feelings. Parents are encouraged to continue this work at home through similar play activities and verbalising/guessing at feelings when reading stories to their child.

With children aged three and older, therapeutic life story work is introduced following emotional literacy work. Although very young children have limited understanding and recall of the complexities in their life story, it is often surprising how much they do understand about having "lived with different mummies and daddies", and how well they respond to acting out their story with miniature figures (e.g., Sylvanians) or soft toys, such as teddies. Naming and validating the feelings they might have had about their moves and other "big things" that happened in their short lives helps them to process these. Some children actively participate by moving figures/teddies around and even adding parts to the story. Using the Sylvanian figures, one four-year-old child spontaneously acted a visit to her birth mother "to have a cuddle" and then "go home with mummy and daddy".

Ethnic diversity is addressed, using miniature figures/soft toys of different colours, so that similarities and differences between the child and birth or adoptive family members can be positively acknowledged. It is essential that the adoptive parents are present at these sessions to witness the child's story and provide acceptance, containment, and validation for her history, associated feelings, and her developing identity. Such therapeutic life story work can enhance attachment, the child using the parent as a secure base when processing his or her often very difficult early experiences.

Such therapeutic family work might sound like child's play, but many traumatised children present with disorganised and intimacy-averse behaviours that need to be contained by the therapist and translated into their underlying emotions. The therapist also needs to "hold" the parents, who are often exhausted and despairing from living 24/7 with a continually rejecting and difficult child.

The parents usually continue to have some sessions on their own to address specific therapeutic parenting challenges and explore necessary changes in their lifestyles to meet their child's developmental needs. The therapist recommends resources (training days, websites, articles, books, CDs, DVDs), and gives some home tasks: Theraplay games, emotional literacy activities, going out on a parents-only date, etc.

The therapist's tasks include liaising with the referring social worker/s, the child's nursery/school, and other professionals involved in the child and family's life. Parents are asked to give qualitative feedback at the beginning of each session. Progress/outcomes are assessed with pre- and post-intervention standardised questionnaires (SDQ, Parenting Scale of Competence, Assessment Checklist for Children

Plus, and PAC's own feedback questionnaires). The therapeutic work is challenging, but generally rewarding.

Conclusion

Adoption, like any other form of parenting, is hard work and a long-term commitment. It can be a mutually enriching experience, lightened by humour and hopefulness, and sustained by parental self-care and support.

Taleb's concept of "anti-fragility" (2012) seems similar to that of bones knitting more strongly after rupture, or that described by Hemingway: "The world breaks everyone and afterward many are stronger at the broken places" (1929). If adoptive parents can honour their own and their child's "lost loss" (Winterson, 2011, p. 190), it is possible for them to build healthy and lasting new attachments, thus helping to end intergenerational cycles of neglect and abuse.

References

Blaustein, M., & Kinniburgh, K. M. (2010). *Treating Traumatic Stress in Children and Adolescents: How to Foster Resilience Through Attachment, Self-Regulation, and Competency*. New York: Guilford Press.

Booth, P., & Jernberg, A. M. (2009). *Theraplay: Helping Parents and Children Build Better Relationships Through Attachment Based Play* (3rd edn). San Francisco, CA: Jossey-Bass.

Bowlby, J. (1953). *Child Care and the Growth of Love*. Harmondsworth: Penguin.

Cairns, K. (2002). *Attachment, Trauma and Resilience: Therapeutic Caring For Children*. London: BAAF.

Cairns, K. (2008). Enabling effective support: secondary traumatic stress and adoptive families. In: D. Hindle & G. Shulman (Eds.), *The Emotional Experience of Adoption: A Psychoanalytic Perspective* (pp. 90–98). London: Routledge.

Casement, P. (1985). *On Learning from the Patient*. London: Tavistock.

Cozolino, L. (2006). *The Neuroscience of Human Relationships: Attachment and the Developing Social Brain* (2nd edn). New York: Norton.

Fraiburg, S., Adelson, E., & Shapiro, V. (1975). Ghosts in the nursery: a psychoanalytic approach to the problem of impaired mother–infant relationships. *Journal of the American Academy of Child Psychiatry*, *14*: 387–422.

Fuller, A. (2011). Unpublished university assignment.

Glasser, H., & Easley, J. (1999). *Transforming the Difficult Child: The Nurtured Heart Approach*. World Publishing.com.

Hayward, G. D., & Salkeld, C. E. (2013). Evaluation of Sing & Grow within adoption (unpublished article).

Hemingway, E. (1929). *A Farewell to Arms*. New York: Scribners.

Lifton, B. J. (2002). *Journey of the Adopted Self: A Quest for Wholeness*. New York: Basic Books.

Lifton, B. J. (2009). *Lost and Found* (3rd edn). Ann Arbor, MI: University of Michigan Press.

Ortner, N. (2013). *The Tapping Solution*. London: Hay House.

Raicar, A. M. (2009). *Child-Centred Attachment Therapy: The CcAT Programme*. London: Karnac.

Raicar, A. M. (2010). When adopted adults are shadowed by disrupted attachments. *The Psychotherapist* (UKCP Journal), *44*(Spring): 6–9.

Salkeld C. (2008). Music therapy after adoption: the role of family therapy in developing secure attachment in adopted children. In: A. Oldfield & C. Flower (Eds.), *Music Therapy with Children and their Families* (pp. 141–158). London: Jessica Kingsley.

Simmonds, J. (2008). Developing a curiosity about adoption: a psychoanalytic perspective. In: D. Hindle & G. Shulman (Eds.), *The Emotional Experience of Adoption: A Psychoanalytic Perspective* (pp. 27–41). London: Routledge.

Taleb, N. N. (2012). *Antifragility*. London: Random House.

Van der Kolk, B. (2005). Developmental trauma disorder. *Psychiatric Annals*, *35*(5): 401–408.

Verrier, N. N. (1994). *The Primal Wound: Understanding the Adopted Child*. Baltimore, MD: Gateway Press.

Wassell, S. (2008). Why is early development important? In: D. Hindle & G. Shulman (Eds.), *The Emotional Experience of Adoption: A Psychoanalytic Perspective* (pp. 42–56). London: Routledge.

Winterson, J. (2011). *Why Be Happy When You Could Be Normal?* London: Vintage Books.

CHAPTER NINE

In a strange country without a map: special needs babies

Julie Kitchener

he title of this chapter is taken from the words of a mother speaking to the psychoanalyst Salo Tischler more than four decades ago. This woman says of her early experience of her son's disabling condition, "My characteristic look was . . . of one who has landed suddenly in a strange country without maps or landmarks" (Tischler, 1971, p. 230). Despite medical, social, political, and therapeutic developments, the overwhelming sense of disorientation conveyed in this description is likely to be familiar to anyone working therapeutically in the field of "special needs", a disorientating description in itself ("I hate SEN," a young patient of mine once complained). Certainly, it has been a recurring theme in my own experience as a child psychotherapist within an integrated, multi-professional service for children with complex disabilities and significant developmental disorders.

I hope here to give voice to the experience of children and their parents in composite vignettes drawn from my clinical experience (disguised to ensure confidentiality). But there is also a growing body of literature in the wider public domain in which parents and young people share their experience of disability: newspaper and magazine articles, internet blogs, and books such as Andrew Solomon's *Far From*

166 SURVIVING THE EARLY YEARS

the Tree (2014), or *The Reason I Jump* by Naoki Higashida (2013). Take, for example, Emily Perl Kingsley's essay, "Welcome to Holland"[1] (now "as iconic to disability as 'How do I love thee?' is to romance", writes Solomon), in which the writer depicts her gradual and ongoing adjustment to having a child with Down's syndrome. "When you're going to have a baby," she suggests, "it's like planning a fabulous vacation trip—to Italy." But then your plane lands and you find you are in Holland: not somewhere terrible, but not Italy. "So you must go out and buy new guidebooks. And you must learn a whole new language." Like Tischler's mother, Kingsley evokes an experience of bewilderment, loss, and dislocation, of challenges to expectations, and the need to find new ways of being in the world.

I will trace this experience through pregnancy, birth, and into the early years, not losing sight of the reality that for most this is a lifelong process, with shifting signs and landmarks. Many families will not need the support of a psychotherapist to find their bearings but, as Tischler suggests, it might be that sometimes parents of children with a disability "need to become extra healthy", to negotiate even the ordinary challenges of development: feeding, sleeping, toileting, separation. Also, some children will need a psychotherapeutic space in their own right. I will touch on the part played by trauma and helplessness, questions of integration and disintegration, the push to omnipotence (the difficulty of accepting the limitations of human capabilities or medical expertise), and the fact that disability brings these children and their families, as well as those who work with them, face to face with existential questions about what it is to be human.

Drawing on the child psychotherapist's twin guides of ordinary child development and psychoanalytic theory and in particular on Winnicott's understanding of early preverbal development, I will consider what the therapeutic task might be (is there a map?), taking into account the work of mourning, the work of noticing, the work of imagination. In doing so, I will rely heavily on the clinical, theoretical, and human insights offered by other psychotherapists working in this field (e.g., Pamela Bartram and Valerie Sinason). Like them, I have come to recognise the particular value—and risks—attached to the psychotherapist's use of the self in this work, that honed capacity for attending to non-verbal communication that we call countertransference responses, but which can so easily slide into attempts to see "with one's blind spot" (Owens, 2005, p. 297).

What, then, are the implications for the child's emotional and psychological wellbeing—particularly in the crucial early years—of the ways in which those on whom he or she depends for care orientate themselves to their child's "special" needs? And what are the factors—affecting the child, the parents, and the professional network—that can lead to a referral for psychotherapeutic support?

Guides and experts

"First you tell me my child's brain is too badly damaged to fix. Then you tell me I'm mental and need a shrink. I mean, come on, what's going on here?" After a complicated labour and traumatic delivery, Denise and her partner, Glen, learnt that their son Raul had cerebral palsy.[2] Suddenly, their world was invaded by specialists and experts, just as Raul's frail body had been subject to seemingly endless—albeit vital—intrusions of intensive care: drips, ventilators, monitors, etc. Yet, to Denise, the wonders of medical science had failed to protect her son in the first place. Once Raul was home from hospital and under the care of the community child development team, Denise could still swing between viewing these experts—doctors, speech and language therapists, physiotherapists, occupational therapists—as holders of a "secret store of answers" (Bartram, 2013, p. 169) or as deeply unskilled, ham-fisted, and ill-informed.

It is easy to see how a distraught and angry mother might pose challenges for a child development team, and it is good to have colleagues on that team who appreciate the input of a child psychotherapist. However, at this point at least, Denise was having none of it. Much later, when she felt able to tell me this story, her blunt words still packed a punch. *See how you like it*, she might have been saying, *when all your assumptions about your capabilities—as a parent, as a professional, as a person—are dealt one knock-out blow.*

Compared with Denise's "fight-or-flight" response, Helen's was more one of "deep immersion". Helen's daughter, Ginny, has a rare genetic disorder that was detected only after she was born. It is a condition with potentially life-threatening complications that affects her physical co-ordination and digestion, as well as her cognitive development. "I knew having a baby would be a major adjustment for someone used to working and being independent," Helen tells me.

"But how could I have begun to get used to the idea of something I'd never heard of before?" Once Ginny was born, there was no chance to reflect or think, "or even experience post natal depression". Ginny's day-to-day care and medical needs required constant attention: tests, surgery, expressing milk because she did not have the muscle control to suck. "On top of that, I suddenly had to become an expert in a condition I hadn't even known existed before." Helen became expert: she researched, she joined online groups, she attended conferences.

Helen ensured Ginny attended every check-up and developmental assessment. Not a single block of occupational therapy or physiotherapy was interrupted, and advice was always followed, intelligent questions asked. However, when Ginny turned two, her speech and language therapist noticed a harshness creeping into Helen's interactions with her daughter. The occupational therapist was bombarded with tearful requests for a weighted blanket, the paediatrician with questions: *Why wasn't Ginny yet able to sleep through the night? What could be done to control her eating, her impulsive behaviour, her tantrums? Should she have further medical investigations?* The team was beginning to feel as overwhelmed as Helen seemed to have become.

Before my first meeting with Helen, I spent hours doing my own research, feeling a pressure to learn all I could about Ginny's rare and complex condition. In truth, my attempt to adopt what the French child analyst Catherine Mathelin calls "the white uniform of knowledge" (1999, p. 177) was a cover-up for my sense of my own limitations. Inevitably, having no medical training, I could not seem to retain a single fact. Frantically, I scribbled a few notes that I could refer to during the session. In the room, I met a rather distracted looking woman, clutching a sheaf of medical papers and letters, which she thrust towards me: she had thought they might be helpful. I dug in my pocket for my glasses. No glasses! Like Helen, I had failed in my manic attempt to counter "a bad bout of helplessness" (Phillips, 2010, p. 127). As Sinason says, "To pretend to more knowledge than you have, rather than face openly what you do not know, is indeed handicapping" (1992, p. 17).

Signposts or dead-ends?

Mathelin notes that a "shrink" tends to be called in at points when "parents decompensate, that is, when they present undue problems for the team" (1999, p. 168). In my experience, "decompensation" is often associated with periods of assessment and diagnosis—as in "this mother is struggling to come to terms with her son's diagnosis".

"I think of diagnosis as an aid to pattern recognition," the mother of a child with autism tells Andrew Solomon. "We could make sense of things that had previously been inexplicable to us" (2013, p. 257). A diagnosis means something has been named and can be spoken about, however painful that might be; it signals the possibility of understanding, clinical guidelines for treatment, "care pathways". But, cautions Solomon, while a diagnosis might be "a revelation" to some, for many parents, it can be "a crossing of the Styx into hell".

Sofia, a refugee from a North African country, weeps as her three-year-old son, Samir, careers around the room: his newborn brother in her lap silent and unseen. "Do you think Samir will ever talk? . . . Do you?" asks Sofia over and over. We have just left the multi-disciplinary team meeting in which, following months of careful assessment, Samir's diagnosis of autism has been confirmed. Samir's assessment team are flummoxed. From Samir's first appointment, Sofia has voiced her suspicions that he has autism. How else could one account for his avoidant eye contact, his obliviousness to danger, his hand flapping, and repetitive door banging? She knows a little about autism: Samir has a cousin in France who has been diagnosed on the spectrum. But throughout this last meeting, Sofia has stared blankly ahead, addressing none of us in particular: "I don't understand. Why is this happening to us?"

The paediatrician explains again, with tact and gentleness, the "facts", as far as they can be known, of Samir's diagnosis. But there is a "confusion of tongues" between the language of social communication disorder, prognosis, and therapeutic intervention, and Sofia's trauma-driven questions. For the team, the diagnosis is a call to action: Samir is still little; plasticity brings urgency. For Sofia, it reignites deep-rooted fears about herself and her family's future. "When they tell me I should be doing this or doing that to help Samir," she says to me later, "I feel not just that they're telling me I'm a bad mother. I feel they're telling me I'm a bad person." She recalls another time when she felt she was getting it all wrong: a hospital in a land foreign to her, a nurse issuing instructions she does not understand. As she talks, I realise Sofia is right back there on the labour ward where Samir was born, behind the plastic curtain, wracked with pain and terror, praying for a doctor she thinks will never come.

Trauma, as Freud recognised (1920g), is an experience that cannot be integrated; it can threaten to remain a raw, unprocessed, lived present, inducing persistent states of helplessness that were an intrinsic element of the original trauma. For Sofia, "states" of helplessness and fear have become "traits" (Perry et al., 1995). Displacement and a prehistory of oppression were compounding factors, but disability itself often entails traumatic experiences, "risk of death and repeated frights and assaults of surgical interventions" (Hoxter, 1986, p. 88). Lost in space and time, Sofia seemed unable to orientate herself to her children.

First find your child

Helen remembers "the moment time stood still" for her. It was at the second birthday party of a friend's daughter. Instead of joining the celebrations, Helen found herself focusing on Ginny's difference from her peers, the milestones she had not yet achieved, and might never achieve. Anniversaries, like diagnoses, can prompt parents to "decompensate". "All I could see were Ginny's disabilities," says Helen. "I thought: this is how it will always be ... For the life of me, I can't remember whether it was a good party or not, or if Ginny enjoyed herself. Though I do remember her meltdown when I said it was time to leave."

Pamela Bartram, a child psychotherapist and former colleague who has pioneered a great deal of integrated work in the field of disability, highlights the risks associated with focusing on knowledge about a symptom or condition at the expense of developing knowledge of a particular child and that child's experience. Disability in babies and young children evokes intense and disturbing feelings in those around them, as many writers have described (e.g., Hoxter, 1986; Manoni, 1970; Sinason, 1992). Bartram detects an unconscious resistance to seeing the child with a disability as a whole as a way of defending against these feelings, a tendency to "split [the child] into manageable pieces: fine motor skills; cognitive ability; speech and language" (2009, p. 2). What usually then follows is a battery of tasks and treatments that mean that even "family mealtimes become exercises in posture, feeding and communication rather than a time to relax and commune with one another, person to person, not person to disability" (Bartram, 2009, p. 2).

Ginny was a child who had been subject to a catalogue of exercise regimes and treatments. "If I stopped to think," Helen said, "I could feel like I was some sort of torturer." Now that Helen had begun to stop and think, and to recognise her difficulties in seeing Ginny for herself, she was also able to use our meetings—and my blindness to technical terminology—as a way of "seeing more of Ginny", exploring ordinary developmental issues, such as those "meltdowns". For, of course, Ginny had reached the "terrible twos" and was learning the meaning of "No"—albeit on her terms, as Helen found it hard to put her own foot down. Ginny had, for example, taken up residence in the marital bed, with her father sleeping on a put-u-up bed in his study further along the landing.

Consciously, Helen was aware that her own anxieties around separation contributed to the problem. She still could not shake off the fear that Ginny might die suddenly in the middle of the night. But there was something else. One day Helen "confessed" that she had caught herself looking at Ginny and thinking, "You great big stupid lummox". Winnicott, as we know, lists eighteen reasons why a mother ordinarily hates her baby, "even a boy". These include, for starters, "The baby is not her own (mental) conception" (1947, p. 201). "You got the wrong boy," as one of my young patients put it. Helen, by her own admission, was struggling to find a way of not "always thinking of what might have been".

The point is, Winnicott tells us, "A mother has to be able to tolerate hating her baby without doing anything about it" (1947, p. 202). Torn between guilt and exasperation, Helen could be both infuriated by Ginny and scared to say "No" for fear of being cruel. "These parents need space for their ambivalence," says Solomon, "whether they can allow for it themselves or not" (2013, p. 21). Indeed, being allowed to recognise her own uncomfortable feelings, without being told she should be doing this or doing that, helped Helen respond more kindly but firmly to Ginny's own developmentally appropriate expressions of ambivalence.

There is no immunity to ambivalence, as I experienced in my work with Sofia. The development team were becoming increasingly concerned about Samir and his baby brother Ahmed—might he be autistic too?—and I found myself ever more critical of this mother. In her profound and moving paper, "Melancholia, mourning, love" (2013), Bartram explores the self-accusatory and judgemental states of mind characteristic of melancholia that can be associated with disability: "All they need is a place to settle, a thinker to think them" (p. 169). I realised I needed support. A colleague agreed to join me to meet with the family. To begin with, we would simply observe and share those observations with Sofia, trying to steer both children into view.

Creative ventures

In our sessions with Sofia and her children, we observed how Samir would flap around the door, yanking the handle and banging it shut, particularly at points when Sofia was tearful or distressed. We noticed, too, how it was possible at times to redirect Samir to games of peek-a-boo. After a while he even dared to be a bit curious about what was going on down the corridor outside, rushing back every now and again, enjoying our "Hellos" and "Goodbyes". If Sofia became tearful at memories of other goodbyes, Samir would resume his repetitive attempts to bang the door. Meanwhile, Ahmed was growing more animated:

> I comment that Ahmed seems interested in his big brother. Sofia looks down at him, then over to Samir. She turns back to Ahmed and smiles. Ahmed's face lights up under her gaze. He wriggles and gurgles. "You talking to mummy?" my colleague says. "You are. You're talking to mummy." Sofia beams and nods at Ahmed, slowly beginning to rock him, humming softly. Samir belts over from the door, clambers on to the arm of her chair and squeezes in close. He wants to be part of that cuddle, too. Sofia chuckles: "It's OK, I know you're there, Samir."

At a review meeting, Sofia says, "I sit in our living room and I look at Samir and I think: your world is so small; it's getting smaller and smaller. I want to help him venture out, have new experiences, to grow and develop, but then I worry: how will he manage without me?" We agree it might be time to see if Samir can make use of his own therapeutic space. Separation was a struggle, but a few months into his individual sessions, for the first time Samir instigated a game of peek-a-boo, using the towel.

He soon engineered another on my lap, leaning backwards so that his head dangled and allowing me to pull him back upright. He slid on to the floor and under my chair, mumbling something that sounded like "Baby crying", and tapped his head. "Crack!" Then he clambered on to my lap again to repeat the exercise. This time he looked up into my face and began to "sing", though I couldn't say there were any words. I picked up the tune and joined in the song: "Humpty-Dumpty sat on a wall . . ." Samir watched my mouth intently.

It was a hatching of sorts, capturing perhaps the fragility of Samir's birth for both mother and child.

Helen arrives for her appointment one day, smiling. She is expecting another baby—oh, yes, she had forgotten to mention last time that Ginny is now sleeping in her own bed. Well, most nights, fingers crossed.

Denise and Glen find their way to me in their own time. Today, they are describing the effort it takes to try to understand Raul. Although they think he is getting better at signing, they struggle to know when his gestures really are attempts at communication, and if so what they might mean, what he might want.

> "We can move his hands to try to get him to sign," says Denise. "But we can't move his tongue for him to get him to speak."
>
> "But you would if you could?"
>
> They smile and nod. They talk about all their efforts to encourage Raul to develop, to play, to move, to walk. I say, listening to them, I have this picture of them trying to build a boy, to build Raul. Glen says, "That's it: that's just what it's like." Then Denise recalls how in the emergency of Raul's birth and his treatment afterwards there was little opportunity for cuddles. It is still hard to hold Raul. Glen reaches for a tissue. "These are not man-sized tissues," he complains.

Flimsy tissues aside (how easy it can be to marginalise fathers), this session suggested to me the possibility of a shift for this parental couple from grievance to grief, a mourning for the missed early pleasures of that "armful of anatomy and physiology" (Winnicott, 1965). In the absence of ordinary opportunities for parent and infant to engage in the process of "holding" and "handling", of the necessary "imaginative elaboration of somatic parts, feelings and functions", they were forced to find new ways of helping Raul develop a "diagram of himself" (Winnicott, 1949, p. 243). Loving our children, writes Solomon, is "an exercise for the imagination" (2013, p. 1).

Conclusion

One of the reasons I find Winnicott so helpful in work with disabled children and their families is his appreciation of paradox. It is a paradox, for example, that when professionals and parents start to focus inwards on the child's experience, in the detailed observation that is intrinsic to the training of child psychotherapists, that child's world can begin to open outwards, and experience become integrated. "A small shift in parents' attitudes can be of great benefit to the child", says Tischler (1971, p. 246). A young girl can begin to sleep in her own bed and her parents once more conceive of the possibility of a creative coupling; a mother can find ways of helping her son to separate and broaden his experience, rather than feeling driven to spend every moment on exercise regimes or trapped in compulsive ruminations.

It is also a paradox, as Solomon discovered, that "parents of disabled children often achieve a feeling of control by making a firm and positive affirmation of their lack of control" (2013, p. 377). This is perhaps one of the ways in which they "need to become extra healthy", in order to be open to the possibility of mourning, noticing, and imagining—likewise practitioners. If anything brings life to the truism that a psychotherapist needs to remain in touch with his or her limitations, to be able to bear not knowing, it is working with children such as Raul, Ginny, or Samir and their families.

"The contemporary psychoanalyst has to recognize the sense in which each person revises—is inevitably a threat to—the available descriptions of what a person is", writes Adam Phillips (1995, p. 8). Such ideas might not sit easily in a world of goal-based questionnaires and brief interventions, but try to draw a therapeutic map for working in the field of "special needs" and you will constantly find yourself blown off course. "Raul doesn't ask questions," Glen says to me one day, "and I know he probably never will, but I go on presenting the world to him as if he does, trying to imagine what might make him curious, what sort of world he is building in his mind."

Notes

1. "Welcome to Holland", by Emily Perl Kingsley, was first featured in Dear Abby's column "A fable for parents of a disabled child", *Chicago Tribune*, 5 November 1989.
2. All names, descriptive details and background information in the clinical illustrations used have been changed.

References

Bartram, P. (2009). The eye of the sea: a response to the article TAC for the 21st Century: a unifying theory about children with multifaceted disabilities. *Tac Journal, 7*: 1–3. Freely available online.

Bartram, P. (2013). Melancholia, mourning, love: transforming the melancholic response to disability through psychotherapy. *British Journal of Psychotherapy, 29*(2): 168–181.

Freud, S. (1920g). *Beyond the Pleasure Principle. S. E., 18*: 7–64. London: Hogarth.

Higashida, N. (2013). *The Reason I Jump: One Boy's Voice from the Silence of Autism*, K. A. Yoshida & D. Mitchell (Trans.). London: Sceptre.

Hoxter, S. (1986). The significance of trauma in the difficulties encountered by physically disabled children. *Journal of Child Psychotherapy, 12*(1): 87–103.

Kingsley, E. P. (2012). Welcome to Holland. In: J. Canfield, *Chicken Soup for the Soul: Children with Special Needs. Stories of Love and Understanding for Those Who Care for Children with Disabilities* (pp. 2–4). Cos Cob, CT: Backlist.

Manoni, M. (1970). A challenge to mental retardation. In: *The Child, His "Illness", and the Others* (pp. 203–225). London: Karnac.

Mathelin, C. (1999). An analyst on a neonatal unit: a different experience. In: *The Broken Piano, Lacanian Psychotherapy with Children* (pp. 167–181). New York: Other Press.

Owens, C. (2005). Moved to tears: technical considerations and dilemmas encountered in working with a 13-year-old boy with acquired quadriplegia. *Journal of Child Psychotherapy, 31*(3): 284–302.

Perry, B. D., Pollard, R. A., Blakely, T. L., Baker, W. L., & Vigilante, D. (1995). Childhood trauma, the neurobiology of adaption, and "use-dependent" development of the brain: how "states" become "traits". *Infant Mental Health Journal, 16*(4): 271–291.

Phillips, A. (1995). *Terrors and Experts*. London: Faber and Faber.

Phillips, A. (2010). *On Balance*. London: Hamish Hamilton.

Sinason, V. (1992). *Mental Handicap and the Human Condition: An Analytic Approach to Intellectual Disability*. London: Free Association Books.

Solomon, A. (2013). *Far From the Tree: A Dozen Kinds of Love*. London: Chatto & Windus.

Tischler, S. (1971). Clinical work with the parents of psychotic children. *Psychiatria, Neurologia, Neurochirugia, 74*: 225–249.

Winnicott, D. W. (1947). Hate in the countertransference. In: *Collected Papers: Through Paediatrics to Psychoanalysis* (pp. 194–203). London: Tavistock (1958).

Winnicott, D. W. (1949). Mind and its relation to the psyche-soma. In: *Collected Papers: Through Paediatrics to Psychoanalysis*. London: Tavistock (1958).

Winnicott, D. W. (1965). Communication between infant and mother, and mother and infant, compared and contrasted. In: C. Winnicott, R. Shepherd, & M. Davis (Eds.), *Babies and Their Mothers* (pp. 89–103) . London: Free Association Books (1987).

PART III

VULNERABLE GROUPS COMING FROM "INTERNAL" FRAGILE CIRCUMSTANCES

In the final part of the book, we look at vulnerable groups of babies—their vulnerability due to "internal" fragile circumstances—and learn what is essential for them to develop in a healthier way. Not only do we have to keep up with new developments in applied psychoanalysis and neuropsychology, we also have to review what has worked in the past. Overall, we need to recognise the power of the relationship and be grateful for the ways we can prevent the occurrence of disorders and difficulties that can be avoided.

CHAPTER TEN

Early recognition of autism

Daphne Keen

Why early recognition?

From a paediatric perspective, early recognition is felt to be important and beneficial for several reasons. First, and most importantly, parents tell us that this is what they want, both to access the best help for their child and to plan as a family.

By the time of the first paediatric consultation, most parents have already recognised the abnormal responsiveness of their infant, and it is an unfortunate fact that generally they have been inappropriately reassured, not only by well-meaning family members, but also by professionals.

Early recognition facilitates access to genetic counselling and advice for parents regarding the risk of autism for future siblings. The advice generally given has been of an increased risk of 3–10%, but recent studies have suggested this to be an underestimate, and a sibling risk for autism spectrum disorder (ASD) of just under 19% has been reported, with a three-fold increase for males and an additional two-fold increase if there is more than one older affected sibling (Ozonoff et al., 2011).

The initial focus of paediatric contact should be to allay or confirm parental concern. This initial assessment will identify any other medical and developmental conditions that may present as co-existing and/ or confounding problems that can complicate the diagnostic process.

Impact of co-existing medical and developmental conditions on delay in diagnosis

It is increasingly apparent that the majority of conditions affecting neurodevelopment can be associated with an increased risk of autism. The range of conditions that may co-exist with autism are consequently quite diverse and the examples given below are by no means an exhaustive list, but illustrate some of the important and clinically challenging scenarios that can make the assessment of suspected autism such a complex process.

Sensory impairment

There is a rich and complex literature describing the intimate relationship between impairment in those key sensory modalities that are essential for the successful integration of information and development of language and social function.

Hearing impairment

In an otherwise healthy child presenting with concerns regarding social functioning, it is essential to ascertain auditory competence. Following the implementation of the neonatal hearing screen, late diagnosis of severe sensorineural hearing loss is now infrequent. Typically, though, when any condition becomes less frequent in the population, the state of knowledge and therefore vigilance declines, and the condition disappears from prominence in differential diagnosis.

It is important to bear in mind that not all children have undergone neonatal hearing screening, especially those born outside the more affluent countries, and also that there are some forms of sensorineural deafness that are progressive and so not necessarily evident in the neonatal period. One recent example known to me was a child who passed the neonatal hearing screen and presented at the age of eighteen months with severely impaired receptive and expressive language associated with apparently typical autistic repetitive behaviours. A further hearing test was inconsistent, but deemed adequate, and it was only after parental insistence that a further referral to a specialist audiology centre confirmed parental suspicion that there was a profound bilateral hearing loss. Subsequent investigation identified a previously unsuspected congenital cytomegalovirus infection raising the possibility that this could have been a progressive hearing loss, a quite uncommon picture. After cochlear implantation, the "autistic" behaviours disappeared.

However, we also know that there is an increased incidence of autism in children with hearing impairment, with a suggested presence of autism in just over 5% (Hitoglou et al., 2010).

Visual impairment

The increased risk of autism occurs in severe visual impairment of a neurological cause (i.e., from damage or disease of the brain, optic nerves, or retina), as opposed to impairment from structural anomalies of the anterior eye structure.

Child psychoanalyst Selma Fraiberg was one of the earliest to describe the progressive diverging patterns of development in blind children (Fraiberg, 1977). The presence of autistic features in blind children has been the subject of considerable interest subsequently over many years, with the emergence of a very complex picture of interrelationship and overlap between developmental and sensory impairments (Ek et al., 1998).

Features termed "blindisms", such as echolalia, pronoun reversal, stereotypical behaviour, and poor symbolic play, have been observed as frequently occurring in blind children, but the association with autism in adults is thought to be weak (Pring, 2005).

However, true autistic regression seen in children with blindness has been well documented and can be catastrophic and the diagnostic picture incontrovertible.

Psychosocial deprivation

The consequences of psychosocial deprivation on brain development have parallels with the effects of sensory impairment through the profound effects on the integration of language and social information and, hence, psychosocial and emotional function.

Children who come into local authority care because of significant psychosocial adversity with a history of neglect or abuse can present with a range of language and communication and other developmental delays, unusual social behaviours, and repetitive or restricted play behaviour. There is a paucity of good quality research on the progress of, and outcomes in, these children who, clinical experience tells us, can change substantially both in the short term following a secure family placement and, indeed, subsequently over several years into early adolescence.

The effects of severe institutional deprivation have been extensively explored in the studies of Romanian orphanage children (Rutter et al., 2007). Rutter's group coined the term "quasi autism" to describe features of the resultant impairment of social interaction and communication and presence of rigid behaviours that they felt had a different quality to that generally seen in children with autism. By the age of eleven years, 25% were assessed as having lost their autistic features. Between four and six years of age, there was a greater improvement in social functioning than generally is seen in autism. At the most recent follow-up at twelve years, 10% showed continuing "quasi autism", but as a group they had more flexibility in communication with a substantial social approach, albeit with an abnormal pattern of social engagement with indiscriminately friendly behaviour similar to that described in "disinhibited" attachment.

The overall message from research and empirical observations of this group is that one should be cautious in diagnosing autism in children who have sustained significant emotional or psychosocial deprivation and it is essential to take a longer term view as they grow and develop, particularly following a long-term fostering or adoptive family placement. This has significant practical implications for those asked to advise prospective foster and adoptive parents, since the picture is more complex and outcome less certain than is generally the case.

Selective mutism

Selective mutism (SM) is a complex, little understood, and poorly described condition that is now felt to be part of a spectrum of social anxiety conditions, reflecting a social anxiety and/or a more specific speech anxiety. In its most severe form, it may present in nursery and school as a socially unresponsive child with severely impaired non-verbal communication skills, emotional unresponsiveness, and poor eye contact in the context of overall lack of communication with peers and all adults (Keen et al., 2008; Standart & Le Couteur, 2003).

The presence or absence of SM is relatively easy to ascertain through clinical history with parents or carers that will elicit description of a child who speaks freely with normal affect in certain situations (char-acteristically, with family members at home). However, the majority of children with SM are known to have associated developmental deficits, especially in language, and it is recognised by clinicians who work with these children that there is an over-representation of children with autism spectrum conditions. However, the presence of social communication deficits might come to light only after prolonged observation and following specific therapy to address the SM.

Attention deficit hyperactivity disorder

There has been increasing realisation of high levels of autism in the attention deficit hyperactivity disorder (ADHD) clinic population, and a growing research now demonstrates this overlap, which is recognised in classification systems such as the *Diagnostic and Statistical Manual of Mental Disorders, Fifth Edition* (*DSM-5*, APA, 2013).

From a population-based twin study of ADHD using the social res-ponsiveness scale (a sixty-five-item parent–teacher questionnaire devel-oped by J. N. Constantino and C. P. Gruber), autistic traits were evident in both inattentive and combined hyperactive–impulsive subgroups. Where both severe attentional and hyperactive–impulsive symptoms were present, up to a third of males and three-quarters of females met clinical cut-offs for autistic symptomatology (Reirsen et al., 2007).

Severely hyperactive and socially impulsive symptoms may mask underlying social communication deficits, and it might be only after successful medical treatment that these areas become sufficiently clear to be diagnosed.

In my experience, the vast majority of two- to three-year-olds presenting to their child development service with a query of ADHD are found to have a co-existing autism spectrum disorder, underlining the importance of ensuring that local care pathways provide for a fully multi-disciplinary assessment of such children.

Intellectual disability and developmental syndromes

The presence of intellectual disability, whether or not within the context of a genetic syndrome, is an important factor affecting the presentation and assessment of autism. The recognition of autistic features of young children with intellectual disability might be hindered because of the child's overall immature level of functioning. This can affect confidence in the assessment of communication skills, leading to delay in diagnosis. Similarly, severely delayed language and communication skills could initially appear to be autism related, but evolve with general maturation into a picture of delay rather than disorder.

The estimated rates of autism in intellectual disability vary, but clearly are increased, although to varying degrees dependent on the condition. The prevalence in a population sample of adolescents was reported as 28% (Bryson et al., 2008), but the incidence in Down's syndrome was reported as being 7% (Kent et al., 1999). The presence of autism in the 22q11.2 deletion syndrome (previously also known as velocardiofacial syndrome) might also be part of a complex, and possibly life-threatening, medical picture involving physical anomalies of vital organs, and occurs at rates considerably higher (up to 50%) than that predicted from intellectual disability, making autism considered to be a part of the syndrome (Vorstman et al., 2006).

The increased rate of autism in a wide range of developmental conditions continues to be uncovered—for example, the recognition of autism in just under 9% of those affected by fetal valproate syndrome (Rasalam et al., 2005)—in a picture characterised by an even sex ratio, absence of regression or skill loss, and language delay in the absence of global delay.

Professional and service responses
affecting delays to early recognition

It is not uncommon to come across parents who have been told that their child cannot undergo a diagnostic assessment until the child is older (say, four or five years of age). This is quite unacceptable in the light of the considerable growing body of work showing that diagnosis around the age of two years is generally stable within the autism spectrum. While some of the instability in formal diagnosis is due to children moving between discrete categories, over time these subgroups are becoming less meaningful to clinicians and researchers (Chawarska et al., 2007; Lord et al., 2006) and, as reflected in the *DSM-5* classification, will tend to be replaced in the future by the term "autism spectrum disorder".

Sometimes, clinical professionals have explained autistic behaviours as being "due to the child's language being delayed" and, therefore, a cause of the child's abnormal social relationships. However, it has been shown that the associated "features" of autism in preschool children generally persist even when language recovers (Michelotti et al., 2002), underlining the intrinsic interrelatedness of all aspects of language and social development.

Another factor in delaying diagnosis is a possible reluctance of clinicians to consider a dual diagnosis in children with a known condition, such as a genetic syndrome with intellectual disability, for fear of creating additional distress for parents already dealing with the implications of one serious disorder. While this reluctance is understandable, the implications of not acknowledging an underlying social communication impairment might not be ultimately helpful for either the family or the child, as access to the most appropriate advice and intervention could be further delayed.

I have experienced the distress of parents who have themselves noticed growing differences between their autistic child with Down's syndrome and their peers encountered in a parent self-help group, but had not had their concerns addressed.

Failure to recognise the social deficits of autism can sometimes be a consequence of a blinkered mind-set in some professionals who prefer to "avoid labelling", or who can be unduly focused on various psychosocial explanations of atypical child behaviour, such as attachment issues in working mothers or families that have live-in child care, families providing little in the way of play experience, or those providing an overwhelming and confusing whirl of activity. Unfortunately, professionals can blame parents for being "desperate for a label". Although it is clearly important to be sensitive to possible factitious reporting, in fact this is extremely uncommon in my experience.

To facilitate early recognition, we should address two key issues. First, there must be a clear understanding of the patterns of normal infant development and identification of disordered pathways. Second, services must be able to respond with flexibility of approach, recognising that children with a high risk of autism will present to professionals in many different services.

It is important, however, to put diagnosis into perspective. There can be a tendency for developmental teams to become very focused on diagnosis in its own right. Diagnosis itself is not necessarily the end point, but a signpost to the next stage. It is more important to identify children who have high risk of autistic development in order to focus both the assessment and intervention. By seeing diagnosis as being part of a broader process, unnecessary and unhelpful interventions (such as medical investigations) can be avoided and access to targeted support facilitated. Although research evidence is still inconclusive, we hope that appropriate intervention at an early stage can alter the trajectory of development, which is the point of the whole process.

The competent infant: developmental milestones of social cognition

The following section brings together our knowledge of how social understanding and communication develop in the early years.

Social understanding

Babies are born with an innate preference for looking at the social stimuli. Although there are gender differences in the strength of interest in object *vs.* person perception, from birth babies show interest in social stimuli and a general preference for looking at faces and representation of faces. In fact, babies are able to discriminate happy and sad faces from around one day old. At three months, they are able to detect biological motion, and at five months, by matching facial and vocal expressions of emotion, are able to discriminate emotion in the voice and face (Table 10.1). A key stage in this period of development is the shift in attention, at three to four months of age, from objects to human beings.

Table 10.1.   Age-related interest in social stimuli.

Interest in social stimuli	0 months
Discrimination between happy and sad faces	1 day
Detection of biological movement	3 months
Discrimination of emotion in voice and face	5 months

Joint attention

The second stage in the development of social cognition is that of joint attention.

From three months of age, the infant actively monitors the gaze of others, translating the perception of biological motion to intention: for example, the purpose of an adult's arms reaching out to the child. A key stage in social development at this age is the initiation of social contact (in distinction to the response to social contact) for the purposes of social interaction. This appears at around six months of age.

Social referencing—searching for emotional expression and regulating behaviour accordingly—develops towards the latter part of the first year of life with the development of joint attention. This is seen in following the gaze of another person, use of gaze to elicit joint attention, and the development of pointing with the index finger for a variety of purposes, including, most importantly, integration with eye contact to indicate and share interest with another (Table 10.2).

The expression of emotion in the human face is delivered particularly in the eyes and the upper part of the face. The importance of this has been carefully demonstrated by Klin and colleagues (2002) in their beautifully illustrated studies of adults with and without autism viewing the emotionally intense film *Who's Afraid of Virginia Woolf*, starring Elizabeth Taylor and Richard Burton. In the illustrations below, one can see the trajectory of eyes over just a few seconds of film recording.

Table 10.2.   Age-related stages of joint attention.

Gaze monitoring	3 months
Detection of human action, e.g., reaching	6 months
Initiation of social contact for social interaction	6 months
Social referencing	9–12 months
Joint attention	9–12 months
True joint attention (going out of field of vision)	18 months

In Figure 10.1, the typical comparison viewer rapidly alternates between the eyes of the husband and wife, whereas the eyes of the viewer with autism slowly move between the lower faces and become distracted towards Elizabeth Taylor's necklace.

In Figure 10.2, which shows a flirtatious engagement being conducted in view of the husband, the typical comparison viewer rapidly tracks over a few seconds between the faces of the three involved, whereas the viewer with autism clearly misses the key content of this triadic situation.

It is easy to see the implications of this failure to observe, monitor, and interpret emotional information over the crucial early years of development. The child with autism persistently misses out on potentially useful sources of social information because of slow processing and failure to instinctively recognise where the social "action" is happening.

Mentalizing

This brings us to the third area of development of the competent infant, that of "mentalizing", or theory of mind (ToM), which is the

Figure 10.1.   Eye tracking of a dyadic interaction—viewers with and without autism.

Figure 10.2.   Eye tracking of a triadic interaction—viewers with and without autism.

intuitive ability to understand that other people have feelings and thoughts that are different from one's own. In humans, socialising and mentalizing seem automatic and effortless. Autism illustrates a fault in the mentalizing process.

In infants, social cognition associated with the development of mentalizing begins at around eighteen months of age and is observed in social imitation and development of pretence and the social skills associated with pretence. Increasing maturity brings new vocabulary and use of cognitive terms associated with mental states. Understanding how another person could know something through the process of inference should become apparent at the age of six years (Table 10.3).

The process of mentalizing is illustrated in the now well-established "Sally–Anne ToM test" (Figure 10.3) (Baron-Cohen et al., 1985). In this simple test, two dolls, Sally and Anne, sit with a basket and a box respectively. Sally puts her marble in her basket and then "leaves" the room. Anne, unbeknown to Sally, removes the marble and puts it in her box and returns to her original position. Sally returns to the

Table 10.3. Age-related effects of the development of mentalizing.

PLAY	
Social imitation	18 months
Begin to pretend	18 months
Deception	18+ months
Varied pretence	2 years
LANGUAGE	
Use of words referring to internal states: want, see, look	2 years
Use of "pretend" and understanding others are pretending	2½ years
Use of cognitive terms: know, think, remember	3 years
Understanding concepts of "seeing", "knowing"	4–6 years
Understanding how another could know through inference	6 years

room and the question put is "Where will Sally look for her marble?" The answer, of course, is where she thinks it is.

Typically, developing children begin to understand this first order false belief task from the age of two or so, and the majority will have established this ability by the age of around five. Some cognitively able children with autism might eventually achieve this level of competence, but not until around ten years and are less likely to ever achieve second order and more advanced ToM tasks.

Early signs of atypical developmental pathways

Despite an increasing interest in the early signs of autistic development and growing understanding of early language and social behaviours, our knowledge in this area is far from complete. The trajectories towards autism are unclear, with different scenarios that could indicate different subgroups: for example, where abnormalities are evident soon after birth, or in the first year of life where there are associated developmental delays, or where there are deficits appearing only after a period of normal development followed by a period of developmental stagnation or following regression.

Recent studies have underlined the importance of considering motor dysfunction as an integral part of the presentation of autism. Both gross and fine motor skills have been shown to be substantially

Figure 10.3. The Sally–Anne ToM test.

impaired among children with autism and highly correlated with autistic severity and IQ. Total motor composite scores of at least one standard deviation below the general population mean were seen in 83% of the group with autism (Hilton et al., 2011).

Growth and neuroimaging studies suggest that prior to the observed behavioural signs of autism, the clinical onset of autism might be preceded by two phases of brain growth abnormality: a reduced head size at birth and a sudden and excessive increase in head size between one to two months and six to fourteen months (Courchesne et al., 2003).

That atypical brain function precedes the behavioural signs and symptoms of autism is further supported by a study of infants exposed to eye gaze. In a prospective study of infants between six to ten months of age at increased risk of autism (Elsabbagh et al., 2012), those who were later diagnosed with autism showed a lack of differentiation in neurophysiological response between a face whose eyes were directed to them and a face with eyes looking away. However, no difference was perceptible in the time at-risk and non-at-risk infants spent fixating on the eyes relative to other regions of the face. The authors link this early perturbation with interference with emergence of typical developmental milestones and a cascading effect "derailing" the development of social cognition.

Early signs in language and social communication

Recent studies are helpful in shedding light on early observable signs of autism. Rhea and colleagues (2011) examined vocal behaviour, observing the pre-speech of younger siblings of children with autism who were rated at six, nine, and twelve months of age. Observations were directed towards the frequency of vocalisation, speech-like and non-speech-like vocalisations, early, middle, and late consonant acquisition, and the production of consonant–vowel–consonant syllables. This study concluded that early vocal behaviour seen in the first year of life is a sensitive indicator of increased risk of autistic symptoms in infants with a family history of autism. The study found no difference in the frequency of vocalisations. The high-risk sibling group showed fewer speech-like vocalisations and more non-speech vocalisations than the control group. Most associated with a future diagnosis of autism was the poor emergence of new speech behaviours, with fewer late consonants and consonant–vowel syllables at nine months and the predominance at twelve months of early consonants.

When followed up at twenty-four months, just over 50% of this study group were diagnosed with an autism spectrum disorder or the broader autism phenotype, a proportion higher than has been described in the past.

The second study of younger siblings of children with autism (Ozonoff et al., 2010) observed early social behaviours, particularly gaze directed to faces, responsive social smiles, and socially directed vocalisation. Figure 10.4 illustrates the trajectories of the control group compared to the group going on to receive a diagnosis of autism, and clearly shows that the behavioural signs of autism are not usually present at birth. In fact, key social behaviours are well established or even better than average at six months of age.

Loss of skills occurred in the majority of children who showed a slow decline in key social communicative behaviours most marked between six and eighteen months. The authors particularly note that

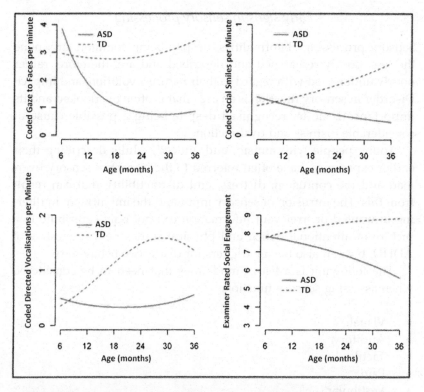

Figure 10.4. Estimated trajectories for coded social communication behaviours and examiner ratings of social engagement (ASD = autism spectrum disorders; TD= typically developing children).

the decline in social communicative behaviours is not related to, or explained by, declining cognition or language.

Importantly, most parents did not, in fact, report this regression, which, as in other infant regressive neurological disabilities, occurs in the context of child growth and development and, therefore, might be disguised because of the opposing trajectories. Parental report methods, as used in formal diagnostic schedules (for example, the ADI-R), do not capture this phenomenon well.

In a study looking specifically at the phenomenon of language loss, 15% of those with autism/autism spectrum experienced this. Loss of language appears to be highly specific to autism and could be hidden in children whose language is delayed (Pickles et al., 2009).

Early signs in sensory processing

Sensory processing abnormalities, despite being common, are, none the less, poorly researched and described and are, therefore, rather poorly understood with regard to their nature, evolution, and impact. Disorder in sensory function is an area that is often overlooked and its importance is under-recognised despite being a possible cause of considerable distress and dysfunction.

Young people with autism, and, indeed, adults describing their earlier experience, have often referred to the impact of sensory overload and the confusion, distress, and distractibility that can result from this. The intrusion of sensory input and the impairment in filtering unwanted or irrelevant information can not only contribute to a picture of attentional deficit and physical restlessness suggestive of ADHD, but can also be key triggers for disruptive behaviours.

The following is a list of modalities that need to be considered when assessing sensory function.

- Visual.
- Auditory.
- Tactile.
- Pain.
- Vestibular.
- Regulation of internal state.
- Oral.

- Gustatory.
- Olfactory.

Disordered sensory integration can lead to hypo-responsiveness or hypersensitivity. It is not unusual for parents to report an unusual ability of their autistic child to turn tiny objects into the focus of obsessive interest. Unusually high visual acuity has been demonstrated in a study using standard optometric tests (Ashwin et al., 2009), which showed an average visual acuity of 20:7 in the autism study group (in other words, being able to see at 6.1m/20ft what the average person can see at 2.1m/7ft) in contrast to the norm described as 20:20 vision. In addition to the high visual acuity is the unusual use of vision, such as a tendency to observe objects at extremely close range, or unusual styles of visual scrutiny—for example, observing out of the corner of the eye or with eyes partially closed.

Studies of auditory function in autism (such as Rosenhall et al., 1999) have demonstrated both the increased risk of hearing impairment and hyperacusis in 18% of children. Auditory hypersensitivity problems may impinge on many areas of life, affecting functioning in the classroom, social gatherings (such as the school dining room, parties, funfairs), exposure to traffic when out and about, or negotiating public transport.

Other areas of sensory functioning have not been studied as systematically. Tactile defensiveness or aversion to contact with certain materials—including cutlery, sand, grass, and sticky or messy material such as food or play items—is commonly observed. A child's extreme reactions due to irritability with, and intolerance of, clothing textures, labels and seams, can be described by parents as a "nightmare". I recall a grandmother who had sought diagnostic consultation for her grandson. Her Internet search for a source of less irritating seamless socks for him led her to being immediately confronted with the term Asperger syndrome. Tactile fascinations may be a notable feature, such as the desire to stroke silky or furry materials—unfortunately, sometimes attached to a stranger in the supermarket.

Vestibular processing problems might be seen in the difficulty in tolerating motion, such as being on a swing or, more extremely, in coping with movement on a bus, as well as a constantly seeking motion through rocking and spinning activities.

Extremes in response can be seen in pain perception with both overreaction to minor discomfort on the one hand and a deep indifference to pain on the other. An example of the latter observed on one occasion was seen in a case of a fifteen-month-old brought to the attention of the safeguarding team. The child's unresponsiveness to a fractured tibia sustained two days previously led to the child presenting to the A&E department with professional concern at the unexplained delayed parental response. The child's autism had not been recognised at that time.

A cluster of sensory modalities appear to operate in association in the body's biological alerting and regulating mechanisms, affecting response to appetite and thirst, illness and temperature, through the oral, gustatory, and olfactory functions. Problems in these areas are seen in abnormal appetite regulation, either with little evidence of signs of hunger and thirst and little pleasure in food, or an inability to regulate the intake of liquids and food: so much so, that parents need to put careful boundaries on intake. Parents might report insensitivity to extremes of ambient temperature or food.

Parents sometimes report that the child, as an infant, never went through the usual stage of oral exploration of the environment or the persistence of infantile mouthing activity into later life, chewing or licking objects (such as metal), or putting inedible objects of various sorts (stones, paper, faeces) into the mouth.

Difficulties in the gustatory modality are seen in the heightened response to food tastes and textures, leading to excessive aversions as well as unusual cravings.

In the olfactory modality, a personal observation has been the common indifference of young autistic children to environmental smells, whether food, perfume, or unpleasantness, which seems to occur far more frequently than hypersensitivity to smell, making ordinary family activities, such as mealtimes, difficult. Fascination with smell may be seen in a propensity to smell foods before eating, and also in exploring objects in the environment, including toys, self, and others.

The autism-related feeding disorders are a fascinating and very poorly understood phenomenon. Feeding disorders have been described in a number of ways, but an accepted classification is

- selective eating (acceptance of a very few food types);

- inappropriate texture for age (failure to wean on to adult foods, for example, continuing to eat only puréed food);
- restrictive eating (unusually small appetite for age).

In addition to these recognised problems can be added "failure to self-feed", a problem related to tactile aversion (to handling food and/ or cutlery) and/or extreme behavioural passivity. I have described a case series where severe feeding disorders manifested in the very early years of life, and prior to the recognition of autism in the individuals, were associated with significant failure to thrive, sometimes involving hospitalisation, nasogastric tube, and gastrostomy feeding (Keen, 2007).

Interestingly, there is also growing literature demonstrating a link with autism in some cases of adult anorexia nervosa (e.g., Gillberg et al., 2007), an area that is very complex.

It is the author's clinical impression that sensory processing abnormalities in these related modalities, combined with social interaction abnormalities affecting the dyadic relationship between mother and child, can interact with early manifestations of behavioural rigidity or obsessiveness in creating abnormal feeding patterns. We know that starvation itself can produce abnormal cognitive–behavioural rigidity and so there might be highly interrelated factors that could direct the trajectory of development.

Promoting early recognition

Knowing what we do about early developmental signs, the question often raised is whether or not to screen for autism. The American Academy of Paediatrics recommends two screens at around eighteen months and twenty-four months of age, but the UK does not.

The UK National Screening Committee is currently considering the evidence for ASD screening in the under-fives. The draft report, at the time of writing in consultation, recommends caution at this stage as the evidence suggests that a third of babies identified with possible "autism" on screening tests conducted before the age of two would lose the diagnosis by the age of four. It would appear that research evidence of the natural history of abnormal signs is not yet robust. Caution is also recommended because the tools used are unacceptable epidemiologically on account of their relatively poor sensitivity and positive predictive value. A further factor is that the existing screening process appears to be unacceptable to parents, with the reported drop-out of a third to a half after an initial failed screening test.

The decision of whether or not to screen for any condition also depends on the implication of a positive finding and, in particular, whether it is possible to make a positive intervention that would change outcome. Unfortunately, the intervention studies of autism thus far are not robust enough (on account of study size, length of follow-up, and the outcome measures used) to provide a level of evidence for epidemiological purposes. At the time of writing, the first randomised controlled trial of a truly "prodromal" early intervention for infants (eight to fourteen months) at high risk of autism is being undertaken through the British Autism Study of Infant Siblings (iBASIS; www.medicine.manchester.ac.uk/IBASIS), which will, it is hoped, begin to build a body of evidence.

At present, then, we have established a great deal of knowledge regarding normal patterns of infant development and the beginnings of defining different pathways leading to a diagnosis of autism. However, there are still many gaps in our knowledge.

The evidence at present would suggest that there are subgroups of infants who follow different pathways. Although there is a subgroup for whom the early indicators are present within the first year of life, this would not seem to be the most common. It would appear that the most common presentation is the progressive deviation from normal patterns of development in the second year of life.

The research evidence tells us there are no clear rules that lead to early recognition of autism, but three key messages stand out.

- First, it is essential that professionals listen carefully to parents' instinctive feelings about their child's social functioning, and particularly with regard to a reduction in use of language and communication.
- Second, consistent evidence for the potential value of screening child populations has come from studies of the Checklist for Autism in Toddlers (CHAT; Baron-Cohen et al., 2000), which demonstrate that at eighteen months children who fail to show gaze monitoring, pointing to share interest, and pretend play are highly likely to go on to be diagnosed with autism.

- Third, a thorough understanding of the development of social cognition will underpin the use of skilled clinical judgement. The clinical judgement of an experienced assessor is still considered the most important and reliable component of the process of assessment (Lord et al., 2006).

References

American Psychiatric Association (2013). *Diagnostic and Statistical Manual of Mental Disorders, Fifth Edition (DSM-5)*. Arlington, VA: American Psychiatric Association.

Ashwin, E., Ashwin, C., Rhydderch, D., Howells, J., & Baron-Cohen, S. (2009). Eagle-eyed visual acuity: an experimental investigation of enhanced perception in autism. *Biological Psychiatry, 65*: 17–21.

Baron-Cohen, S., Leslie, A., & Frith, U. (1985). Does the autistic child have a "theory of mind"? *Cognition, 21*: 37–46.

Baron-Cohen, S., Wheelwright, S., Cox, A., Baird, G., Charman, T., Swettenham, J., Drew, A., & Doehring, P. (2000). The early identification of autism: the Checklist for Autism in Toddlers (CHAT). *Journal of the Royal Society of Medicine, 93*: 521–525.

Bryson, S., Bradley, E., Thompson, A., & Wainwright, A. (2008). Prevalence of autism among adolescents with intellectual disabilities. *Canadian Journal of Psychiatry, 53*: 449–459.

Chawarska, K., Klin, A., Paul, R., & Volkmar, F. (2007). Autism spectrum, disorder in the second year: stability and change in syndrome expression. *Journal of Child Psychology & Psychiatry & Allied Disciplines, 48*: 128–138.

Courchesne, E., Carper, R., & Akshoomoff, N. (2003). Evidence of brain overgrowth in the first year of life in autism. *Journal of the American Medical Association, 290*(3): 337–344.

Ek, U., Fernell, E., Jacobson, L., & Gillberg, C. (1998). Relation between blindness due to retinopathy at prematurity and autism spectrum disorders: a population-based study. *Developmental Medicine and Child Neurology, 40*: 297–301.

Elsabbagh, M., Mercure, E., Hudry, K., Chandler, S., Pasco, G., Charman, T., Pickles, A., Baron-Cohen, S., Bolton, P., Johnson, M. H., & the BASIS Team (2012). Infant neural sensitivity to dynamic eye gaze is associated with later emerging autism. *Current Biology, 22*(4): 338–342.

Fraiberg, S. (1977). *Insights from the Blind: Comparative Studies of Blind and Sighted Infants*. New York: Basic Books.

Gillberg. C., Råstam, M., Wentz, E., & Gillberg, C. (2007). Cognitive and executive functions in anorexia nervosa ten years after onset of eating disorder. *Journal of Clinical and Experimental Neuropsychology, 29*: 170–178.

Hilton, C., Zhang, Y., White, M., Klohr, C., & Constantino, J. (2012). Motor impairment in sibling pairs concordant and discordant for autism spectrum disorders. *Autism, 16*: 430–441.

Hitoglou, M., Ververi, A., Antoniadis, A., & Zafeirou, D. (2010). Childhood autism and auditory system abnormalities. *Pediatric Neurology, 42*: 309–314.

Keen, D. V. (2007). Childhood autism, feeding problems and failure to thrive in early infancy: seven case examples. *European Child & Adolescent Psychiatry, 17*: 209–216.

Keen, D. V., Fonseca, S., & Wintgens, A. (2008). Selective mutism: a consensus based care pathway of good practice. *Archives of Disease of Childhood, 93*: 838–844.

Kent, L., Evans, J., Paul, M., & Sharp, M. (1999). Comorbidity of autistic spectrum disorders in children with Down syndrome. *Developmental Medicine & Child Neurology, 41*: 153–158.

Klin, A., Jones, W., Schultz, R., Volkmar, F., & Cohen, D. (2002). Defining and quantifying the social phenotype in autism. *American Journal of Psychiatry, 159*: 895–908.

Lord, C., Risi, S., DiLavore, P., Shulman, C., Thurm, A., & Pickles, A. (2006). Autism from 2 to 9 years of age. *Archives of General Psychiatry, 63*: 694–701.

Michelotti, J., Charman, T., Slonims, V., & Baird, G. (2002). Follow-up of children with language delay and features of autism from pre-school years to middle childhood. *Developmental Medicine and Child Neurology, 44*: 812–819.

Ozonoff, S., Iosif, A., Baguio, F., Cook, I., Hill, M., Hutman, T., Rogers, S. J., Rozga, A., Sangha, S., Sigman, M., Steinfeld, M. B., & Young, G. S. (2010). A prospective study of the emergence of early behavioral signs of autism. *Journal of the American Academy of Child and Adolescent Psychiatry, 49*: 256–266.

Ozonoff, S., Young, G. S., Carter, A., Messinger, D., Yirmiya, N., Zwaigenbaum, L., Bryson, S., Carver, L. J., Constantino, J. N., Dobkins, K., Hutman, T., Iverson, J. M., Landa, R., Rogers, S. J., Sigman, M., & Stone, W. L. (2011). Recurrence risk for autism spectrum disorders: a baby siblings research consortium study. *Pediatrics, 128*: e488–495.

Pickles, A., Simonoff, E., Conti-Ramsden, G., Falcaro, M., Simkin, Z., Charman, T., Chandler, S., Loucas, T., & Baird, G. (2009). Loss of language in early development of autism and specific language impairment. *Journal of Child Psychology and Psychiatry, 50*: 834–852.

Pring, L. (2005). *Autism and Blindness. Research and Reflections.* London: Whurr.

Rasalam, A., Hailey, H., Williams, J., Moore, S., Turnpenny, P., Lloyd, D., & Dean, J. C. (2005). Characteristics of fetal anticonvulsant syndrome associated autistic disorder. *Developmental Medicine & Child Neurology, 47*: 551–555.

Reirsen, A., Constantino, J., Volk, H., & Todd, R. (2007). Autistic traits in a population-based ADHD twin sample. *Journal of Child Psychology and Psychiatry, 48*: 464–472.

Rhea, P., Fuerst, Y., Ramsay, G., Chawarska, K., & Klin, A. (2011). Out of the mouths of babes: vocal production in infant siblings of children with ASD. *Journal of Child Psychology and Psychiatry, 52*: 588–598.

Rosenhall, U., Nordin, V., Sandström, M., Ahlsén, G., & Gillberg, C. (1999). Autism and hearing loss. *Journal of Autism and Developmental Disorders, 29*: 349–357.

Rutter, M., Kreppner, J., Croft, C., Murin, M., Colvert, E., Beckett, C., Castle, J., & Sonuga-Barke, E. (2007). Early adolescent outcomes of institutionally deprived and non-deprived adoptees. III. Quasi-autism. *Journal of Child Psychology and Psychiatry, 48*: 1200–1207.

Standart, S., & Le Couteur, A. (2003). The quiet child: a literature review of selective mutism. *Child and Adolescent Mental Health, 8*: 154–160.

Vorstman, J., Morcus, M., Duijiff, S., Klaasen, P., Heineman-de Boer, J., Beemer, F., Swaab, H., Kahn, R., & van Engeland, H. (2006). The 22q11.2 deletion in children: high rate of autistic disorders and early onset of psychotic symptoms. *Journal of the American Academy of Child and Adolescent Psychiatry, 45*: 1104–1113.

CHAPTER ELEVEN

The power of the relationship to awaken positive emotional potential

Stella Acquarone

Introduction

Relationships are important in normal development. When there are difficulties in forming relationships with parents and infants, how can we help to create one that pulls development in the right social way? The power of the relationship creates a potential space where reflection and empathy will lead to the possibility of integration of experiences in the mother–infant dyad.

"There is no such thing as a baby ... If you set out to describe a baby, you will find you are describing a baby and someone. A baby cannot exist alone, it is essentially part of a relationship" (Winnicott, 1952, 1964).

What if there is a lack of relationship?

What happens when it does not seem as if there *is* a relationship, when the mother feels numb, or feels that her baby is "numbed"? How do we therapists and clinicians go about making the relationship an enjoyable one, and helping normal development to take place?

Meet Martha, four months old (Photo 11.1), one of triplets—all girls, all beautiful—whose mother brought her for consultation because she felt she could not get through to her. Unlike her other two baby girls, who were communicative (cooing, arching their stomachs forward to be picked up, and moving their arms and legs joyfully whenever they heard their mother speak), Martha seemed aloof, not there. She did not seem interested in what was going on around her, not in her mother, her sisters, music, songs—and not a single smile had been seen from her. With increasing worry, Martha's mother had brought her in to ask if I could help. She wanted to be connected to Martha, to have the same happy relationship she enjoyed with her other two daughters (Photo 11.2).

We will talk further about Martha, keeping in our minds this baby girl and her mother, but if we are to help the relationship develop and move the baby from at-risk to mainstream, we need to pause for a moment and examine some of the underlying premises (or hypotheses) about relationships in general.

All professional clinicians know that relationships between parents and infants are important (this is certainly one of the central messages of the colleagues who have written chapters in this book). We know that these relationships do not develop at the same speed and neither

Photo 11.1. Martha, aged four months.

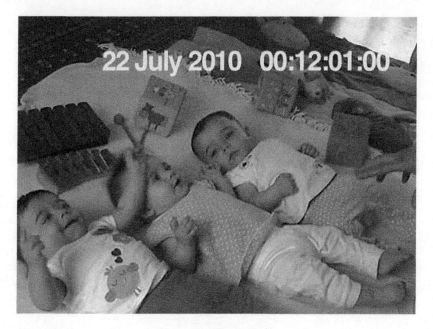

Photo 11.2. The triplets.

do they develop in the same way—parenting is different, each parent's personality is different, the baby, too, has a unique personality and presents special challenges that must also be taken into account.

So, when we speak about helping parents and their infant to understand each other and be able to love, we are speaking specifically about the *early* intervention: an intervention that can happen from pregnancy to three years old, is psychoanalytically informed, and is focused on bringing understanding to the unhappiness between the mother/father and a baby. This specific kind of early intervention we called parent infant psychotherapy (Acquarone, 2004).

Because the causes of unhappiness can be so varied, there are different ways of approaching and working out the problems or difficulties. However, the overall aim is to find the lost links necessary to establish positive, healthy, happy, enjoyable, and fun parent–infant interactions (Brazelton et al., 1974; Murray, 2014; Murray & Andrews, 2000; Murray & Trevarthen, 1985; Trevarthen, 1998a,b, 2001, 2004, 2010; Trevarthen & Delafield-Butt, 2013; Trevarthen & Hubley, 1978).

Parent infant psychotherapy is the process of finding and re-establishing these lost links, and avoiding or correcting difficult development and relationships that can become pathological and entrenched, as in, for example, the autistic evolution, described in the case treatments below. It should come as no surprise that because the process includes the unconscious and an understanding of life's known and unknown emotions, the core of parent infant psychotherapy is psychoanalytic. An early intervention is needed when negative interactions upset emotional balance and limits development.

So, how do we create a relationship that makes sense, that pulls the infant and parents closer towards each other and leads to better outcomes?

Before we can establish a focus of the early intervention, we first have to find out where the main difficulties lie.

If the difficulties centre on the mother, we must determine the degree of severity and then consider the best approach to take. This might be:

- *Insightful*, where what is required is one of the following interventions: a crisis intervention (one or two sessions), a short intervention (six to twelve sessions), or an intensive intervention (two to four weeks for thirty hours per week followed by once a week for a year or more, as needed).
- *Supportive* to the borderline mother (with emphasis on the emotional and individuality of the infant).
- *Part of the existing network*, as in the case of psychotic mothers. This network could be the system of care already in place for the mother and her baby. For example, if the mother is an inpatient or outpatient, we work with the hospital staff, or if there is an "arrangement" for the care of the baby, we work with the child minder, or perhaps it is the extended family that need our support to "hold" the mother and baby.

If the difficulties centre on the baby, we have to keep in mind the following: the emotional state of the child, and the way the baby has (so far) internalised the relationship with the parents (inner object relations). The emotional states and mental representations can present in a variety of ways:

- *Developmental crisis,* where parents feel and see a marked change of behaviour in their child when there has previously been normal development (for example, extreme anxiety to strangers at around eight months, crying excessively when teething, etc.).
- *Reactive disorder,* when the infant's behaviour changes at around two months after a big change in the family's ordinary life (for example, moving house, nanny leaving, mother starting work, etc.).
- *Avoidant and attachment disorder,* when infants show overt signs of not wanting to be with the mother or, conversely, wanting to be constantly held in her arms and cannot stand being on their own.
- *Slow processing of perceptions,* when infants show signs of being confused and upset about the content of their perceptions (for example, visual, auditory, tactile, olfactory, etc.).
- *Psychosomatic disturbance,* when physical symptoms—which can vary in appearance—manifest in specific situations (for example, when the mother is with the siblings, the baby might develop eczema one day but breathing difficulties another day).

After determining whether the relationship difficulties are centred on the mother or on the baby, our focus is then to try to establish an enjoyable relationship while the baby's brain is still "wiring up", in the first three years of life. Figure 11.1 shows the necessity of intervening early to facilitate the maximum potential of the brain.

The brain: connections and relationships

The brain is formed and adapts to rivers of knowledge coming from many ages and sources:

- the information that comes from the evolutionary past is called *genetics*;
- the information that comes from hundreds of years ago is called *culture*;
- the information that comes from decades ago and in the womb is called *family*.

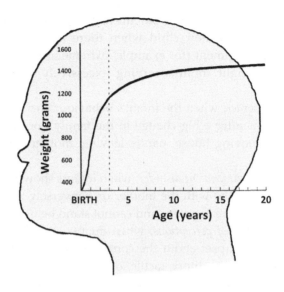

Figure 11.1.   Brain development in the first three years of life.

Our thoughts and skills are moulded by all the tributaries of these rivers that contribute to the functioning of the brain with its 100 billion nerve cells, each having one axon and some with as many as 100 thousand dendrites over which information passes. Nerve cells migrate and settle in specific parts of the brain as activity becomes more organised and the foetus (and then the baby) responds to input from the environment. To satisfy needs and make demands, many of the connections are enlisted for specific jobs, such as smiling, babbling, seeing, remembering, and playing. In the crucial first years, the connections that are not used are pruned (nerve cells will die in the absence of proper stimulation), so the more relationships and fun encounters in the first three years of life the better, helping to avoid unnecessary pruning while producing more connections that are useful for the growth of brain connectivity.

The point I want to make is that in the first years, babies develop neural connections through the ability to form relationships. That is why it is crucial to intervene at the first signs that the normal development is breaking down and evolving pathologically. As Figure 11.2 illustrates, the parent–infant relationship is crucial in facilitating this development. In fact, the central premise of our clinical work is to use

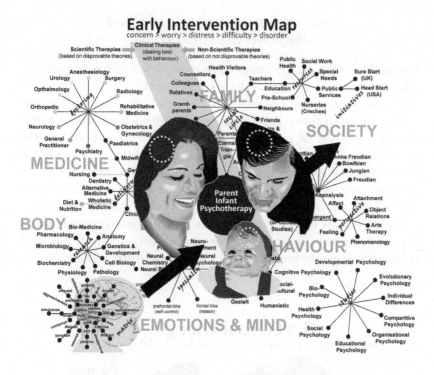

Figure 11.2.   How the infant–parent relationship develops..

and work through the relationship to redirect and if necessary re-start development.

As I envision it, the use of the parent–infant relationship goes like this: babies are born emotionally complete. In the first years, they develop "inner" connections to be able to manage their "outer" relationships. In other words, babies develop from their emotional matrix (housed deep in the brain) through family relationships (the "eternal triangle") into the larger matrix of society. Through relationships, as infants progress into adulthood, what they do not have on the inside, they pull from the outside, seeking lines of physical or psychological help until they are emotionally balanced.

All of these roles have emerged in response to a parent's (and society's) escalating sense that "something is wrong": an early concern that becomes a worry, which, if not attended to, is transformed into distress, which leads to a difficulty and, in time, becomes a disorder.

How humans relate: the quality and
the power of the relationship

The quality of the parent–infant relationship results from "provision", what the parents—as well as the infants—provide. As their provision increases, so does their capacity for "reverie", the "potential space" created between them, the way they relate to each other and within their own individual provision (Figure 11.3). The quality of the relationship can also be assessed by examining the "reflective function" in the mother and gauging the infant's "emotional development". Is the child developing an ability to integrate experiences, or is the child on a path I call an "autistic evolution", which I shall describe below.

Relationships can be thought of as human constructs that satisfy the needs of both infants and parents, accompanied by pleasure, enjoyment, fun, and gratitude—a powerful construct indeed.

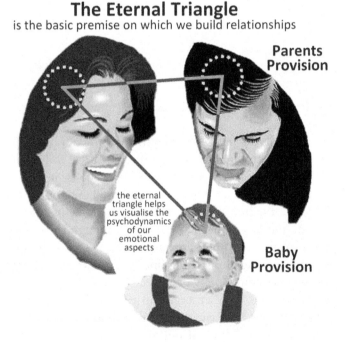

The Eternal Triangle
is the basic premise on which we build relationships

**Parents
Provision**

the eternal
triangle helps
us visualise the
psychodynamics
of our
emotional
aspects

**Baby
Provision**

Figure 11.3.   The eternal triangle.

Parent provision

As described above, parents provide reverie, potential space, and reflective function. The main provision parents make and have is their (internal) "emotional preparation" in the development of "reverie"— that state of preoccupation that both parents immerse themselves in when preparing for the birth of their child.

After birth, some mothers prolong the relationship in a state of illusion about still being together, and will create later on in the relationship the "potential space" for the baby to separate and still feel in a relationship with her. This space is an area of psychological experience located between fantasy and reality and between the parents' inner and external world. It is also the hypothetical locale for the emergence of the transitional phenomena, allowing the internalisation of the holding and the containing functions performed by the mother during pregnancy (Winnicott, 1958, 1960, 1975).

While the potential space operates interpersonally, the "reflective function" operates intra-psychically. Coming from another body of thought, the reflective function describes the capacity to represent mental states. As a provision of the parents, it is used to optimally adapt the orientation of the self in relation to others. In other words, parents use their reflective function to best position themselves to others.

Infant provision

Infants come with provision, too. Infant researchers such as Trevarthen, Brazelton (1973, 1974), and Stern (1985. 2006) have shown us what many mothers know intuitively:

- that infants are born *ready to relate*, with a passionate world of strong emotions;
- that they are *social from birth*, as seen in their eye contact and their intentional and prospective movements of arms, hands, fingers, legs, and body;
- that their senses have *as much multi-modal capacity as adults*: looking, touching, hearing, smelling, etc. all demonstrate individual differences and individual processing timings and preferences;

- that infants *can adapt to any culture* they are born into: to the differing temperaments and ways of handling, and can even teach their parents and family what they like, what they prefer, and what makes them happy.

In addition to these provisions, the infant must also develop tolerance, attunement, and protective mechanisms.

Even from foetal life, the infant must integrate new sensations in order to make sense of the external world (Delafield-Butt & Trevarthen, 2013; Piontelli, 1992; Rascovsky, 1971). But these sensations have to be tolerable for the infant to be able to incorporate them in their store of "good memories" that are essential to moving forward securely.

The newborn has plenty of needs. These needs are coupled with other requirements, and timing and delivery become mixed up—little wonder that parents become confused when trying to read into their baby's demands and prioritise an appropriate response. Babies will often demonstrate blind frustration before they know they can trust their carer(s). The emotions appear raw and might be seen as tremendous or dramatic, but as they are understood and held calmly by the mother they become tolerable and tamed into a trusting relationship.

As the relationship develops, the newborn experiences pleasure and, in turn, is able to give pleasure to the parents. This attunement provides a smooth ride between needs and satisfaction in the appropriate manner.

Along the way, newborns can develop a number of protective mechanisms in an effort to cope when life becomes "too much":

- averting their gaze, looking away, or closing their eyes; even going to sleep manifests itself as allowing infants to have time-out when they feel overwhelmed;
- protesting by crying (mainly whining), fighting (making the body rigid or pulling back, extensive movement of the arms, vomiting), or simply dissociating, which might take the form of other somatic expressions, such as holding their breath, coming out in rashes, etc.;
- self-comforting mechanisms, such as clasping their hands firmly together in front of them, sucking their thumb (or fists, or toys, or blankets), or focusing on something outside themselves, such as a toy, a light, or hanging mobile.

Emotional development: internal interference in the relationship

If you have read this far, no doubt you now realise that it is the relationship that carries development. However, because of internal reasons, some babies cannot find the objects to relate to (the mother) and need to be helped to acquire this important ability. Without professional help, development will follow a different path.

Internal factors can derail emotional development. When we talk about emotional development, we can see that the same process could have different outcomes. Bion (1962, 1965), an important figure in psychoanalysis, envisions a child's mental apparatus emerging from a "process of transformations" where primitive sensory elements change into elaborated elements. This "process" allows mothers (and therapists) to attune themselves to the sensory and proto-thoughts of children (and patients), helping them to progress. But what happens if this process becomes complicated by overexposure to overwhelming tensions or sensations that can feel traumatic for the (hypersensitive) baby? Interference enters the relationship. To further complicate matters, we have to keep in mind that what is traumatic for the baby might be unseen or unknown to the mother/family.

As I mentioned above, in some cases, development is shifted from the ability-to-integrate-experience path to the "autistic evolution" channel. I use the word "evolution" in the same way Darwin did when referring to "the need for organisms to survive in their environment" in his work *On the Origin of Species* (1859, p. 503). Assume, for the moment, that the pre-autistic baby (my label for babies with autistic behaviours) is struggling to survive in an environment which other babies have no difficulty with. This environment includes the reciprocity and reverie in basic good mothering, as well as receiving, containing, elaborating, modifying, and returning—in a transformed state—the baby's projections and projective identifications vital to normal emotional development (Bion, 1970; Winnicott, 1945, 1960, 1965). The following are just some of the internal factors that can interfere with the usual path of development.

- *Too much sensory information.* Observing that "autistic children often shun many kinds of physical contact", Ratey theorised that sensory information might come to autistic children too fast for their brain to process and they are simply overwhelmed (Ratey,

2001). They "shut down" or fall back on a primitive reflex to regulate or limit their exposure to a confusing external world. Because they cannot prioritise the deluge of incoming signals, information is just fragmented data and is poorly processed. Healthy babies, for example, shift their gaze from the eyes to the nose to the mouth of the mother within a fraction of a second. However, pre-autistic babies can take up to six seconds just to process the nose. They cannot take in the whole face at once, only parts of it, missing social cues such as a smile or a frown, suggesting that perhaps mental processes have been shifted to the autism evolution channel.

- Early coping habits become entrenched. Studies in neuropsychology show that the early experiences and faulty processing mechanisms of the pre-autistic child become imprinted on the growing connections of babies' cells, and development can spiral into difficulty:
- A need to generate object relations (relationships with the internal parents). As a result, the infant's mental and emotional capacities become compromised.

What we often see, too, is that if their mother (or psychotherapist) tries too hard to bring the infant into a relationship, it can backfire, antagonising them further rather than bringing them closer.

Later in this chapter I present two cases using an approach we have developed to treat babies caught in the autism evolution channel.

Infantile sensuality and sexuality

The sensual system starts early in pregnancy and by birth consists mainly of taste, sight, touch, smell, hearing, and balance. The tactile receptors in the skin sense all sorts of vibrations and pressures, producing pleasure (and oxytocin) and pain: a process that does not require learning or experience. Stimuli like colour, rhythmic sounds, sweetness, balance—even the human face—are pleasurable unless there are negative circumstances that interfere in the mother–baby relationship.

We can see clearly from birth how ordinary babies with good enough mothers are deeply connected to each other. We can see that infantile sexuality based on pleasure is the driving force that relates the external and the internal, the relationships on the outside to the object relations on the inside (internal parents relationships), which lead to the development of neural connections in the brain (neurobiology). What makes this bridge possible? The answer is simply the strong nature of babies.

Tactile sensations and attachment

Infant researchers like Spitz (1962), Escalona (1963), Kleeman (1965, 1976), and others further observed that these sexual/sensual tactile sensations underlie emotional regulation in early neonatal life, which in turn supports the developing system of mother–baby attachment. Working with 1,248 babies between birth and the first year of life in a women's prison and in ordinary homes, Spitz found that the presence of autoerotic behaviours varied depending on the quality of the relationship with the attachment figure. Good attachments led to autoerotic behaviours. Conflictive attachments led to little autoerotic behaviour, self-harming, and self-aggression. In neglectful relationships, development fell behind and there were no autoerotic behaviours. It seems that autoerotism is expressed through experiences with "other people"—in other words, real people trigger, activate, and stimulate predetermined conditions.

When troubling factors impede the reverie and the development of attachment, Selma Fraiberg and colleagues (1975) called them "ghosts in the nursery", the "unconscious obstacles to the parent being sensitive and responsive to the baby". They pioneered the idea of a "helping relationship", in which observation and reflection are used as tools to address obstacles rooted in the parents' inner, subjective world.

However, there could be more than just "ghosts in the nursery" troubling the development of attachment. There could be obstacles in the baby as well, when traumatic experiences (birth, mother unavailable due to illness, prematurity, or mysterious sensibilities, etc.) cut off attachment, causing the baby to dissociate and the relationship to wither (Acquarone & Jimenez Acquarone, 2016, in press).

Tools for understanding primitive— sometimes non-verbal—communications

We need the proper tools—and the skills to use them—to tackle these internal interferences in the relationship. With the right set of tools, we can help the relationship by adjusting the communication to new information, by understanding, and by talking about it.

- *Observation*: a tool and skill set acquired after two years of observation of the same infant, through weekly one-hour observation sessions that are written up and discussed in a small group so that we can understand the details of the communication between mother and infant.
- *Patience*: a tool and skill set acquired from waiting and understanding all that is going on without imposing our thoughts or administering advice. We call this "containment" by internal and external holding.
- *Openness*: a tool and skill set acquired in receiving feelings and emotions that are known and unknown to the different individuals in the parent–infant relationship.
- *Capacity for attunement*: a tool and skill set acquired by working with the feelings transmitted to psychotherapists who understand about their own reactions. This allows invaluable information and insight into the inner life of the parents and the baby to come forth.

Our approach: developing a relationship

Based on everything we know about how the brain develops, how humans relate and the resulting emotional development, we developed an approach—largely based on psychoanalytic theory and neuroscience—that aims to awaken a positive emotional response in the parent–infant relationship, leading to a reflective function in the mother and a meaningful relationship for the baby. Our approach hinges on both "deeper" or not-known (unconscious) emotions as well as the known (conscious) emotions "closer to the surface". Our approach recognises that these unconscious and conscious emotions can be stimulated and transmitted between individuals—baby, parents, and others—and are largely dynamic and changing all the time. It is important to note that because we are researchers and academics, in addition to being clinicians, we are always testing and developing our approach, evaluating it, and looking for ways to improve it.

Unlike other, more behaviourally based, approaches, we recognise and work with the inner world of the infant and the family by looking at how satisfaction and pleasure become associated with, or attached to, pain and uncertainty, and how a sense of self and of others is formed. We look beyond the behaviour to the motivations behind interacting and learning. We want to intervene early so that a natural growth of emotions is re-established, facilitating secure attachment. This is why, in our approach, we recognise the importance of observing the following:

- each child's biological challenges and strengths;
- each child's emotional development (Fraiberg, 1980, 1982);
- the effect on the parents, and the effect of the parents' frustrations and/or happiness towards their child;
- the effect on the professionals and the use of our own emotional reactions to understand the child and parents so that we can help them out of the vicious circles of communication and behaviours.

The effectiveness of our approach depends upon communicating our understanding through words and actions that promote the basic steps of interaction (Acquarone, 2004).

Babies at risk of developing autism

When babies start showing repetitive behaviours—especially self-soothing behaviours coupled with no interest in people (mother, father, siblings, and others)—our thinking is that this is a family affair and must be treated as such. Our experience shows that if the family is prepared to get into a planned programme to understand emotions in everybody, they can become attuned to, and better able to help, the baby who has mysterious sensibilities and finds family relations intolerable.

So, for babies at risk of developing autism, our approach is as follows:

- first, it requires us to think of the treatment as a family affair;
- second, we think of the intervention and training as a laboratory.

To understand those with difficulties forming interpersonal relationships, we need a laboratory for personal relationships. The psychoanalytic thinking and setting provides an ideal laboratory to observe and understand relationships at different levels of consciousness and depth. Also, for training purposes, the laboratory metaphor allows us to think of the disciplines using laboratory methods: observation, reflection, and being able to understand the feelings that are not spoken but are deeply related to emotional processes.

We have combined what we know about parents and infants, the brain (how it works, its connections and plasticity), relationships, a family affair, and a laboratory to create an infant–family programme that is intensive in different degrees. Individual features and emotions are encountered and family dynamics are observed and worked through. The idea is to explore sensitively, to be able to re-start intricate processes that are already becoming engrained, and that respond to inner forces that are not yet known but that need to be brought into the light. We also incorporate other theories as necessary, such as Bowlby's attachment theory (1988) and family systems theory, and we use art and music as tools to express and communicate.

We assess each child and treat him according to his needs and his age. Some cases will benefit from a series of six to eighty treatment sessions that can be weekly or monthly, and others will benefit from an intensive course of six hours per day involving the whole family and other important people in the life of the child. I will present two cases as examples.

An example vignette: Stephanie and her son, Cosmo (two months old)

The mother, Stephanie, asked for a consultation as her son, Cosmo, never looked at her and slept all the time. She was worried and anxious and requested to come without the father as he had to work a lot. We told her she could come, but that we also welcomed fathers.

On her first visit to us, Stephanie began by apologising deeply that her husband was not present before showing me her sleeping baby. She said that the pregnancy had been a planned and happy one and that the problems had only started when she went for a check-up and was told that the baby should be born immediately via C-section as she had eclampsia. From that moment, she lost control of events. Things spiralled out of control as she became seriously ill and ended up in the intensive care unit. Her husband and family were afraid she might die, and left the baby to be changed and fed by the nurses. While Stephanie was telling me this, Cosmo woke up and fussed. Stephanie picked him up and held him precariously. While in her arms, Cosmo was half-asleep, seeming in a state of lethargy.

After finding out more details about her feelings, her worries, and discontents, and the terrors of the events during and after the birth, a hypothesis began to form in my mind: Stephanie had not been able to complete the natural process of pregnancy—it had been interrupted. She had gone from a blissful state into one of panic and almost dying. The sudden delivery and serious postnatal complications had left Stephanie extremely ill and unable to look after her baby. This trauma had left her paralysed, frightened, and with complete amnesia.

Cosmo had been part of this experience—a tiny baby held in unknown arms. But neither mother nor baby could share their pain and fears. The mother's reflective function could not develop because she was still stuck in the aftermath of the delivery, in the fifteen days filled with a disintegrating fear of death. Cosmo refused to attach to his mother or to communicate in any meaningful way, rejecting any social interaction.

What was the connection between the interruption of Stephanie's maternal reverie and her reflective function and how could we connect the internal growth of the reverie with the external capacity of understanding one's own emotions and the one from the baby and/or others?

Consultation and treatment

By working through the mother–baby relationship, our objective was to help Stephanie and Cosmo develop a consciousness of the trauma by encouraging them to share and talk about theirs directly. From the very first consultation, our treatment proceeded along three inter-twining strands: (i) the process of talking to the baby; (ii) creating a space for the relationship to grow; (iii) finding a way for mother and infant to attune to one another, and integrate the father in this process.

To catalyse the "process of talking to the baby", we clinicians seek to produce a kind of specialised maternal reverie in which we act as the primary reverie person. We are constructing a "space" so that we can accompany the mother into the reverie and, proceeding with the nega-tive experience, we can "hold her hand" by expressing all feelings that were there without prejudice, theories, or expectations. We do the same with the infant, feeling the thick wall of terror and negativity genera-ted between them simply as a "lost momentum" that has occurred.

From the first consultation, "attunement" replaced this "lost momentum", as words expressed their reciprocal feelings of being "frozen" in the traumatic delivery and its aftermath. For the first time, both mother and son cried together. Seeing his tears, Stephanie felt guilty for the times she had ever stuffed the dummy in his mouth with hate. However, in the new "space" created in the relationship, she could now speak about her feelings of hate and anger towards the baby who had almost killed her. Cosmo showed despair. He wanted to get rid of his dummy as well as his bottled-up feelings surround-ing the desolation he had experienced, abandoned by his mother and left to drift in a wild sea of traumatic events without anchor, sense, or meaning. Now *attuned* to her baby, Stephanie could hear both sides; the process of talking had "struck a chord" between them, holding them together—with greater ease—in a different world of under-standing. Slowly, facial gestures became interesting to Cosmo, he felt secure when held, and he wanted to reach people outside, to look, smell, touch the other, and feel curiosity.

Seven more sessions followed, some of which the father attended. Stephanie developed her capacity to take, feel, reflect, talk kindly, and enjoy her relationship with Cosmo, who became alert and able to guide her in his desires and needs.

Discussion and summary

What can we say about the internal world of Cosmo and his mother? Cosmo would dissociate when held precariously in his mother's arms, or he would sleep incessantly. He found it difficult or impossible to integrate experiences, given the amount of trauma he and his mother had suffered. Stephanie's hidden hate, anger, and resentment were communicated non-verbally: in her holding, in her stuffing the dummy in her baby's mouth to make him quiet, not letting him cry, and not listening to his cues.

But in the initial consultation and over the following sessions, Cosmo found enough experience of being loved to enable him to trust the external world and to grow internally.

Another (more detailed) example vignette: Thomas (four months old)

In this next case study, because of the tangled family dynamic, the whole family had to be involved in the primary treatment process. Since our treatment model works through the relationship to re-start development, and since here the child–parent relationship did not exist, we had to pursue another line of treatment that included the siblings. Brothers and sisters are part of a mini-society called "Family", and because dealing with family in treatment adds so much complexity to the treatment, measured in hours per day and many hours and days in succession, we add the word "intensive" to the family programme. This vignette is an example of our intensive family treatment programme.

Four-month-old Thomas and his family lived in the north of Scotland. His mother, Jacqueline, came for a consultation and left with a list of insights as to how to proceed. She had a husband who worked long hours and two other children, a four-year-old girl, Chloe, and six-year-old boy, Luke. We maintained telephone contact for six months of trials to help to socialise Thomas and support him to feel less overwhelmed. However, there was no progress, as Thomas became more isolated and more reluctant to relate to anyone. It was recommended that the family underwent our intensive infant–family programme, as we kept hearing about family incidents that were difficult to ascertain over the telephone.

The Re-start intensive infant–family programme

A little digression is appropriate here to talk about our special programme for babies or toddlers at risk of developing serious autistic behaviours.

We call it the "intensive infant–family programme" because we think that autism is a family affair where all members should be collaborative in changing how they interact, and come to understand and respect the behaviours that seemed avoidant and frightening. Our focus is on observing and working on the family constellation so that we can

- explore and assess the impact of having a pre-autistic child in the family. For example, a brother with pre-autistic behaviours that does want to relate to his siblings and so avoids them, a mother whose energy is almost completely focused on her pre-autistic son, and, in some cases, an absent father;
- replace feelings of impatience in the siblings with an understanding of their young brother's deficits and capacities.

This work is all done in parallel, and continues once a week for a year or two as necessary. In addition, as the child gets older and starts nursery, we help with his or her integration in the nursery setting.

The intensive Re:Start programme starts with a thorough paediatric assessment. It lasts for three weeks, each week comprising five six-hour days in the clinic and one day (usually Saturday) in the home.

We work with a multi-disciplinary team that consists of a developmental paediatrician, adult and child psychotherapists, music therapist, paediatric physiotherapist, speech therapist, parent–infant psychotherapist, and a dietician.

The assessment and treatment focus on: observations with the child and the parents at home, at nursery, or with others through play, interactive time informed by psychoanalysis and neuroscience, and a blind evaluation with a chart at the beginning and at the end of the treatment to monitor progress and to see if there are any areas that still need special attention.

The stages in the treatment are:

- Phase I: three full days of assessment and formulation;
- Phase II: the intensive therapeutic intervention;
- Phase III: last three days for integration of feelings and assessment of progress.

After Phase III comes the "follow-on" treatment. This includes weekly or twice-weekly parent–child psychotherapy and, if necessary, social integration in mainstream nursery for a year. After that, we follow up with the child and the family every six months.

Unique features

- It is intensive—six hours a day, six days a week for one to four weeks.
- We provide a "follow-on" programme. Once the intensive treatment is complete, our follow-up work concentrates on consolidating the achievements of the intensive phase; this includes one-to-one specialised support in the crèche or nursery for a year for help with social integration
- It has an emotional focus. We "talk" all the time: to the baby using psycho-dynamic skills, and to the family. We also perform actions that speak to the inner needs of the child, such as holding and scaffolding the child, as well as other techniques.
- We work with each family member: siblings are also involved, as well as the parents, so that we can come to understand their inner world.
- We help bring about a different family integration by adjusting the dynamics.
- We request total commitment from the family: this is an important condition that the family must agree to before we help the family, otherwise the treatment does not take place.

Ten-month-old Thomas, and his parents and siblings (continued)

Thomas's parents were both British, and were living in Scotland. His mother, Jacqueline, was born in a small town in Yorkshire, his father in Edinburgh. They met through mutual friends at a party twelve years ago, and were married after three years.

Thomas's father was an investment banker, and often travelled abroad for work. His mother was a graphic designer who gave up work to care for the children. She planned to return to work part time when the children were older.

Family history

Luke and Chloe were both born after planned pregnancies and uncomplicated natural deliveries. They met routine developmental milestones and no concerns about their development had been raised. Chloe attended nursery school, though she initially found it difficult to settle. Luke had attended the same nursery and was now in primary school, where he was doing well.

Thomas was conceived as soon as his parents decided to try for a third child. The pregnancy was uncomplicated and the natural birth without note. The maternal grandmother came to help care for the older children for a fortnight during the period of Thomas's birth.

His parents first had concerns about Thomas's behaviour at around seven months: there was a lack of eye contact, and a strong preference to play with objects rather than people (Figure 11.4). They had been advised by their GP to "wait and see", and routine tests for deafness had come back normal. However, the family decided to seek a private medical opinion and arranged to see a developmental paediatrician. He concurred with the parents' concerns and referred them to the clinic.

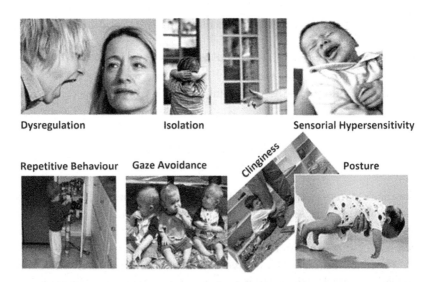

Figure 11.4. The signs of pre-autism are shown in the parents' concern about their child: isolation, sensorial hypersensitivity, repetitive behaviours, clinginess or active avoidance, body posture, and others.

After the initial consultation process with the family, it was agreed that the intensive treatment programme would benefit the baby and the family and we set a start date for when Thomas had reached a year old.

After the paediatric assessment, we met the family as a team of three to see how the family utilised the professional resources available.

The signs of pre-autism are shown in the parents' concern about their child: isolation, sensorial hypersensitivity, repetitive behaviours, clinginess or active avoidance, body posture, and others

Thomas presented himself as serious and avoidant, and would sleep all the time. His body was floppy and he would cry as soon as anybody picked him up, extending backwards with his arms. He never looked at his mother, not even when he was being breastfed.

Luke (the eldest sibling) appeared as the boss. Luke took over the attention of the therapist with his imaginary play, and when near Thomas would dangle teddies in front of his face or, without realising, throw the ball too hard or push a car too loudly. Meanwhile, his sister, Chloe, followed, marginalised. She hovered on the periphery, quiet and shy, yet sweetly smiling all the time.

It was made clear that Luke and Chloe must enter the programme as part of their brother's treatment. The parents were cautioned not to worry about the effect this would have on the two siblings, on their emotional understanding of the situation. There were no concerns about the two children. The only intriguing factor was that Luke had slept with his mother since he was born, and his father was forced to sleep in a different room. Both Thomas and Chloe had slept in their own bed since birth.

The therapeutic programme includes:

1. Work with the parents as a couple and as parents with a child that is difficult to reach.
2. Work with the infant with behaviours that could became autistic.
3. Work with the siblings.
4. Work with the different family relationship combinations.

The work with the parents as a couple includes exploration of:

- obstacles in the way of relating to the avoidant (pre-autistic) infant;
- emotions: shock, shame, guilt, loss, and fear for the future;
- trans-generational patterns of relating and attachment: how internalised past family dynamics are played out in the present family;
- difficulties in the couple: sometimes arising from such issues as the father sleeping in another room because the pre-autistic child will not let his parents sleep together;
- problems attuning to and playing with the infant with specific needs.

I shall talk about each of these elements.

We begin with assessments of the infant and of the mother/carer, in this instance, of Thomas and his mother (Figures 11.5 and 11.6).

We re-start by going back to the beginning, in a darkened room (like the womb) with the mother and the father: we tolerate any feelings evoked, and go at a slow pace. We help the parents to stay with the experience and, in the quietness of the room, tell them to focus on the relationship and gather their thoughts about themselves as parents and about their baby. The parents take the first steps towards this exploration of themselves as individuals, facing up to the "ghosts" of their childhood, sharing the pain, staying with it, and talking about it.

We observe the mother breastfeeding Thomas in an awkward position. The baby does not mould himself to his mother's body, and the reverie in the mother becomes interrupted by memories of her own father reprimanding her.

To the baby or young toddler, we talk about their fears and what we think might have caused it. We try to reset the child's basic self-soothing patterns by creating a secure space with each parent and with the siblings, where his individuality is accepted, respected, and helped to develop. Slowly smiles start to appear . . . the spice of life.

One can feel the release of fear as trust begins to develop—the basis of social experience. Thomas can start to feel and recognise what pleasure is (he already knows too well about pain and fear). Thomas could find fun and enjoyment with his mother and the father, learn how to relate, interact, and find peace.

In the relationship with the mother and father, the psychotherapist finds out about Thomas's likes and dislikes. We help parents to enter

ACQUARONE DETECTION SCALES FOR EARLY RELATIONSHIPS®
EARLY SIGNS OF ALARM – pre-Autism

ASSESSMENT – INFANT/CHILD

name: **THOMAS**
age: 8 months   date of this observation: DD MMM YYYY

		NEVER	RARELY	FREQUENT	ALWAYS	OBSERVER REACTIONS
INTERPERSONAL	**1. GAZING** Eye-to-eye contact within a relationship and the maintenance of this contact	●				
	2. BABBLING Making sounds for the benefit of the partner in the parent-infant relationship		●			
	3. CALLING – The facial expressions – Noises or gestures that seek to produce an affectionate response from the partner		●			
	4. IMITATING – Moving mouth, tongue, etc., in imitation of mother's (or another) – The repetition of a sound or a movement heard or seen by the child	●				
	5. PROVOKING Inciting the person into interacting, not just to use as an instrument to do something for him/her	●				
	6. POINTING Indicating with index finger to a person about an object of interest					
	7. FEEDING Child's attitude during the intake of food, including anticipatory behaviour (e.g. head-turning, moving arms the food/breast)			●		... fast anxious
	8. JOINT ATTENTION Looking in the same direction	●				
	9. PLAY – Capacity to play the same game for more than 5 minutes, and share with another person – Take turns and stay with a person – Children		●			
	10. ALONE				●	
	11. RELATING Behaviours indicating the capacity to relate & accept emotional warmth. – Mother, Father		●			
	– Other caregivers		●			
	– Other unfamiliar adults		●			
	– Siblings		●			
	– Other unfamiliar children		●			
	12. REACTIVE BEHAVIOURS tolerance to frustrations, including: – a) Capacity to accept emotional warmth – b) Capacity to bounce back after stressful event – c) Capacity to adapt to changes...please indicate	●				
SENSORIAL	**TOUCHING** **13.** Skin-to-skin contact initiated by infant for play or affection	●				
	14. Does the child touch paint, foam, sand, water, playdoh, plasticine and other messy substances	●				
	RESPONSE **15.** Response to sounds		●			
	16. Response to noise		●			
	17. Response to name		●			
	18. Response to light & patterns		●			
	19. Response to smells		●			
	20. COMFORTING Child's ability to find relief from distress by themselves (e.g. thumb sucking, touching hands, playing with one car, others)...specify		●			
MOTOR	**HOLDING** **21.** The posturing of the child when he is supported in the arms of the mother (e.g. floppy, rigid, restless) – General muscle tone when sitting or standing		●			
	22. Stereotypic movement of arms, eyes, etc. – Walking: on tiptoes or sluggish		●			
	23. Use of hands: for grasping, for helping himself – Use of body: to reach, to climb, to hide, other...		●			
AFFECT	**24. EXPRESSIVENESS** The body or facial expression of emotional states (e.g., sad, worried, anxious, bland, happy, or others)...specify		●			... looked away, cut off
	25. SELF HELP DEVELOPMENT – Ability to cope independently with the environment, (e.g., dress) – Eating – Being careful with him/herself or others	●				

ANY OTHER OBSERVATIONS NOT LISTED ABOVE:

© Acquarone 2013

Figure 11.5.   Initial assessment of Thomas.

ACQUARONE DETECTION SCALES FOR EARLY RELATIONSHIPS®
EARLY SIGNS OF ALARM – pre-Autism
...*affecting the baby or being affected by the baby*...

ASSESSMENT – MOTHER/caregiver

name: **NAME**
child: THOMAS   age: 8 months

	NEVER	RARELY	FREQUENT	ALWAYS	OBSERVER REACTIONS
1. GAZING — Eye-to-eye contact with the baby and the maintenance of this contact			●		... mothers anxiety transmitted
2. BABBLING – Making sounds for the benefit of the parent-infant relationship – Talking			●		... high pitch tone, persistent and repetitive
3. CALLING — Facial expressions, noises or gestures seeking to produce an affectionate response from the infant			●		... Mother looked frightened
4. FEEDING Mother's attitude towards infant's hunger and need to feed: – Does she anticipate behavior and have meal or breast easily available? – Does she pay attention, talk with the baby and enjoy feeding? – Does she interrupt with any excuse (e.g., talks to others and looks away)? – Is she fearful, full of anguish or has any delusions? – Is she apathetic?		●			... mother breastfeeding ... mother talked a while ... in spite of baby's posture ... being outward
5. GAMES / PLAY – Playful encounters, including songs and teasing	●				
6. RELATING — Behaviours indicating the capacity to relate & accept emotional warmth towards the baby			●		... fast anxious
7. REACTIVE BEHAVIOURS including: – Tolerance to frustrations – Capacity to accept emotional warmth – Capacity to bounce back after stressful event – Capacity to adapt to changes			●		
8. TOUCHING – Skin-to-skin contact initiated by infant for play or affection			●		... little contact
9. COMFORTING – Mother's ability to find relief for the baby's distress			●		... constant
10. POSTURE The posturing of the mother when the infant is supported in her arms or any other way (e.g., other, rough, balanced precariously)		●			... good and welcoming
11. EXPRESSIVENESS – Expression of emotional state (e.g., sad, worried, anxious, bland, happy, others)...specify			●		... very clear anxious, worried and sad
12. UNDERSTANDING OF EMOTIONS – in themselves – in the baby	●		●		... wanted to know about baby internal world
13. PAST – Psychiatric illness – Other difficulties	● ●				... sleeping with her children rather than husband

ANY OTHER OBSERVATIONS NOT LISTED ABOVE:

Preoccupied since Nicola 4th month about not being able to understand and have a relationship with her

© Acquarone 2013

Figure 11.6.   Initial assessment of Thomas's mother.

into his space that they do not recognise, that feels like a place of rejection; it is daunting, but they need to stay there. This space is called the "pre-autistic space". Their attitude could change with their baby changing. They must learn to feel part of his "re-forming".

The avoidant infant is quiet, but his non-verbal communications through his body movements and transmitted feelings speak loudly to us. Feeling overwhelmed, unable to make sense of his surroundings, feeling pain on hearing certain sounds, such as mother's voice (high pitched) and other noises (too many for him to take in), including his siblings talking, the television, traffic, toys. At times, he shows us that he is confused about different colours and shapes, as if they, too, were too much. He does this by looking down and sucking on his hands. Then his mother, feeling desperate, becomes intrusive, unable to control the surge of discontentment and anxiety that comes over her.

Further on in the treatment, we undertake more exploring experiences with the mother. She sits on the floor with the parent–infant psychotherapist, who presents simple string and pentatonic instruments: we follow the idea of feeling the urge to communicate in a different way, slowly and with patience, and from a distance; we use made-up songs. There is no place for judging or expecting things to happen. This idea makes for a different experience for the mother and her child, where expressions of different states can be felt, shown through the body, and enjoyed.

The mother experiments with the instrument, producing different sounds. Through these actions, she starts to experience a new sensation of being happy, and feeling trust. Thomas might feel different being with her like this, but at least her anxiety is in a different mode. They are exploring in the company of one other rather than in the merge and confusion of both. There is now a clear, calmer feeling.

The instrument (the lyre) is sounding simple and sweet: one person produces sounds and awakes interest in the other, a motivation to look, to seek, to pursue.

Allowing the father into the bedroom and into the relationship: central for emotional development

For the eternal triangle (oedipal relationship) to form in this relationship, it seemed that the family needed help, and that the father had to find his place. The father accepted his involvement in the programme and made himself available for the duration of the treatment. He was keen to find a way to communicate with his son, with whom he found it so difficult to relate compared with his other two children. Gradually, the father learnt to talk to Thomas. He felt awkward at first, as did Thomas, who suddenly felt the need to rock (a new experience). He was disconcerted and looked away, but the father stayed with the moment. He picked up Thomas and decided to recover his space in the family. Closeness was experienced for the first time and there was a discovery of each other as a new space evolved to enrich and relieve the mother–baby relationship.

On one occasion when the father was in the room, Thomas became interested in a big round mirror in which both of them were reflected. In the new space of observation and talking

- there develops respect and differentiation of individuals, even of oneself;
- the space between parent and child offers a new stage;
- the father needs the experience first and words to integrate it second.

Patterns of attachment

Thomas seemed largely oblivious to the chaotic family interactions around him. At times, he would sit on the rug looking down at a book, turning the pages. At other times, Thomas seemed to be watching his family from a distance. His response to anyone who attempted to engage with him or expand on his play was to move round and turn his back on them.

Luke seemed to be in a dominant position in the family—bossing his sister, choosing games, demanding attention—while Chloe was more withdrawn, playing quietly on the periphery.

A busy chaotic atmosphere reigned when all three children were together.

Luke, the eldest, appeared at first to have a secure attachment. However, during the treatment it became apparent that he had an insecure attachment resulting in a merging between him and his mother. Luke began life in his parents' bed and, by the age of six, had still never slept apart from his mother. His father, relegated to life outside of the matrimonial bed, slept on his own, or with his daughter. Luke's bedroom was never used.

Chloe could be seen as ambivalently attached. While having a loving relationship with her parents, it seemed as if she was more self-sufficient and separate. Chloe went to her parents at times for comfort, but on the occasions when she got upset or angry or even hurt, she appeared to retreat into her own world.

Sibling rivalry

In the family sessions, Luke was often terribly competitive for his mother's attention. This made him aggressive and pushy with his "distant" baby brother. Meanwhile, Chloe appeared frightened and subdued. The rivalry between the siblings needed to be attended to, and as Houzel points out, the ". . . fantasies and emotions [of] brothers and brothers may be even more primitive and violent than those concerning the parental couple" (Houzel, 2001).

Tustin's "nest of babies" fantasy explains how infants' awareness of their own identity gives rise to a distinction between themselves and others, as well as the fantasy that there are "special babies" who are given "special food" (Tustin, 1972). In this case, the siblings had formed a complicated rivalry because they had a younger brother who appeared to occupy more space in his parents' mind than was usual. This resulted in different responses from the two siblings: Luke was in the centre of the "nest" clamouring more loudly for food, while Chloe was pushed to the side of the "nest", as if unable or unwilling to make herself seen.

The interventions with the siblings comprised a combination of directive and non-directive play. A range of toys, games, and activities were made available, such as dressing-up, shops, playhouse, dolls and babies, paints, playdough, drawing materials, bubbles, zoo animals, crafts, storybooks, musical instruments, and outings.

Progress with the siblings

Both siblings changed their patterns of attachment and means of relating to other people and with Thomas. We had to employ the skills of the individual child psychotherapist to help Luke come down from his narcissistic manner of relating to the family and to learn to acknowledge other people's needs as well. Concerning the relentless fear he felt of losing his mother, Luke had to acknowledge the father's role in the family, and control his feelings of rivalry with regard to his mother and his siblings.

Once he overcame the shock of not being obeyed, Luke acted in a far more gentle way. He learnt to take turns and deal with his overwhelming feelings in a controlled way. As for Chloe, she found her voice, became more assertive, and better able to express her own will and desires.

How the siblings and parents found a way of being with Thomas

The family had to learn how to talk more softly, or even whisper, to

Thomas. They had to give him space, watch his cues, no longer put toys too close to his face. Most importantly, they had to accept that Thomas had his own way of wanting to be part of their family.

For this to happen, Thomas's siblings and parents practised and supported the new playing guidelines we set out for them. By doing so, they saw results and realised that everybody could have a good time and enjoy a fun relationship with Thomas.

Obstacles in the work with siblings

Any obstacles encountered had to do with a reactivation of other conflicts. Just as the siblings had to share their parents, so, too, did they have to share a therapist. The therapist had to prioritise their needs and assist each child in developing their own mental capacities to wait for the attention they deserved. At times, there was a need for strict behavioural interventions and working with the two children could be emotionally draining.

Progress with Thomas

Thomas's progress manifested itself in his smiles and laughter (Photo 11.3. In addition, he

- became interested in people, and was happy to interact;
- was able to form relationships;
- developed curiosity;
- had a new-found capacity to play;
- overcame his fears.

The big turning point in the family dynamics came with the change in family bedtime habits—the father reclaimed his place in the parental bed and Luke learnt to sleep apart from his mother.

The siblings became able to cope with being separate from one another—to play different games, or with different people—and they learnt to play *with* Thomas and not just *to* him.

Summary

In this case study, it was essential for the parents to first recognise the "ghosts" (Fraiberg et al., 1975) from their own pasts and from the

Photo 11.3. The big turning point.

family intergenerational transmission of values. Only then were they able to understand the differing needs of their children: Thomas with his hypersensitivities, fears, likes, and need for a slower pace; Luke's strong feelings of rivalry and bossiness over the family, almost representing the mother and father's internal "Almighty Father" figure; Chloe, who had to be supported to speak up and voice her thoughts and wishes. But one of the most important and necessary achievements was to rescue the "real" father in the family.

Figures 11.7 and 11.8 show the results from Thomas's and his mother's charts completed at the follow-up to the programme, and Figures 11.9 and 11.10 show the results for both Thomas and his mother at the end of the programme.

Thomas's follow-up every six months showed his increasing security in forming relationships, becoming a happy member of his family, as well as enjoying life at nursery and then school. Thomas is now seven years old and in mainstream education. He has three close friends and likes to socialise with others. He plays football and the violin, which is going from strength to strength.

ACQUARONE DETECTION SCALES FOR EARLY RELATIONSHIPS®
EARLY SIGNS OF ALARM – pre-Autism

FOLLOW-UP – INFANT/CHILD

name: **THOMAS**

age: **8 months**   date of this observation: **DD MMM YYYY**

	NEVER	RARELY	FREQUENT	ALWAYS	OBSERVER REACTIONS
INTERPERSONAL					
1. GAZING			●		
2. BABBLING			●		
3. CALLING			●		
4. IMITATING			●		
5. PROVOKING			●		
6. POINTING			●		
7. FEEDING			●		
8. JOINT ATTENTION			●		
9. PLAY			●		
10. ALONE			●		
11. RELATING – to other children			●		
– to adults			●		
12. REACTIVE BEHAVIOURS capacity to... a) accept emotional warmth b) bear stressful event c) adapt to changes			●		
SENSORIAL					
TOUCHING 13. Skin-to-skin			●		
14. Textures					
RESPONSE 15. Sounds			●		
16. Noise					
17. Name			●		
18. Light & patterns					
19. Smells					
20. COMFORTING			●		
MOTOR					
HOLDING 21. Posturing			●		
22. Stereotypic movement			●		
23. Use of hands/Use of body			●		
AFFECT					
24. EXPRESSIVENESS			●		
25. SELF HELP DEVELOPMENT			●		

ANY OTHER OBSERVATIONS NOT LISTED ABOVE:

© Acquarone 2013

Figure 11.7. Thomas's assessment at follow-up.

ACQUARONE DETECTION SCALES FOR EARLY RELATIONSHIPS®
EARLY SIGNS OF ALARM – pre-Autism
...affecting the baby or being affected by the baby...

FOLLOW-UP – MOTHER/caregiver

name: **NAME**
child: **THOMAS**   age: **8 months**

	NEVER	RARELY	FREQUENT	ALWAYS	OBSERVER REACTIONS
INTERPERSONAL					
1. GAZING			●		... with joy
2. BABBLING			●		... nicely in a glare tone
3. CALLING			●		... learn to wait and see
4. FEEDING			●		... nicely resting
5. GAMES / PLAY	●				... learn the signs to start game
6. RELATING			●		
7. REACTIVE BEHAVIOURS			●		
SENSORIAL					
8. TOUCHING			●		... carefully
9. COMFORTING			●		... when necessary
MOTOR					
10. POSTURE			●		... calm, nice and firm
AFFECT					
11. EXPRESSIVENESS			●		... Continue to be able to show and talk. And feelings now
12. UNDERSTANDING OF EMOTIONS – in themselves – in the baby			● ●		... constant
13. PAST – Psychiatric illness – Other difficulties			● ●		... understanding family dynamic

ANY OTHER OBSERVATIONS NOT LISTED ABOVE:

© Acquarone 2013

Figure 11.8. The assessment chart for Thomas's mother at follow-up.

Emotional development

We end this account of two different kinds of parent infant psychotherapy with thinking about emotional development as the ability to cope with a variety of emotional experiences and not to feel overwhelmed by them, being able to enjoy and learn in the relationship, and to communicate in a passionate way.

We can also say that rather than feel frightened of encountering the mother, father, and others, these infants learnt to cope with them, and to trust that relationships can bring joy, excitement, and fun. We

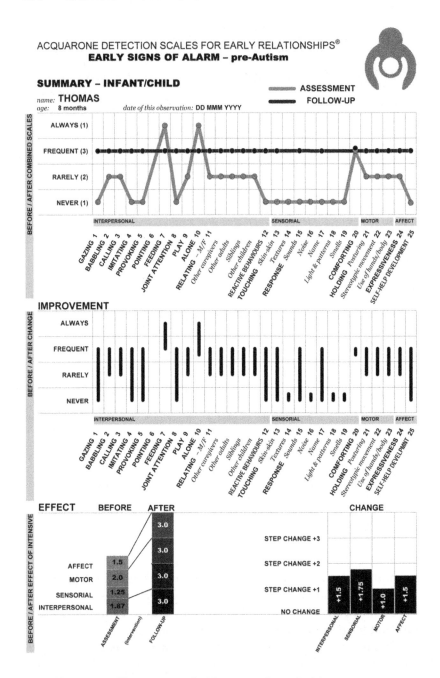

Figure 11.9. The summary for Thomas at the end of the programme.

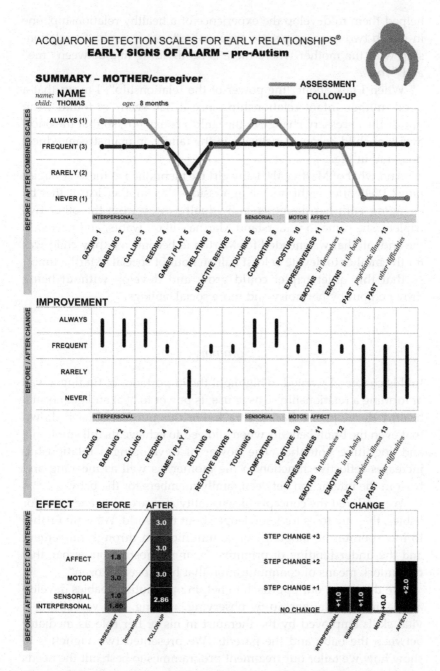

Figure 11.10. The summary of Thomas's mother at the end of the programme..

helped them to develop the experience of a healthy relationship, one in which two or more people are involved, not a symbiotic relationship with the mother where there is no dividing line between "me" and "you".

When I talk about "the power of the relationship", I mean that a good mother–infant relationship, once it has been "re-found", can power the necessary change in the child's behaviour, so that the once-avoidant child becomes inclusive in the family, in mainstream education, and in life.

And what of Martha, the baby girl we mentioned at the very beginning? Well, after eight hour-long sessions, her mother learnt that by engaging with her daughter individually, away from the other two triplets, she came to understand Martha's likes, wants, and needs. In the end, all that was needed for Martha to become a happy child was for the mother to devote at least half an hour of special "Martha time", so that this quiet triplet could grow and develop without being drowned out by her noisy and more social siblings.

Summary

In this chapter, I wanted to highlight the importance of finding a way of forming a relationship so as to use its power to heal and get normal healthy development back on track. For this purpose, I have shown that even the brain benefits when allowed to achieve its full emotional and cognitive potential. The power of developing a relationship increases reflective function in the mother, as well as meaning and trust in the interaction between family members for the baby.

We explored the concepts of sensuality and sexuality and how, for babies, they are tools for knowledge about the world. We went further to incorporate the language of communication through movement and the understanding of primitive feelings, mostly non-verbal, that can unlock means of communication that have been "frozen".

We discussed our approach to helping pre-autistic babies develop a meaningful relationship by observing, waiting, and verbalising—vital skills employed by the therapist in his or her role as mediator between the baby and the parents. We presented two vignettes to show how we tailor our treatment programmes to best suit the needs of each family: the first was a two-month programme where we worked with the mother (and sometimes father) and baby for eight one-hour sessions; the second was a three-week intensive treatment that involved the whole family for six hours a day. For the latter programme, our approach was multi-disciplinary in nature, incorporating parent–infant, individual, couple, and family therapy. The results were astonishing, as not only was the infant able to develop a relationship with the mother and father, but each member of the family benefited from understanding and forming better and healthier relationships with each other. This intensive treatment was followed by weekly sessions to support progress, and maintain the same level of interest, novelty, and joy.

The social and interpersonal positive results demonstrate the importance of intervening early and involving the whole family as a means of understanding, creating, and maintaining healthy bonds.

Acknowledgement

I would like to thank the charity International Pre-Autistic Network for the funding of these treatments.

References

Acquarone, S. (2004). *Infant Parent Psychotherapy: A Handbook*. London: Karnac.

Acquarone, S., & Jimenez Acquarone, I. (2016). *Changing Destinies: The Re-Start Intensive Family Programme for Young Children with Autistic Behaviours*. London: Karnac, in press.

Bion, W. R. (1962). *Learning from Experience*. London: Heinemann.

Bion, W. R. (1965). *Transformation: Change from Learning to Growth*. London: Tavistock.

Bowlby, J. (1988). *A Secure Base: Parent–Child Attachment and Healthy Human Development*. New York: Basic Books.

Brazelton, B. (1973). *The Neonatal Behavioural Assessment Scale*. London: MacKeith Press. [reprinted 1976].

Brazelton, T. B., Kozlowski, B., & Main, M. (1974). The origins of reciprocity. In: M. Lewis & L. Rosenblum (Eds.), *The Effect of the Infant on its Caregiver* (pp. 49–76). New York: Elsevier.

Darwin, C. (1859). *On the Origin of Species*. An Electronic Classics Series publication. Pennsylvania State University. 2001–2013.

Delafield-Butt, J. T., & Trevarthen, C. (2013). Theories of the development of human communication. In: P. Cobley & P. Schultz (Eds.), *Theories and Models of Communication* (pp. 199–222). Berlin: De Gruyter Mouton.

Escalona, S. (1963). Patterns of infantile experience and the developmental process. *Psychoanalytic Study of the Child*, 51: 360–397.

Fraiberg, S. (1980). *Clinical Studies in Infant Mental Health. The First Year of Life*. London: Tavistock.

Fraiberg, S. (1982). Pathological defenses in infancy. *Psychoanalytic Quarterly*, 51: 612–635.

Fraiberg S., Adelson E., & Shapiro, V. (1975). Ghosts in the nursery. A psychoanalytic approach to the problems of impaired infant–mother relationships. *Journal of the American Academy of Child & Adolescent Psychiatry*, 14(3): 387–421.

Houzel, D. (2001). The "nest of babies" fantasy. *Journal of Child Psychotherapy*, 27: 125–138.

Kleeman, J. A. (1965). A boy discovers his penis. *Psychoanalytic Study of the Child*, 20: 239–266.

Kleeman, J. A. (1976). Freud's view on early female sexuality in light of direct child observation. *Journal of the American Psychoanalytic Association*, 24(Suppl.): 3–27.

Murray, L. (2014). *The Psychology of Babies*. London: Constable & Robinson.

Murray, L., & Andrews, L. (2000). *The Social Baby*. Richmond: CP.

Murray, L., & Trevarthen, C. (1985). Emotional regulation of interactions between two-month-olds and their mothers. In: T. Field & N. Fox (Eds.), *Social Perception in Infants* (pp. 177–197). Norwood, NJ: Ablex.

Piontelli, A. (1992). *From Fetus to Child: An Observational Psychoanalytic Study*. London: Tavistock/Routledge.

Rascovsky, A. (1971). *El Psiquismo Fetal*. Buenos Aires: Paidos.

Ratey, A. (2001). *A User's Guide to the Brain: Perception, Attention, and the Four Theatres of the Brain*. New York: Knopf Doubleday.

Schore, A. (1994). *Affect Regulation and the Origin of the Self. The Neurobiology of Emotional Development*. Hillside, NJ: Lawrence Erlbaum.

Spitz, R. A. (1962). Autoerotism re-examined: the role of early sexual behavior patterns in personality formation. *Psychoanalytic Study of the Child*, 17: 283–315.

Stern, D. (1985). *The Interpersonal World of the Infant*. New York: Basic Books.

Stern, D. (2006). Introduction to the special issue on early preventative intervention and home visiting. *Infant Mental Health Journal*, 27: 1–4.

Trevarthen, C. (1998a). *Children with Autism: Diagnosis and Interventions to Meet Their Needs*. London: Jessica Kingsley.

Trevarthen, C. (1998b). Passionate observers and imitators: joys and deceptions of companionship with infants. Presented to the Baby Brain Conference, School of Infant Mental Health at the Tavistock Clinic, London.

Trevarthen, C. (2001). The neurobiology of early communication: intersubjective regulations in human brain development. In: A. F. Kalverboer & A. Gramsbergen (Eds.), *Handbook on Brain and Behavior in Human Development*. Dordrecht: Kluwer.

Trevarthen, C. (2004). Brain development. In: R. L. Gregory (Ed.), *Oxford Companion to the Mind* (2nd edn). Oxford: Oxford University Press.

Trevarthen, C. (2010). What is it like to be a person who knows nothing? Defining the active intersubjective mind of a newbon human being. *Infant and Child Development, 20*: 119–135.

Trevarthen, C., & Delafield-Butt, J. T. (2013). Autism as a developmental disorder in intentional movement and affective engagement. *Frontiers in Integrative Neuroscience, 7*(49).

Trevarthen, C., & Hubley, P. (1978). Secondary intersubjectivity: confidence, confiding and acts of meaning in the first year. In: A. Lock (Ed.) *Action, Gesture, and Symbol* (pp. 183–229). London: Academic Press.

Trevarthen, C., Murray, L., & Hubley, P. A. (1981). Psychology of infants. In: J. Davis & J. Dobbing (Eds), *Scientific Foundations of Clinical Pediatrics* (2nd edn) (pp. 211–274). London: Heinemann.

Tustin, F. (1972). *Autism and Childhood Psychosis*. London: Hogarth.

Winnicott, D. W. (1945). Primitive emotional development. *International Journal of Psychoanalysis, 26*: 137–143.

Winnicott, D. W. (1952). Anxiety associated with insecurity. In: *Collected Papers: Through Paediatrics to Psychoanalysis* (p. 99). London: Tavistock 1958.

Winnicott, D. W. (1958). The capacity to be alone. *International Journal of Psychoanalysis, 39*: 416–420.

Winnicott, D. W. (1960). The theory of the parent–infant relationship. *International Journal of Psychoanalysis, 41*: 585–595.

Winnicott, D. W. (1964). *The Child, The Family and the Outside World*. Harmondsworth: Penguin.

Winnicott, D. W. (1965). *The Maturational Process and the Facilitating Environment*. London: Hogarth Press.

Winnicott, D. W. (1975). *Through Paediatrics to Psycho-Analysis*. London: Hogarth Press.

CHAPTER TWELVE

Early paediatric intervention: to see or not to see, to be or not to be—with others

Jo Winsland

Introduction

Most babies under the age of three months prefer faces to toys. Their innate capacity to relate seems to be primed to practise during those first few months. The fine-tuning of the interactional process in the weeks and months after birth is probably vital for increasing the chances of long-term survival for that individual and their family group.

Occasionally, something seems to get out of "synch", and parents can find themselves with a baby who fixedly refuses eye contact and interaction, or who simply seems not to see them. Often unsure of how much to expect from a very small baby, many parents in this situation will say to themselves that the baby probably cannot see properly yet. None the less, they will usually be disturbed and worried by the lack of interaction with their baby. A non-interacting baby can awaken deep feelings of insecurity and rejection, which can be difficult to talk about. To avoid such feelings, the natural tendency can be for the parents themselves to look away and interact less with their baby, waiting, as such, for a sign that their baby is interested in them— an invitation that the baby might not at that point be able to initiate.

In this way, a vicious circle can begin; a waiting game that can over-run the baby's developmental readiness to relate. Three months is a very long time for a baby, and a very short time for an adult.

Regular contact at the right time, with sensitive, appropriately trained health professionals in whom the family has established trust, can be sufficient to change the course of events. I try to illustrate this with the case histories of three babies followed up from birth in southern France. There are two short introductory cases, and one longer, more detailed case history.

The context

In France, after their eighth day postnatal check-up, babies are seen monthly from birth until twelve months, and then every two to three months until the twenty-four-month check-up. In this way, early child health and development is closely monitored, by independent paediatricians, general practitioners, or the PMI (Protection Maternelle et Infantile). It should be noted, however, that this practice is becoming increasingly difficult to maintain as numbers of paediatricians fall, and public funding for the PMI and associated services diminishes.

Founded in 1945, to counter horrific post-war infant and child mortality figures, the PMI is a publicly funded medico-social service for family planning and pre- and postnatal parental support that local councils legally have to provide. The PMI works hand in hand with social workers, educators, and psychologists, and is also responsible for quality control of all childcare provision for the under-sixes. In many parts of France, since the decentralisation of the 1980s, when services were transferred from the state to the *département* level (roughly equivalent to a British county council), generous funding for high quality ongoing professional training has been available for these public sector staff working directly with children and their families.

On the clinical side, doctors specialising in child health and protection work with specialist paediatric nurses (*puéricultrices*) who, like the midwives, do home visits. The clinics are free, open to all, and provide regular developmental and preventative follow-up, including vaccinations, for all children from birth to six years. After two years, children are seen less often, depending on need, but many parents return once a year, or if in difficulty with their child. A screening and developmental check by the PMI is available to all three- to five-year-olds at school.

The ready availability and generally welcoming environment of the PMI, coupled with the French tradition of frequent follow-up from birth, creates a context in which trained and experienced professionals can often find themselves in the right place at the right time for very early preventative intervention, which, in this conducive environment, is often very simple and short-lived.

Two short cases: Samuel and Emma

Samuel and Emma were both babies placed in pre-adoption foster care one after the other. The job of the foster mother who took in first Samuel and then Emma was to collect abandoned babies from the hospital and care for them over the two-month waiting period prior to adoption. Samuel was the first baby I came across in the clinic who refused eye contact.

Recently trained to detect the early warning signs possibly predictive of autism, I was particularly concerned when I met Samuel in the clinic with his carer. He would not make eye contact with either of us. I shared my concern with his particularly warm and intelligent newly qualified foster mother. We were both unsure of what to expect from a baby who had already lost all that was familiar to him once. He was four weeks old, born at term without complications, and was the result of a teenage mother's hidden pregnancy.

His foster mother asked me if she should get attached to this baby who would have new parents in four weeks' time: would it not be easier for him to move on if they were not too close? This question had not been addressed by any of my training. I could only answer from the heart: "Yes!" I replied with conviction, "Get attached to him." I was unable to see how further attachment would be possible for Samuel if primary bonding had not yet begun. A baby cannot survive alone. My response seemed to reassure Samuel's carer at some intuitive level. I arranged to see them at the clinic a week later.

A few days later, Samuel's young biological mother changed her mind, and took him back. I never saw him again, but he had sparked off a thought process that gave us a head start for the following case.

Within a very short space of time, there was another baby up for adoption: Emma. She came to the clinic at the age of three weeks. Her first week had been spent on the paediatric ward, waiting for her mother to decide whether or not to give her up for adoption. During the wait, the foster mother could not visit, and her biological mother did not want to see the baby if she was to give her up. Emma was named and cared for by the nurses taking turns on eight-hour shifts, but she had no mother for seven days.

Like Samuel, she was born at term without complications. She was the fifth child of a depressive mother with a tendency to serial hidden pregnancies and neglect of her own and her children's needs. Her mother finally decided to give her up, and she was taken into pre-adoption foster care at the age of one week.

When she came to the PMI at the age of three weeks, Emma was so unresponsive to eye contact or voice that there was concern that she might be either blind or deaf or both. Hearing and vision tests were being carried out. Her foster mother, this time keen to bond with this little girl, was increasingly frustrated by the lack of response. A week later, the sight and hearing test results were found to be normal, but Emma remained unresponsive. There was now concern all round regarding her capacity to relate. There were no other signs of ill health, and Emma was feeding and growing normally.

Emma was now four weeks old. I encouraged the foster family to continue trying to attract her attention, and to become attached to her, and within a few days we had a joint consultation with a psychologist colleague, a specialist in infant psychology.

At five weeks, Emma began to respond intermittently to members of the foster family. A second joint consultation with the psychologist took place when Emma was six weeks old. At this point, Emma was beginning to look at everyone and relate. She had a tendency to squint at times.

Adoptive parents were found for her, and she met them aged seven weeks. She remained responsive and communicative. Progressive contact with her new parents was arranged over a week. They were informed of her initial delay in relating and her progress since. She was adopted at eight weeks. Her new mother responded positively to the information about Emma's tendency to squint as she herself had a squint.

Emma was seen regularly at the PMI clinic in another area by one of my colleagues. She continued to relate. By the time she was five years old, her development was recorded as normal.

Long case history: Kevin

Kevin was seen at the PMI clinic from age six weeks to twenty-one months. He was the second child in a stable family, with a big sister of nine years. Both parents were at home at the time of his birth. He was born at term by normal delivery without complications.

First clinic visit: six weeks old

Kevin came to the clinic with his mother and sister. His mother was concerned about his frequent feeds, regurgitation, and constant crying. His posture was rigid, mostly in hyper-extension (arched backwards), and there was total avoidance of eye contact. In contrast, his visual attention for objects was abnormally good for his age. The medical examination was otherwise normal, as was his weight gain. His mother seemed attentive, though reserved.

While examining Kevin, I tried hard to get his attention and eye contact, but to no avail. I mentioned this to his mother, asking, "He won't look at me—does he look at you?" "No, not at anyone," was the reply.

I shared my concern about his lack of eye contact and posture with his mother and sister, and advised them to try to attract Kevin's attention and communicate with him as much as possible, while not allowing him to remain for long periods in his hyper-extended posture (this posture seems to exacerbate relating difficulties).

Kevin's mother seemed perplexed, but, none the less, agreed to return in two weeks at my request.

Second clinic visit: eight weeks old

This time Kevin's mother came alone with him. There had been little change since the last appointment; Kevin continued his active avoidance of eye contact and remained in hyper-extension. His mother was worried that he might have a "problem".

On this occasion, seeing them outside normal clinic hours, I took the time to ask detailed questions about the family context at conception, during pregnancy, and birth. I learnt that Kevin's was a desired pregnancy, although it had gone unnoticed for the first two months. His mother, unaware that she was pregnant, underwent a general anaesthetic at one month for a minor surgical procedure. Her pregnancy was subsequently dominated by an overriding fear of anaesthetic-induced malformations, despite normal test results, ultrasound images, and reassurance from the doctors, whom she did not believe. This fear had grown even more acute over the past two weeks because of my concern about eye contact and posture.

Disturbed at having exacerbated her fears and concerned at the lack of change in Kevin's behaviour, I was unsure of how to react, and asked a rather random question about the mother's siblings. She replied that she had two sisters, and should have had a little brother when she was six, but he was stillborn due to cardiac malformation. She only learnt much later as an adult what happened and did not know as a child why her mother returned from hospital without the baby. At this point, things began to seem clearer to me.

I shared the following thoughts with Kevin's mother: that perhaps there was a connection between the loss of her brother and her intense fears around the birth of her first son, and that the buried childhood memory of the unexplained loss could somehow have left her with a subconscious conviction that having a boy was dangerous.

I insisted on the physical normality of all aspects of her baby boy, and explained that subconscious anxiety can affect all babies, and could be temporarily delaying eye contact in Kevin's case. She seemed to find my suggestion hard to believe, but, none the less, listened attentively. She agreed to return in two weeks.

Third clinic visit: ten weeks old

This time Kevin was visibly more relaxed, smiling, gurgling, and maintaining a flexed forward posture throughout. He had become very responsive to his mother's voice, and interaction *with* eye contact was now possible some of the time, but he remained easily distracted by objects and lights.

Kevin's physical strength was impressive and now no longer focused on arching backwards constantly. He was feeding less frequently, and sleeping through the night. All aspects of the medical examination remained normal. His mother was reassured—as was I.

Fourth clinic visit: three months old

Two weeks on, Kevin was now maintaining eye contact most of the time, smiling, vocalising, and communicating, even when tired. He was expressing frustration clearly and crying when his father left for work. He was growing fast, and his mother was clearly impressed by her baby, and close to him. It seemed reasonable from this point to see them monthly instead of every two weeks.

Fifth clinic visit: four months old

A month later and Kevin had made remarkable progress; he was remaining available for social interaction all the time, with eye contact, and there were no further instances of eye contact avoidance at all.

There was still some occasional harmless regurgitation, but he was now able to hold his own bottle of water and drink from it unaided (this is extremely rare at four months). He could also play with his feet, putting them in his mouth (this normally happens at around six months). His co-ordination and strength was unusually good for his age. His mother and sister were in continuing admiration of his skills.

Development from four to twenty-one months

Kevin's further developmental milestones can be summarised as follows:

- five months—sitting (early);
- six months—belly crawling. Pulling himself up to standing (very early);
- nine months—crawling, dancing, furniture walking;
- ten months—walking alone (early);
- twelve months—saying several words, talking to himself in the mirror, making faces, laughing, sharing the joke;
- fourteen months—very active but able to play calmly; attentive, communicative, very cross when forbidden something;
- seventeen months—refusing to go to bed before the parents;

- nineteen months—potty trained at his request;
- twenty-one months—elaborate language capacity (for both understanding and expression), climbing on everything and out of his cot, moving furniture, turning keys, sleeping in his parents' bed. His mother was by now finding him hard work.

Summary

By twenty-one months, Kevin had become a difficult child for his family. His overdeveloped capacity for exploration, and unusual strength and co-ordination were complicated to manage, and his rapid progress took everyone by surprise.

His very normal need for clear and firm boundaries came before his family was ready, swinging him into an unhealthily dominant role in the family. His parents, with a relaxed attitude to life in general, and not in the habit of over-stimulating their children, were ill-equipped to deal with Kevin's excessive curiosity and determination. Providing appropriate boundaries for Kevin was going to require a concerted effort.

Observation

It would seem that from the moment his mother's fears were reconnected to their probable roots, when he was two months old, Kevin's capacity to relate became safe to practise, and his posture lost its imperative to "self-hold". (As pregnancy progresses and there is less space, a baby stretching out in the uterus is increasingly but gently maintained in a position of flexion by the firm but flexible uterine walls against the baby's back. It could be that arching the back is a way of looking for a lost environment associated with a previous feeling of safety. Some autistic children specifically seek positions where their backs are in contact with a wall or other fixed surface.) If constantly arching backwards is a baby's attempt to return to the lost comfort of the womb (which seems likely), Kevin lost this tendency surprisingly quickly at the time when he began to relate. From this point onwards, he was able to bond with the three members of his direct family, for whom he rapidly became the centre of attention, and which no doubt led to his rapid progress.

Kevin's early obsession with objects as a refuge from the dangers of relating to people would, none the less, appear to have left its mark in his overdeveloped imagination and capacity for attention to detail, which he retains to this day.

It is easy to postulate that a lack of early intervention in this case would have left Kevin in need of his autistic-style defences for much longer, with diminishing ease of reversibility with time.

It is worth noting the remarkably rapid turnaround observed with Kevin: from an incapacity to relate at two months, to normal social interactions at four months. Change for Emma also occurred within a few weeks, as for many other cases that I have followed up.

In my experience, this rate of change is consistently observable when intervention takes place in the first few months or weeks of life, before anything becomes fixed. The longer defences remain in place, the more likely it becomes that we will miss the boat, the sensitive period for each developmental stage, which, like building blocks, build upon each other. Development can happen late, even very late, but it takes exponentially longer, and is increasingly difficult to facilitate.

In particular, the very specific environment necessary for safe bonding is fairly easily and naturally available to very small babies, but is infinitely more difficult to create and maintain around bigger children or adults.

Conclusion

When things go wrong, babies develop coping strategies to minimise their discomfort. Different babies have different thresholds for discomfort and different coping strategies, but a useful short-term defence mechanism can become a long-term handicap. Put simply, and with reference to the title of this chapter, most babies can see, and most babies can be (in a relationship), but sometimes something gets in the way. A non-relating baby makes everyone insecure, normal bonding and development can be interrupted, and things can get stuck in a vicious circle.

There are simple things that can be done very early to break a vicious circle, and it is important not to miss the boat. Timing is everything.

CHAPTER THIRTEEN

Working in a National Health Service setting with toddlers at risk of autistic spectrum disorder

Maria Rhode

For a variety of reasons, both personal and practical, some families find themselves unable to participate in the kind of intensive intervention described elsewhere in this volume. My aim is to describe a conjoint intervention within an NHS setting for toddlers at risk of autism and their parents in which they are seen for one, or at most two, sessions a week.

This intervention grew out of a pilot study of outcomes achieved in a home-based therapeutic observation for toddlers at risk of autistic spectrum disorder. I have described this pilot study[1] in detail elsewhere (Rhode, 2007), and have referred to the growing recognition among practitioners and teachers of infant observation that a modified, "participant" observation often proved supportive for the parents as well as their baby. Infant observation, which involves once-weekly visits to a baby and its family in their own home (Bick, 1964), is seen as an essential part of many trainings in psychoanalysis, psychotherapy, and social work.

Houzel (1999) has outlined the principles of modified "participant" observations, which he introduced into the French child psychiatry service in Brittany and, later, in Normandy; a particular practical advantage of this intervention was the possibility of reaching families who might not be able to attend clinic appointments. Individual reports have been published that illustrate good outcomes for a variety of young children in difficulty; these include children at risk of being taken into care, children who are failing to thrive or who have suffered from life-threatening illnesses, and children at risk of autistic spectrum disorder (e.g., Cardenal, 1998; Delion, 2000; Houzel, 2011). More particularly, a six-month-old baby who had been diagnosed with West's syndrome by a paediatrician was found to have a normal EEG after six months of a therapeutic observation (Lechevalier et al., 2000). West's syndrome is characterised by epileptoid seizures and a characteristic abnormal EEG ("hypsarrhythmia"); it is usually treated with cortisone, and a high proportion of children suffering from it develop autistic features. The authors were careful not to generalise from one case, but this was obviously a striking result. It seemed to us both worthwhile to carry out therapeutic observations of children at risk of autism, and essential to follow these up systematically.

Fortunately, a screening measure exists that shows excellent specificity in detecting toddlers at risk, though it picks up only 27% of those who later receive a diagnosis. The CHAT (Checklist for Autism in Toddlers: Baron-Cohen et al., 1992) is a simple measure designed for use in primary care. It is based on a combination of questions to the parents and observation of the child's response to the professional's request to carry out three simple tasks. These target the child's capacity for joint attention (gaze following and proto-declarative pointing) as well as for pretend play. Children who do not engage with any of these tasks fall into the high risk category: they have an 85% chance of a diagnosis of autism at the age of three and a half, or, to phrase it differently, they have only one chance in six of not receiving such a diagnosis. Children who engage with one task but not with the other two fall in the medium risk category: approximately half of them are later diagnosed with autism, while most of the rest are diagnosed with developmental delay. A child who is seen to be in the high risk category is obviously in need of intervention. Equally, a likelihood of only one in six of such a child not being diagnosed with autism at three and a half means that even a small number of toddlers who had undergone the intervention and did not subsequently receive a diagnosis would provide a strong argument for undertaking a larger, more rigorous study.

In our pilot project, we administered a range of measures before and after a year-long therapeutic observation offered to families with toddlers in the high risk category. These measures included a separation–reunion task based on the strange situation as well as a questionnaire assessing parental anxiety. The fact that the CHAT is valid only between sixteen and twenty months meant that work could not begin until later than we would have wished. (According to a recent study, Ouss et al., 2014, simple observations of interactions between nine-month-old babies with West's syndrome and their mothers correlated completely with the predictions according to the CHAT of a later autism diagnosis. If this correlation were confirmed for a population without West's syndrome, an observation could be offered substantially earlier.)

However, despite the fact that observations did not begin until the children were nearly two, the very preliminary results are encouraging. At the time of my earlier report (Rhode, 2007), three children had been recruited. Of these, one left London after a few months. Another was only twelve months old and was, therefore, too young for the CHAT, but we felt unable, on ethical grounds, to refuse the mother's urgent request to begin at once. This child had avoided eye contact with his mother since birth, and showed a number of worrying bodily stereotypies that are unusual at such a young age. In spite of this, at the end of the year's intervention, the referring paediatrician assessed him as developing normally in all respects, including the use of language. His attachment category had changed from avoidant to secure, and his mother's anxiety levels had decreased by 50%. The third child, Adam, fell in the high risk category of the CHAT and was observed from the age of just under two. When he was three and a half, an independent child psychiatrist reported that his behaviour did not justify a diagnosis of autism, in spite of a very worrying early history and some residual delay in expressive language. As I mentioned earlier, the chance of this outcome, according to the CHAT, was one in six. As had been the case for the one-year-old boy, Adam's attachment category changed from avoidant to secure in the course of the year and his mother's anxiety levels diminished by 50%. A detailed account of the therapeutic observation of Adam can be found in Gretton (2006).

Since then, a further child in the high risk category has been offered the intervention. Unfortunately, his diagnostic assessment at a

Child Development Centre began soon afterwards, which meant that his mother cancelled the equivalent of four months' observations (a third of the total provided) in order to accommodate her son's assessment without missing out on the respite provided by his time at nursery. In the setting of the Child Development Centre, about halfway through the observation, he satisfied the behavioural criteria for an autism diagnosis, although his mother said at the end of the observation that he sometimes seemed so much improved that she half-wondered whether the diagnosis was accurate. This illustrates the co-existence of autistic and normal behaviours in the same child, a point that many authors have stressed (see, for example, Alvarez, 1999).

Therapeutic observation: some components of the process

In his paper describing therapeutic infant observation for young children at risk of autism, Houzel (1999) proposed that the presence of a participant observer who avoided the role of "expert" could go a long way towards counteracting what he called the "vicious cycle of the mother's feelings of incompetence". Parents can easily feel invalidated when faced with a child who does not respond in expectable ways: the feeling of being an incompetent mother in turn undermines the capacity to respond to a child who needs special care that would tax the capacities of any adult. Well-meant advice can inadvertently make this feeling of incompetence worse, whereas the observer's receptive stance can counteract it.

Houzel outlined three levels of the observer's capacity for receptivity. Her perceptual receptivity concerns her careful attention to everything that takes place, whereas her emotional receptivity is self-evidently to do with her openness to the impact of what she witnesses. The most important level of all, according to Houzel, is the observer's unconscious receptivity, which, by virtue of being unconscious, is beyond her control. This level is obviously related to the capacity for what Bion called "reverie", and which he thought was central to the mother's role in transforming her baby's communication of distressed states of mind and in making these bearable (Bion, 1962).

A qualitative analysis of the process of our pilot intervention (Rhode, 2007) highlighted a number of additional factors. We could observe another vicious circle—a "vicious circle of discouragement"—that obviously overlaps with Houzel's "vicious cycle of the mother's feelings of incompetence" but is more specifically concerned with despair and hope in both mother and child. We saw numerous sequences in which the mother and child seemed to have given up on the possibility of making contact with each other, although it was clear that both continued to desire it (Rhode, 2007). As hope dwindled on either side, attempts to make contact could become progressively eroded, which undermined hope yet further.

We also looked at possible functions of the observer. On the most basic level, the observer functioned as a witness: receiving, containing, and validating/verbalising communications from both parents and children. She facilitated the inclusion of all people present, with the paramount aim of making links between parents and child. She was often called upon to experience (and to contain to the best of her ability) feelings of aloneness and rejection. She modulated separations by referring verbally to the mother when she was absent, and by explaining the reason for this absence (for example, "Mummy's gone to turn on the washing machine"). All these functions might be thought of as the observer's response to the communications she was called upon to receive, as the behavioural outcome of Houzel's various levels of receptivity. By these means, the observer provided containment of emotional experience for the parents as well as the child, fostered links between them by means of her descriptions and comments, supported the child's capacity to keep an absent parent in mind, and conveyed, by supplying reasons for people's behaviour, that experience was meaningful rather than random. These functions of the observer have informed my clinic-based work with toddlers at risk of autism and their families.

Clinic-based work with toddlers and their parents

The pilot project I have described has put me in touch with children for whom this intervention was not suitable for a number of reasons, and with whom I have instead worked in a National Health Service (NHS) setting. I will begin by outlining some of the principles underlying this work, and then discuss these in relation to the case of Isabel, whose family was not offered the outreach intervention because she fell in the medium risk category of the CHAT rather than the high risk category. I have worked in similar ways with children in the high risk category who have not later been diagnosed with autism, but whose treatment I cannot discuss in detail here, partly for reasons of confidentiality.

The intervention within the setting of an NHS clinic is informed, as I have said, by what we have learnt from the pilot study so far. It is an observationally based intervention in which interpretation is absent or minimal; it is not primarily focused on making links with the past, and it does not involve video feedback. (This is not meant to imply that video feedback would not be useful: merely that the families I have seen did not give their consent to being filmed.) Instead, the work with toddlers and their parents is grounded in an observational approach. I was probably somewhat more active than a participant observer in the child's own home might have been, but I did not make interpretations or focus on the parents' past. My aims were similar to those of a child psychotherapist assessing a child with autism and his family with a view to later individual work (Reid, 1999; Rhode, 2000). These aims include finding ways to help the child to engage, as well as responding to the parents' anxieties and concerns.

The therapist describes the child's actions and, together with the parents, considers possible meanings they might have: this is more in the service of encouraging communication between parents and child than of offering insight. The therapist validates satisfying interactions between parents and child, points out to the parents things that the child is doing that they might not have noticed, and engages with them in reflecting on the context and possible meaning of difficulties so that they can use their own unrivalled knowledge of the child to find solutions. She encourages the parents' own capacity for observation, both in the clinic and at home; parents generally seem to identify quite quickly with the therapist's observing function, which they are in a position to witness during the sessions.

The setting, which consists of the toddler, the parents, the therapist, and the toys, provides a network of possibilities for interaction: at any given moment, the main interaction may be taking place within a dyad, a triad, or a group. The toys serve as mediators of contact before they take on a truly symbolic function: in my experience, appropriate toys often provide a bridge to children with autism or at risk of it before they can tolerate more direct contact with another person (Rhode, 2001).

Such an approach has obvious overlaps with parent–infant psychotherapy (as well as with observation), but there are equally obvious points of difference. The chief of these is the absence of insight-based interpretation. Instead, the therapist's function consists largely of making links between parents and child, as well as providing acceptance and understanding of what the parents are going through.

Many authors, including Frances Tustin (1972, 1992b), have stressed that the parents of children with autism elicit feelings of sympathy and the wish to be of help to them, and this was certainly true of Mr and Mrs B, the parents who consulted me together with their little girl, Isabel. I have found myself working in what Daniel Stern (1995) has aptly called the "good grandmother transference": as he and many others have pointed out, the birth of a child reawakens the parents' own childhood experience, and their relationship with their own internalised parental figures takes on a heightened importance. New mothers tend to find that external support from their own mothers or mother surrogates means a great deal, and that it reinforces the internal support they derive from their relationship to "internal working models" of helpful maternal figures. Such external support is often practical, but the implicit message is that the parents' own parents recognise their achievement in producing and caring for a thriving child, and take pleasure in that achievement.

However, all of us harbour discouraging internal figures as well as supportive ones, and serious difficulties in a child can seem to confirm the power of those presences that undermine the parents' confidence in being able to produce and look after a flourishing baby (Tischler, 1979). A therapist working in the "good grandmother transference" can dilute the impact of these malign presences. By making links between parents and child, by pointing out the child's strengths, by encouraging the parents' sense of competence and their observational capacities, and by opening herself to their communications, she conveys the message that they have something unique to offer their child and that it is her wish to support them in their parental role.

Such a stance was described as long ago as 1966 by Martha Harris, in a paper on a brief consultation with the family of a toddler who, as it happened, was not speaking at the beginning of the process, though he did not have autism. Unlike authors such as Dugmore (2013), I do not make interpretations addressing difficulties that the parents might be experiencing with me as a transference figure: I do not believe that parents who come to see me because of concerns over their child's failure to communicate have given me licence to work in that way, though obviously I would respond to anything of that nature that they brought up themselves. Although I might ask casually whether they think that their own previous experiences could be exerting any influence on the way they approach the questions about child-rearing that they raise with me, I address any difficulties they might be having with me personally as issues to be resolved between us in the present, not as reflections of their relationship to internalised parental figures.

That relationship may, in fact, develop substantially in the course of our contact, though not as the result of insight-based interpretations. The experience of being listened to with respect has a profound influence, and so does the experience of having their child's capacities taken seriously, attended to, and pointed out to them. But, perhaps most importantly, every improvement that the child makes and the hope that this brings with it weakens the influence of discouraging figures in the parents' minds and strengthens their growing belief in their own capacities and in the therapist as someone who welcomes this belief. Every such development, no matter how seemingly minor, in turn helps them to connect more creatively with their child and to manage the inevitable setbacks and disappointments. In this way, a benign cycle is set in motion, and gradually it comes to replace the vicious circle of discouragement that we had observed in the pilot study of participant observation

Clinical illustration: Isabel

Isabel's parents, Mr and Mrs B, brought her to the clinic when she was seventeen months old because it had been suggested to them during a visit to their country of origin in South America that she might be at risk of developing autism. At that point, she did not babble or make eye contact; instead, she stared blankly into a corner or out of the window. She could sit up, but was not yet crawling. She clutched a spoon that she used as what Tustin (1992a) calls an "autistic object": a hard object that provides reassurance by means of the sensations it generates and can, therefore, make it easier for the child to manage transitions, but that is not valued for its own intrinsic qualities or used for proper play. In the way that is characteristic of children with autism, Isabel had the habit of reaching for an adult's hand to perform a function that she could not carry out herself.

The parents told me that their older daughter, Ana, was developing well. Isabel had apparently developed well, too, until she was about seven months old. At that time, her mother had suffered from a minor illness. This was not related to an earlier, potentially life-threatening one that she had had before the children were born and from which she had recovered completely. Although the doctor had reassured her, the mother remained worried that Isabel might have been harmed at seven months by the medicine that she herself had had to take.

Both parents felt that they had lost Isabel at that point. They did not think that she recognised them or that they mattered to her in any way. They described her as "a vegetable", though they told me that professionals could sometimes get a better response from her than they could. I said how painful that must be for them, but the father disagreed: they were overjoyed that she responded to anyone. She would have to be a lot better, he added a bit wryly, before they could indulge in the luxury of feeling jealous.

Isabel's parents were devoted and highly proactive, and they investigated anything that they thought might help her. At the same time, the father expressed a worry that if Isabel were, as he put it, "resuscitated", it might interfere with her older sister's "oxygen supply". He seemed to doubt that there could be enough of the "breath of life" for both the little girls, and, indeed, I was to hear later that he was an only child, and had grown up without a father for reasons that I did not think fell within my brief to explore. At the same time, he obviously had good memories of his own childhood: for example, he mentioned with an affectionate smile that, as a boy, he had played with the same kind of doll's house that I provided for Isabel. The mother told me that she came from a close family, and she spoke warmly both of her parents and of her numerous siblings. However, one of these siblings had unexpectedly died tragically young, so that she had reason to share the father's fear that there might not be room for everyone. Again, this was not something she gave me licence to talk about: she told me explicitly that she was dealing with the effect of her bereavement in another setting, and that she did not want to go into any of this with me.

I mention these facts concerning the parents' background in order to illustrate that serious difficulties encountered by their younger child could well have reawakened particularly painful experiences for both of them and, in this way, made it harder for them to sustain hope in the extremely distressing circumstances they faced. (This, of course, in no way implies that Isabel's problems were "caused" by events in her parents' past.) Another reason for mentioning these biographical occurrences is to distinguish the kind of approach I am describing from those kinds of parent–infant work in which the parents' representations constitute the "port of entry" (Stern, 1995).

As Isabel fell into the medium risk category of the CHAT (where the risk of an autism diagnosis is about 50%), she and her parents were offered an intervention at the clinic rather than a home-based observation as part of our pilot project. I should stress, however, that, at the age of seventeen months, she showed the traits I have already mentioned that are characteristic of children on the autistic spectrum, and that the professionals' reports that her parents showed me at this stage referred to her as a child with numerous autistic features.

As with many such children, contact with Isabel first became possible through the medium of the toys. She was drawn to a pop-up toy in which little cylindrical wooden people could be pushed downwards into holes in a wooden block, only to spring back or even jump out when they were released. Often, she merely pressed the two ends of the block between her hands as though bracing herself, but sometimes she used the toy appropriately after I had modelled this. Joining in with her and imitating what she did while describing what was happening made it possible for me to elicit very fugitive eye contact. She also seemed interested in a transparent humming-top in which farm animals could be seen to move in a circle when the handle was pushed down, to the accompaniment of the nursery rhyme "Old MacDonald Had a Farm". The handle had to be pushed hard to make the top work. Isabel needed a great deal of encouragement from her parents and me before she could venture to be sufficiently forceful, and it took even longer before she could begin to enjoy banging the handle and growling loudly in unison with the adults. She seemed drawn to the animals inside the top, and later began to pull herself up by holding on to the table and to edge round it in a circle, as though she were imitating the animals' revolving action. However, for quite some time she recoiled from the teddy in her toy box, which perhaps, by virtue of its size, softness, and facial features, might have been too reminiscent of an actual baby.

Although Isabel initially seemed so detached from her parents and me, she was exquisitely tuned to the atmosphere between us. This atmosphere changed suddenly on one occasion when we were discussing the parents' refusal to allow me to liaise with colleagues, and our tones of voice became sharper. Isabel had been practising pulling herself up to a standing position, as I have described, while holding on to the circular table between her parents and me on which the larger toys were arranged. Now, as it seemed to me in response to our changed tone, her knees buckled and she collapsed on to the floor as though she had been suddenly deprived of the support she needed. I described this sequence to the parents, who disagreed with the idea that there could be any connection between our sharper tone of voice and Isabel's collapse. However, they did very tentatively begin to offer their own observations of her. For a while, it was as though one of them could take the risk of ascribing meaning or intention to her behaviour, while the other would deny the possibility or even react as though it as were deluded to entertain it. They continued to respond to my own suggestions as though these were fanciful, bordering on the ridiculous. For instance, Isabel had from the beginning often stared blankly into a particular corner or out of the window. Soon, the blankness was replaced by a look of terror, as though a malign presence in these two places might interfere with the little sequences of play at the table that she was gradually beginning to develop. When I described what I had noticed and what it suggested to me, the father said that perhaps Isabel just looked at the window because she was drawn to straight, vertical lines. The idea that their little girl's behaviour might be meaningful still often struck both her parents as mad, a measure of the repeated instances of profound disappointment they had had to endure.

Early in our work I was to witness a particularly striking example of the "vicious circle of discouragement". The parents had been telling me about a medical appointment they had attended with Isabel. She was sitting on the floor between us, and their absorption in what they were saying prevented them from noticing her when she turned round towards them as though trying to catch their eye. When her first delicate glance did not attract their attention, she immediately gave up and proved impossible to engage for the rest of the session. I described this sequence to the parents and they responded eagerly to a picture of their little girl that tallied with their own knowledge of her: "She's always been like that." They now began to be less consistently sceptical of the idea that Isabel's behaviour could be meaningful and communicative, and they also felt more able to risk believing in each other's observations of the developmental steps she was taking at home.

At the clinic, Isabel's play moved forward steadily while her parents talked to me about their fears for her. These were more than understandable in view of the many shocks to their confidence that they had sustained. However, discussing them in Isabel's presence meant that I could usually point out a bit of progress that counterbalanced the parents' worries to some extent. Obviously, we had no way of knowing what the ultimate outcome might be: all we could say was that, so far, Isabel seemed to be moving in the right direction. She smiled at me at the beginning of each weekly session; she began to babble, to imitate the intonation of her parents' singing, and to point. At the end of a session in the second term of work, when her parents were clearing up and not focusing their attention on her, she pretended to "feed" the teddy she had previously been frightened of with one of the little people figures from the pop-up toy. I pointed this out to her parents, and her mother, clearly overjoyed at this new development, bent over Isabel to take a closer look. At that moment, Isabel was pressing her hands against the two ends of the wooden pop-up toy in the gesture that had become familiar to us as an example of how she often tensed up as though bracing herself, as though she were holding herself together by relying on her own muscles, as Bick (1968) describes. No doubt sensing her mother's pleasure, she lifted up her hands from the sides of the block in a graceful gesture, and gently clasped the two sides of her mother's face instead. It was impossible at that moment for the parents to maintain the belief that they meant nothing to Isabel, and their delight was moving to witness.

Isabel's representational play continued to develop. The little wooden people began to go into the doll's house after she had "rung" the doorbell. Her first words appeared in the sessions: "Mummy" and "Daddy". Her parents told me that her very first word, at home, had been "light" (in Spanish), and that she had accompanied it with a completely appropriate point at a lamp. It seemed to me a touching representation of the lessening gloom that surrounded her. In the third term, she identified two of the pop-up people as "Mummy" and "Daddy" on the basis of the colour of her parents' clothes on that day. The two "parent" dolls kissed at length while the two remaining dolls were casually dropped on the floor. On other occasions, the dolls jostled each other for possession of one of the holes, which all of them seemed to want. The parents explained to me that Isabel regularly came into their bed at night, and that they felt unable as yet to be firm about this in case it drove her to retreat from them again.

In the third term, Isabel threw the parent dolls away repeatedly after making them kiss, then retrieved them. She was now nearly two and a half, and her physiotherapist had thought for some months that she was just on the verge of walking. In the next session, for the first time, she proudly took some steps towards me along the corridor. In the therapy room, she threw the parent dolls away, crouched to retrieve them, and stood up independently, holding one doll in each hand. She seemed to be showing us that she could now trust in being able to retrieve helpful parental figures who supported her in standing on her own two feet, even if she sometimes felt excluded by their relationship and threw them away in annoyance (Rhode, 2013).

Interestingly, in this same session, the parents told me that they had decided to return to their country of origin. This was something they had long wanted to do, but had so far not felt able to because they had not wanted to lose the many professionals who were caring for Isabel and whom they trusted. Their own increased confidence in the future coincided with Isabel's increased confidence in supportive internal figures. When she regressed slightly under the impact of the family's preparations for leaving, I was heartened to see that her parents were able to keep this in perspective, to view it as something that was understandable in the circumstances, and to maintain their belief, based on past experience, that she would recover.

Discussion

Isabel's family had many strengths; chief among these was the love and understanding between her parents. Both came from close and supportive families of origin, even if their lives had been marked by the losses I have mentioned. In the year during which I saw the family, there were perhaps only three or four appointments that both parents did not attend together. The strength of the link between them and of their joint commitment to their children's welfare was, I believe, central to the surprisingly rapid progress of our work, in the course of which Isabel seemed to blossom naturally. The "good grandmother transference" was easy to establish and maintain, and I found no difficulty in attending both to Isabel and to her parents. At the end of the year, they said that what they had valued most was the opportunity to think about their own experience of the various interventions she was having as well as about their hopes and anxieties concerning her future.

A number of reservations remained in my mind. One of these concerned the fact that there had been no opportunity to work directly on any of Isabel's hostile feelings. Although she did manage to represent her anger towards the parent dolls whom she threw away and retrieved, her real parents and I always had to reassure her by being emphatically friendly as well as reliable. Even small babies can understand the use of "marking": the process by which an adult indicates, often by means of raised eyebrows, that their own distressed expression is meant to "mirror" sympathetically the distress felt by the child and does not reflect what they themselves actually feel (see, for example, Beebe, 2006; Gergely & Watson, 1996). Isabel remained unable to make use of "marking"; my face frightened her unless I smiled, as though she could not trust that I would remain friendly if she felt cross or upset. In retrospect, I wondered how far my own anxiety about not having worked enough on Isabel's anger could have mirrored her parents' doubts about whether progress could be maintained, as well as her own preoccupation with being able to retrieve the parent dolls she had thrown away.

In the event, Isabel's capacity to internalise my voice reassured me. While these doubts were in my mind, I said, "Great stuff!" in response to something she had done for the first time and, with a roguish grin, she repeated back to me, "Great stuff!" Clearly, Isabel had managed to establish the primary division between good and bad that Klein (1946) saw as the necessary forerunner of later integration. This division, as Rodrigué (1955) has pointed out, means that substantial areas of goodness can be preserved. Isabel was showing me, as she had when she retrieved the parent dolls, that she could hold on to good experiences even if much work on her fears related to anger still remained to be done.

I have chosen to discuss the intervention with Isabel's family partly because of confidentiality issues, but chiefly because it was less complex than the treatment of children in the high risk category of the CHAT who were also later diagnosed as not having autism. Isabel's parents made the "good grandmother transference" easy to establish and maintain, and I did not feel a pressing need for a colleague with whom to collaborate. (Like their daughter, they might have felt the need to establish a relationship that was kept safe from anything potentially problematic: it was not until Isabel's progress was securely established that they allowed me to liaise with other professionals.) With a number of children in the high risk category, it has also been possible to achieve an outcome that was rewarding both in terms of the children's developmental progress and in terms of the absence of a later autism diagnosis. However, these children's more serious condition meant that the presence of a parent worker was essential to my capacity to function. Ongoing discussion with a colleague made it possible to entertain and integrate a variety of points of view, and in that way to attempt to bring together the experience of different family members. Most of all, however, these consultations helped me to manage the despair that I often felt.

I never experienced such despair with regard to Isabel, though I could well understand why her parents did so initially. In fact, for a long time they found it hard to believe that their little girl did not have autism, even when doctors had reassured them and they had witnessed her progress. This is a problem that often afflicts professionals as well, as I know from personal experience: it can be hard to remember and believe in important developmental achievements in the face of disheartening manifestations of the "autistic" part of the child's personality. Co-operation between colleagues can help to manage this problem, and can underpin the collaboration with parents that is so essential to progress. This provides a safe structure for the child to grow into.

Much remains for us to learn about autism, and about how to provide the kind of support that will best suit each family. We cannot predict how much progress each child will make, and the "vicious circle of discouragement" can have a powerful effect on professionals as well as on parents. However, I often recall the words of the nanny who helped to look after one of the high risk children I saw. This child did not in the end receive an autism diagnosis, but it was not clear for a considerable time what the outcome would be. As the nanny said while things were still uncertain, giving up hope means not putting in the necessary work. A central task for professionals is to provide support and consultation for each other in order to be able to maintain an attitude of realistic hopefulness.

Note

1.   Besides myself, the partners in this pilot study were Professor Judith Trowell, Dr David Simpson, Dr Elizabeth Nevrkla, and Dr Martin Bellman. We wish to express our gratitude for financial support from the Winnicott Trust.

References

Alvarez, A. (1999). Disorder, deviance and personality: factors in the persistence and modifiability of autism. In: A. Alvarez & S. Reid (Eds.), *Autism and Personality: Findings from the Tavistock Autism Workshop* (pp. 62–78). London: Routledge.

Baron-Cohen, S., Allen, J., & Gilberg, C. (1992). Can autism be detected at 18 months? The needle, the haystack and the CHAT. *British Journal of Psychiatry, 1961*: 839–843.

Beebe, B. (2006). Co-constructing mother–infant distress in face-to-face interactions: contributions of microanalysis. *International Journal of Infant Observation, 9*: 151–164.

Bick, E. (1964). Notes on infant observation in psychoanalytic training. *International Journal of Psychoanalysis, 45*: 558–566.

Bick, E. (1968). The experience of the skin in early object relations. *International Journal of Psychoanalysis, 49*: 484–486.

Bion, W. R. (1962). *Learning from Experience*. London: Heinemann.

Cardenal, M. (1998). A psychoanalytically informed approach to clinically ill babies. *International Journal of Infant Observation, 2*: 90–100.

Delion, P. (2000). The application of Esther Bick's method to the observation of babies at risk of autism. *International Journal of Infant Observation, 3*: 84–90.

Dugmore, N. (2013). The grandmaternal transference in parent–infant/ child psychotherapy. *Journal of Child Psychotherapy, 39*: 59–75.

Gergely, G., & Watson, J. S. (1996). The social biofeedback theory of parental affect-mirroring: the development of emotional self-awareness and self-control in infancy. *International Journal of Psychoanalysis, 77*: 1181–1212.

Gretton, A. (2006). An account of a year's work with a mother and her 18-month-old son at risk of autism. *International Journal of Infant Observation and its Applications, 9*: 21–34.

Harris, M. (1966). Therapeutic consultations [part of a paper written jointly with Helen Carr]. *Journal of Child Psychotherapy, 1*: 13–19.

Houzel, D. (1999). A therapeutic application of infant observation in child psychiatry. *International Journal of Infant Observation, 2*: 42–53.

Houzel, D. (2011). L'observation à domicile: une méthode thérapeutique en psychiatrie du nourrisson. *Dialogue, 193*(3): 125–137.

Klein, M. (1946). Notes on some schizoid mechanisms. In: *The Writings of Melanie Klein, Vol. 3, Envy and Gratitude and Other Works* (pp. 1–24). London: Hogarth, 1975.

Lechevalier, B., Fellouse, J.-C., & Bonnesoeur, S. (2000). West's syndrome and infantile autism: the effect of a psychotherapeutic approach in certain cases. *International Journal of Infant Observation, 3*: 23–38.

Ouss, L., Saint-Georges, C., Robel, L., Bodeau, N., Laznik, M.-C., Crespin, G. C., Chetouani, M., Bursztejn, C., Golse, B., Nabbout, R., Desguerre, I., & Cohen, D. (2014). Infant's engagement and emotion as predictors of autism or intellectual disability in West's syndrome. *European Child & Adolescent Psychiatry, 23*(3): 143–149.

Reid, S. (1999). The assessment of the child with autism: a family perspective. In: A. Alvarez & S, Reid (Eds.), *Autism and Personality: Findings from the Tavistock Autism Workshop* (pp. 13–32). London: Routledge.

Rhode, M. (2000). Assessing children with communication disorders. In: M. Rustin & E. Quagliata (Eds.), *Assessment in Child Psychotherapy* (pp. 9–32). London: Karnac.

Rhode, M. (2001). The "sense of abundance" in relation to technique. In: E. Edwards (Ed.), *Being Alive: Building on the Work of Anne Alvarez* (pp. 128–140). London: Routledge.

Rhode, M. (2007). Helping toddlers to communicate: infant observation as an early intervention. In: S. Acquarone (Ed.), *Signs of Autism in Infants: Early Detection and Intervention* (pp. 193–212). London: Karnac.

Rhode, M. (2013). Learning to walk down the corridor: body image, catastrophic anxieties and supportive internal figures. In: A. Varchevker &

E. McGinley (Eds.), *Enduring Migration Throughout the Life Cycle* (pp. 19–38). London: Karnac.

Rodrigué, E. (1955). The analysis of a three-year-old mute schizophrenic. In: M. Klein, P. Heimann, & R. Money-Kyrle (Eds.), *New Directions in Psycho-Analysis* (pp. 140–179). London: Tavistock.

Stern, D. (1995). *The Motherhood Constellation*. New York: Basic Books.

Tischler, S. (1979). Being with a psychotic child: a psycho-analytical approach to the problems of parents of psychotic children. *International Journal of Psychoanalysis*, 60: 29–38.

Tustin, F. (1972). *Autism and Childhood Psychosis*. London: Hogarth Press [reprinted London: Karnac, 1995].

Tustin, F. (1992a). Autistic objects. In: *Autistic States in Children* (2nd revised edn). London: Routledge.

Tustin, F. (1992b). *Autistic States in Children* (2nd revised edn). London: Routledge.

Conclusion

Stella Acquarone

T he ending of this book comes as a relief in a strange kind of way, as we can see that the dangers of the natural development of good mother–child relationships can so easily be jeopardised by external or internal traumas. However, the expertise of the clinicians and their trials has shown how and what is important to support the infant and their mother or family to improve relations and repair what has been damaged by trauma.

Physical survival and resilience are essential, but to be able to survive psychologically and emotionally, the fears and residues of traumatic beginnings have to be calmed. This is best achieved through the availability of the appropriate services and professionals who can offer a space to "tell the story/experience" and accompany them on the process of rehabilitation or habilitation, as some of these persons did not have the opportunity of being able to grow and develop given the state of the shock they endured and despair they now feel. This help could be just the beginning of a better integrated life, the best possible in spite of the storms of stress or circumstances that endanger mental, emotional, and physical life.

It all appears to be dramatic and hopeless and, in most cases, simply a matter of survival, with the consequences of suffering from severe post traumatic stress disorder if they do survive. I think that what is expected is that resilience will protect all babies in trouble. However, we know that even with the most resilient babies, there will be a heavy weight on their shoulders throughout their life.

Drawing on their wealth of experience, the authors of this book discuss themes important to the development of parent–infant relations. We hear from the experts in clinical specialities whose areas of work—from refugees to mothers in prison—are charged with horror and pain, and learn of the unique programmes that use early intervention methods to treat early signs of autism. Each chapter shines a different light on the field of working with children and parents.

All the clinicians come to share their experiences in how to help, what to look for, and how to make a better world by transforming horrific experiences into manageable ones as situations change. In the words of Zack Eleftheriadou, "We cannot expect people to 'manage' or ever forget their experience, but, through reflection, they are able to acknowledge their impact and 'keep them at bay' so that they can get on with everyday life".

The idea of focusing on sharing the circumstances, the traumas, the losses, and the pain goes a long way to helping to heal by becoming a sympathetic and understanding listener who stays with the experience. However, there are some difficult experiences that can be as problematic for the one who describes it as for those hearing it; even though they are in a place of freedom, choice, and comfort, the reactivation of the trauma makes the suffering unimaginable again.

> Forthwith this frame of mine was wrenched,
> With a woeful agony,
> Which forced me to begin my tale;
> And then it left me free
>
> (Coleridge, Part III, p. 99)

And the listener feels out of place, trying to comprehend, and a state of reflexion is triggered.

What is important is to understand how all this affects the professionals involved: how many of the thoughts and feelings provoked can be held and not spill over into their everyday life and other relations? We talk here not only about the support and network of care provided to the carers, but also to the professionals. They, too, need support—in the form of weekly discussion sessions and individual personal psychotherapy—if they are to provide the best care to traumatised patients for whom pride and respect have long been lost and stepped on.

Acquiring a long view about the implications of surviving, to intervene as early as possible means not only to become aware of all the awful circumstances that could have affected the babies in the womb, but also of the immense support network necessary for the clinician who, using the words of Coleridge, might be left feeling like the Wedding guest "turned from the bridegroom's door":

> The Mariner whose eye is bright,
> Whose beard with age is hoar,
> Is gone: and now the Wedding-guest
> Turned from the bridegroom's door.
> He went like one that hath been stunned,
> And is of sense forlorn:
> A sadder and wiser man,
> He rose the morrow morn.
>
> (Coleridge, Part III, p. 100)

The feelings of being stunned and becoming sadder and more reflective makes for a good member of a team that can offer creative, holding, and helpful insights into how best to help the traumatised mother who sits before them. All these professionals have to work within a supportive and caring group of experts who understand the depth of the projections and can help in the sharing of ideas.

I leave the reader with their own thoughts in the hope that they might feel more aware of their views on babies, small children, and their parents if they in any way have had a traumatic early beginning.

Reference

Coleridge, S. T. (1996). *Selected Poems. The Rime of the Ancient Mariner.* Harmondsworth: Penguin Classics.

INDEX